CONFIDENT IDENTITIES, CONNECTED COMMUNITIES

Building Cohesion through Shared Experiences

CONFIDENT IDENTITIES, CONNECTED COMMUNITIES

Building Cohesion through Shared Experiences

Editors

Chan-Hoong Leong
Kantar Public, Singapore

Clarence Lim

Helena Yixin Huang
S. Rajaratnam School of International Studies, Singapore

World Scientific

NEW JERSEY · LONDON · SINGAPORE · BEIJING · SHANGHAI · HONG KONG · TAIPEI · CHENNAI · TOKYO

Published by

World Scientific Publishing Co. Pte. Ltd.
5 Toh Tuck Link, Singapore 596224
USA office: 27 Warren Street, Suite 401-402, Hackensack, NJ 07601
UK office: 57 Shelton Street, Covent Garden, London WC2H 9HE

British Library Cataloguing-in-Publication Data
A catalogue record for this book is available from the British Library.

CONFIDENT IDENTITIES, CONNECTED COMMUNITIES
Building Cohesion through Shared Experiences

ISBN 978-981-12-8537-0 (hardcover)
ISBN 978-981-12-8538-7 (ebook for institutions)
ISBN 978-981-12-8539-4 (ebook for individuals)

For any available supplementary material, please visit
https://www.worldscientific.com/worldscibooks/10.1142/13651#t=suppl

Desk Editor: Sandhya Venkatesh

Typeset by Stallion Press
Email: enquiries@stallionpress.com

ABOUT ICCS 2022

We have many identities. Faith, ethnicity, culture, nationality — all intertwining and defining us as individuals. How can we unite despite our differences? How do we form bonds and bridge divides?

ICCS 2022 was held from 6th to 8th September 2022 at a pivotal time for conversations, as the world emerges from a pandemic where polarisation and social isolation have come to the fore. Through the theme "Confident Identities, Connected Communities", The International Conference on Cohesive Societies (ICCS) 2022 examined our multiple identities and the connections with our communities, covering the key aspects of faith, identity and cohesion.

The Conference also cast a spotlight on youth as future leaders in an increasingly digitalised world and their immensely important role in fostering social cohesion.

Background

The ICCS is the preeminent event for interfaith and multicultural dialogue. Mooted by Madam Halimah Yacob, the former President of Singapore, the Conference was held in Singapore for the first time in 2019, showcasing the tropical island-state's unique approach to managing communal ties within a diverse population. It is organised by the S. Rajaratnam School of International Studies (RSIS) and supported by the Ministry of Culture, Community and Youth (MCCY).

ICCS Secretariat

The S. Rajaratnam School of International Studies (RSIS) is a global think tank and professional graduate school of international affairs at the Nanyang Technological University, Singapore. An autonomous school, RSIS' mission is to be a leading research and graduate teaching institution in strategic and international affairs in the Asia Pacific. With the core functions of research, graduate education, and networking, it produces research on Asia Pacific Security, Multilateralism and Regionalism, Conflict Studies, Non-traditional Security, Cybersecurity, Maritime Security and Terrorism Studies.

The Ministry of Culture, Community and Youth seeks to inspire Singaporeans through the arts and sports, strengthen community bonds, and promote volunteerism and philanthropy. Since its inception in November 2012, MCCY has been actively engaging the arts, heritage, sports, and community and youth sectors. The Ministry aims to bring into sharper focus the efforts to build a more cohesive and vibrant society, and to deepen a sense of identity and belonging to the nation. MCCY works with its stakeholders to create an environment where Singaporeans can pursue their aspirations for a better quality of life and together, and build a gracious and caring society we are proud to call home.

ABOUT THE CONTRIBUTORS

Amanda Wise is Professor of Sociology in the School of Social Sciences, Macquarie University. She researches global cities, urban diversity, migrant workers, sociology of work, and craft. Amanda teaches Living Diversity: Understanding racism and Co-existence, The Urban Century, and Social Movements and Policy Ideas.

André Azoulay, Counsellor to H.M. the King Mohammed VI, is an ardent ambassador of Morocco throughout the world. He is a strong advocate for peace and dialogue between the Arab Muslim World and Jewish Communities in Europe, USA, Morocco, as well as the global Arab and Jewish diasporas. He is also well-known for contributions to the peace process in the Middle East and for the many interfaith cross-cultural initiatives he spearheaded.

Professor Catherine Gomes (School of Media and Communication, RMIT University, Melbourne) is internationally renowned for her research on the lived experiences of international students, their digital engagements and their wellbeing. She is editor of the Media, Culture and Communication in Migrant Societies book series with Amsterdam University Press and founding editor of Transitions: Journal of Transient Migration with Intellect Books. Catherine is also a recipient of an Australian Research Council Discovery Early Career Researcher Award Fellowship.

Clarence Lim is an English teacher. He is passionate about sharing creative writing and research skills with students. A social activist and change maker, he has published in scholarly outlets on migration and integration related issues. Clarence has previously worked for a think tank, the government, and in the education sector.

Farish A. Noor, PhD, is a Professor at the Department of History, Faculty of the Arts and Social Sciences, University of Malaya. His research focus is on the impact of colonialism in Asia. He was previously Associate Professor at the S. Rajaratnam School of International Studies (RSIS) at Nanyang Technological University in Singapore and coordinator of the RSIS doctoral programme. He is also a member of the United Nations Panel of Experts on Religion and Politics.

Father Philip Larrey is currently Dean of the Philosophy Department, Pontifical Lateran University. His publications deal with the philosophy of knowledge and critical thinking. For years, he has been following the philosophical implications of the rapid development of artificial intelligence. He has also published several books concerning the effects of the new digital era on society.

Fritjof Knier's multilingual information platform, Integreat, provides understandable information for refugees and migrants arriving in a city. It has been implemented in collaboration with over 90 of Germany's 400 municipal governments throughout the country and was most recently launched in Lesvos, Greece, as well.

Ghil'ad Zuckermann (DPhil Oxford; PhD Cambridge, titular; MA Tel Aviv, summa cum laude) is Chair of Linguistics and Endangered Languages at the University of Adelaide, Australia. Since the beginning of 2017, he has been the President of the Australian Association for Jewish Studies.

Helena Huang Yixin is an Associate Research Fellow with the Executive Deputy Chairman's Office at the S. Rajaratnam School of International Studies (RSIS), Nanyang Technological University (NTU), Singapore. Prior to joining RSIS, she held several positions in the government sector. She holds a Master of Science in International Relations from RSIS and a Bachelor of Arts (Honours) in English from NTU. Her research interests cover digital impact, transnational crimes, human rights, and international law.

Imam Uzair Akbar is a well-known respected scholar, dynamic speaker, and prominent leader in the Muslim community of Australia. Imam Uzair has been gifted with a unique way of connecting to the common audience through his Islamic lectures, Tafseer, and sermons. His forte includes connecting with the youth and giving common life analogies that really strike into the heart of his listeners.

Iyad Abumoghli has more than 35 years of experience with international organisations, the private sector, and scientific institutions. His expertise focuses on strategic planning, sustainable development, natural resources management, interfaith collaboration, and knowledge and innovation. He is also the Lead Principal Advisor on Engaging with Faith-Based Organisations at UNEP.

Jasvir Singh is a prolific community activist and a leading figure within the British Sikh and British South Asian communities. City Sikhs is one of the main Sikh organisations in the UK and provides a voice for over 10,000 members across the country. He is also the former Co-Chair of the Faiths Forum for London that encourages and promotes interfaith social initiatives.

Katherine Marshall, a senior fellow at Georgetown University's Berkley Center for Religion, Peace, and World Affairs, leads the centre's work on religion and global development. She is also professor of the practice of development, conflict, and religion in the Walsh School of Foreign Service, teaching diverse courses notably on the ethics of development work and mentoring students at many levels. She helped create and serves as the executive director of the World Faiths Development Dialogue, an NGO that works to enhance bridges among different sectors and institutions.

Leong Chan-Hoong, PhD, is Head of Policy Development, Evaluation, and Data Analytics at Kantar Public, a global policy advisory firm headquartered in London that specialises in government affairs and the non-profit sector. Prior to this, he held various academic positions including Associate Professor, Singapore University of Social Sciences (2019–2022) and Senior Research Fellow and Head of Social Lab (2016–2019, Dy Head, 2013–2016) at the Institute of Policy Studies, National University of Singapore (NUS). His research focuses on immigration, inter-racial relations, national narratives, and human–environment interactions.

Lily Kong is widely known for her research on urban transformations, and particularly, social and cultural change in Asia. She has published a large body of work on religion, cultural policy and creative economy, urban heritage and conservation, national identity, smart cities and education. Her work has earned her international awards, including the Association of American Geographers Robert Stoddard Award for Distinguished Service, a Fullbright Fellowship (at University of California Berkeley), a Commonwealth Fellowship (at University College London), and a Humanities Research Fellowship (at Australian National University). In a 2020 Stanford University study, Professor Kong was ranked among the top one percent of scientists in the world in her discipline.

Lord John Alderdice was the founding Chairman (now Emeritus Chairman) of the Centre for Democracy and Peace Building in Belfast and now heads up the Changing Character of War Centre at Pembroke College, University of Oxford. He is also a Senior Research Fellow at Harris Manchester College, University of Oxford, Director of the Conference on the Resolution of Intractable Conflict, and founding Chairman of The Concord Foundation, an independent peacebuilding organisation.

Master Benjamin Tan was initiated into Taoism ZhengYi Sect in 2013, ordained as a Luo generation ZhengYi Taoist priest in TianShi Mansion Mount Longhu (Jiangxi China) in 2018. He has represented the Taoist Federation (Singapore) at prayers, engagements, conferences, seminars, and interfaith work. In addition, he is a leader of the Taoist Federation (Singapore) Prayer and Blessing Group, the Council Member of Inter Religious Organisation representing Taoism, and a mentor to the 3rd batch of Ambassador of Roses of Peace and Eunos IRCC Chairman.

Mohammad Hannan Hassan specialises in the History and Philosophy of Islamic Higher Education, Muslim-Jewish relations, interfaith relations, and the history and philosophy of Islamic law in the Malay Archipelago.

Nazhath Faheema is a social harmony advocate actively engaged in inter-faith and intercultural conversations to strengthen social cohesion. She is the Founder of hash.peace, which is a youth movement in Singapore cata-lysing conversations about race, religion and identities. She initiates various efforts to counter extremist ideologies and exclusivist narratives harmful for the peacekeeping within multicultural societies. Currently, she serves full-time as Director of Development and Community Relations at Hope Initiative Alliance, an NGO in Singapore serving the welfare of vulnerable and marginalised communities. She is also the Team Lead for Sowing Care Together, an interfaith youth initiative focusing on common good efforts.

Patrice Brodeur is an associate professor at the Institute of Religious Studies at the University of Montreal (Canada). His expertise includes contemporary Islamic thought and interreligious dialogues. He is also Senior Consultant at the International Dialogue Centre (KAICIID), Lisbon, and has lectured academically to a variety of audiences and con-ducted training sessions on different forms of dialogue in over 50 coun-tries around the world.

Sadhvi Bhagawati Saraswati is a renowned spiritual leader, author, and social activist based in the Himalayas, India. She is Secretary-General of Global Interfaith WASH Alliance, President of Divine Shakti Foundation and Co-President of Religions for Peace. She serves on the United Nations Advisory Council on Religion and on the steering committees of the International Partnership for Religion and Sustainable Development (PaRD) and the Moral Imperative to End Extreme Poverty, a campaign by the United Nations and World Bank.

Selvaraj Velayutham is Associate Professor in the Discipline of Sociology, Macquarie University. His research interests are in the area of race relations and racism in Singapore, migration work, and informal sports and everyday multiculturalism.

Shashi Jayakumar was previously Head of the Centre of Excellence on National Security and Executive Coordinator of Future Issues and Technology, S. Rajaratnam School of International Studies.

Sister Julia Walsh is a Franciscan Sister of Perpetual Adoration and part of her congregation's formation team, serving women who are discerning their vocation. Along with another Franciscan Sister, she co-founded The Fireplace, an intentional community and house of hospitality on Chicago's southside that offers spiritual support to artists and activists.

Swami Samachittananda is the President of Ramakrishna Mission Singapore, a branch of the Ramakrishna Order of India, a worldwide spiritual and welfare organisation. Like the other branches in Asia-Oceania, North and South America, Europe, and Africa, the centre is a self-sustaining unit that looks to the Ramakrishna Order for spiritual guidance.

Venerable Chi Kwang Sunim, an Australian Buddhist Nun for over forty years, lived and trained for twenty years in South Korea. In 1998, after cultivating knowledge in textual studies and meditative experience, she returned to live in Australia and established a Buddhist Temple in Kinglake, Victoria. Here, she serves a local and multicultural Buddhist community. Chi Kwang Sunim has co-founded several Buddhist organisations and chaired the Australian Sangha Association (ASA) and the Buddhist Council.

Venerable You Guang is the Secretary-General of the Singapore Buddhist Federation and Abbot/President of Samantabhadra Vihara. He is also 1st Vice President of the Metta Welfare Association, serving the community's special education, welfare and social needs. He received Higher Ordination at TzuYun Temple, Taiwan. Venerable received both Dharma transmissions of the Hua-Yen Lineage and CaoDong-Zen Lineage. He guides Buddhists and like-minded ones on the path to a harmonious way of life through sharing, classes and consultations and meets people from different walks of life.

Yoshiko Ashiwa is Visiting Professor at National Graduate Research Institute for Policy Studies and Emeritus Professor of Hitotsubashi University. Her research interests include religion, arts, culture and values, modernity, globalisation, and social movements mainly in Asia, especially Sri Lanka, China and Japan. She is co-author (with David Wank) of The Space of Religion: Temple, State, and Communities of Buddhism in Modern China (Columbia University Press 2023) and co-editor (with David Wank) of Making Religion, Making the State: The Politics of Religion in Modern China (Stanford University press 2009).

FOREWORD

The International Conference on Cohesive Societies (ICCS) brings together thought leaders, community leaders, religious leaders, as well as policy makers and practitioners engaged in strengthening social cohesion in different nations around the world to discuss and promote ideas that will advance communal unity.

As a diverse society of many ethnicities and religions, Singapore offers itself as a suitable venue where we can have meaningful conversations, build lasting relationships — if not, partnerships — and exchange experiences in this endeavour.

Singapore has much to learn and contribute. The sharing of best practices from other cultures will bring valuable insights for further strengthening community's resilience and cohesion.

As I reflected on how the ICCS is a microcosm of strength in diversity, my hope is that these ideas and values are now translated to the macro-world, to each community that the participants go back to.

Keeping Our Bearings

More than ever in our history, we need to understand the driving forces that shape cohesion, and the types of policies and interventions that can prevent ruptures in human civilisation.

As Madam Halimah Yacob, former President of Singapore, pointed out in her opening address at ICCS: "The pandemic (has) deepened fault lines in societies across the world, when what was urgently needed to recover from the pandemic was collective action and cooperation…social cohesion is a necessary condition for our collective security. Societies cannot survive, let alone thrive, without the social glue that bonds people together".

In prolonged periods of uncertainty and insecurity, such as the COVID-19 outbreak and geopolitical conflicts, social tensions will grow and the trust quotient within communities will come under threat. Our contemporary approach to addressing these emerging fault lines and the seismic implications may no longer be sufficient. Fostering tolerance and empathy, and reinforcing cohesion across diverse communities become a social imperative, whether in the physical or virtual realms.

Professor Lily Kong defined social cohesion as the "enduring sense of trust, a strong sense of community, a sense of shared loyalty, and a sense of solidarity".

While social cohesion as a resource has helped prevent interracial and religious tensions from escalating, developmental trends in global polity and human geography have also birthed new paradigms and nuances in how pluralism and connections should be managed.

As Prof Kong noted, "inter-racial and inter-religious relations must be expanded to include greater understanding and management of intra-racial and intra-religious diversities".

ICCS 2022 is an invaluable platform to discuss these dynamic changes.

Harnessing Shared Legacy and Aspirations

Notwithstanding existing fractures, there is reason to believe that humanity can overcome the forces that tear us apart.

Beyond the rhetoric, we have much in common with people from the other end of the political spectrum if only we pay enough attention to our shared legacy. Cultures and civilisations are woven together through the passage of time. The animosity towards the 'Others' can be disarmed and soothed if we recognise that they too have a place in history.

Mr André Azoulay revealed to us what it means to be a Jewish living in Morocco, his native country and a predominantly Arab Muslim society in North Africa/the Middle East. The Jewish and Muslims have had a long history of conflict in this part of the world even as both communities considered themselves as descendants of the land.

Mr Azoulay recounted a most poignant moment in his hometown of Essaouira-Mogador, at the inauguration of *Bayt Dakira* — a Jewish heritage house — where His Majesty King Mohammed VI of Morocco officiated the event.

> "He entered the synagogue in *Bayt Dakira* with me and opened the sacred place where the scrolls of the Torah were kept. He placed his hand on the scrolls for an unprecedented moment of emotion and meditation in the heart of the synagogue. This happened in an Arab country, in the land of Islam, in Morocco".

Indeed, as Professor Katherine Marshall has pointed out, urban diversity — including religion and race — need not be a zero-sum contest, and that dissimilar communities can "benefit both from shared common values and from the rich differences that different traditions bring".

All faiths in the world share a singular commitment to bring peace and harmony. This aspiration is neither exclusive nor contradictory to the other social values practise by mankind. We should harness the thrust for this common goal instead.

Southeast Asian Social Cohesion Radar: A Step Towards Understanding Social Cohesion

The findings of an inaugural social cohesion study were presented at the sidelines of the ICCS 2022. Called the "Southeast Asian Social Cohesion Radar Study", this is a review of social cohesion, between ASEAN member states using the Bertelsmann Stiftung framework.

This is the first time an in-depth empirical study on social cohesion is conducted in this part of the world using this framework. The approach recognises inherent geographical complexity and diversity, and how the various demographic contours inform social cohesion in this region and hence, interfaith dialogue and outreach separately for each country.

The Southeast Asian Social Cohesion Radar study surveyed respondents from each ASEAN member state, covering various segments in the respective communities including the academia, government, non-profit sectors and business enterprises.

Besides providing an overview of regional social cohesion, this primary resource attempts to lay out country-specific feedback for further sense-making and investigation. Taken as a whole, the results offer the beginning of a strategic blueprint to guide policymakers, religious leaders, and community practitioners on interfaith dialogues and peace engagement.

With future iterations, the Southeast Asian Social Cohesion Radar study could provide fresh empirical and analytical updates to help inform ICCS discussions.

ICCS: Thought Leadership in Diversity Management

We put together a book after each ICCS not just to serve as a record of the quality of discussions contributed by participating scholars, policy makers, and community and religious leaders, but also to reach out to the many who could not join us for the in-person event, notwithstanding our efforts to provide live streaming on Internet of the proceedings in Singapore.

This book is not just a collection of speeches, but it has contributions from renowned academics and practitioners. The S. Rajaratnam School of International Studies (RSIS) is proud to be a partner in this endeavour and we aim to elevate this learning journey to new heights in every successive conference.

The issues covered in the 2022 conference on addressing potential forms of cultural polarity, such as religion, race, and immigration, have become even more poignant and critical. And beyond tolerance amongst various racial and religious groups, there should be greater impetus to tap on diversity as a force for good, in particular, as a means to forge stronger cohesion in this region.

Dr Iyad Abumoghli spoke on how faith actors can work together for good for environmental and social causes. For Imam Uzair Akbar, he talks about accommodation and big-heartedness. There is space at the table for everyone, he said.

If we all take ownership to come to the table to discuss our differences with a genuine and sincere heart, and with the hope of bettering our society and community, the walls of prejudice and stereotypes will crumble. Collectively, we can usher in a more united and cohesive society for all.

This prescription for community building is a versatile and powerful blueprint. It works well in our daily rituals within the confines of our neighbourhoods as well as in the cyberworld, connecting strangers who are miles apart.

Mr Jasvir Singh, a community leader of the ethnic minorities in the United Kingdom, shared a delightful case study of how the South Asian community leveraged information technology and social media to raise awareness of the South Asian heritage, which consequently fostered bridging capital for all.

Pondering the Possible in Building Cohesive Societies

The ICCS is committed to establish the main cardinal points of social cohesion for Singapore and beyond. It is a venue for us to learn as individuals and as a collective.

We can take away many learning points, and certainly I have. In the tapestry of cohesion, relationships matter, and this is why ICCS is important. How do we strengthen relationships with faith, social beliefs, and the will to apply what we learnt. We should continue to nurture and cultivate the "sweet spot" we have found together. It is a safe space for such partnerships to be carried out.

The efforts of all speakers and participants in sharing their respective experiences and perspectives have enriched our mutual learning. This has reinforced our resolve to continue the work of the ICCS.

I would like to thank President Halimah Yacob (2017–2023) for her encouragement and guidance as well as our partner, the Ministry of Culture, Community and Youth for their enduring support in making the ICCS 2022 possible.

Ong Keng Yong
Executive Deputy Chairman
S. Rajaratnam School of International Studies
Nanyang Technological University, Singapore

CONTENTS

Part 5 Technology   **249**

Part 6 Youth   **317**

Part 1

SPEECHES AND PROCEEDINGS

Chapter 1.1

OPENING ADDRESS

Her Excellency Madam Halimah Yacob

Former President of the Republic of Singapore

6 September 2022

Mr Teo Chee Hean, Senior Minister and Coordinating Minister for National Security Ministers

Ambassador Ong Keng Yong, Executive Deputy Chairman of RSIS

Distinguished Guests

Ladies and Gentlemen

Good morning. Welcome to the International Conference on Cohesive Societies (ICCS). To our friends from overseas, a warm welcome to sunny Singapore!

I am delighted to host such a diverse gathering of great minds and influential voices for this second edition of the ICCS. When we held the inaugural ICCS three years ago, it was a vastly different time. Participants from all around the world came together to discuss faith, identity, and cohesion. Since then, COVID-19 has changed our world. This year, we continue to focus on the same three pillars, but with a different lens informed by lessons from the pandemic.

The pandemic was a public health crisis with serious social implications. People were confined to their homes, constraining the basic human need for social interaction. Religious communities also faced difficult decisions as houses of worship worldwide had to limit or suspend their activities in order to comply with public health measures. Perhaps the most heartrending accounts were of those who could not bid a proper farewell to the loved ones they lost to the pandemic.

In a period of heightened social anxiety, tensions rose and in certain cases triggered hate, bigotry, and xenophobia. This descended into violence in some places, with reports of hate crimes against people of Asian ethnicity who were blamed for the spread of the virus. Even public health measures like vaccinations became points of contention.

Singapore too was not immune to such challenges. The pandemic deepened fault lines in societies across the world, when what was urgently needed to recover from the pandemic was collective action and cooperation. This reminds us that social cohesion is a necessary condition for our collective security. Societies cannot survive, let alone thrive, without the social glue that bonds people together. National resilience and stability are the result of people working together towards a common cause, united in the face of challenges and threats facing a country. Cohesive societies do not exist spontaneously. They are borne of choice and conviction. The pandemic has reinforced this.

To address these challenges, we need to understand factors that contribute towards social cohesion. A regional study by the S. Rajaratnam School of International Studies (RSIS), the organiser of this conference, found that 69% of those surveyed in Southeast Asia believed that their country is socially cohesive. According to the study, the level of trust and acceptance between each other and the social networks that people build over time are elements that help strengthen social cohesion. Harnessing these aspects can provide a useful springboard towards action. Such insights presented in the Southeast Asian Social Cohesion Radar study can help inform our discussions to develop meaningful approaches towards building cohesive societies. Indeed, the study recommended that the engagement of community and religious leaders and other relevant stakeholders are critical to this effort. RSIS will share more about these findings this afternoon.

In view of these findings, initiatives like the Commitment to Safeguard Religious Harmony have become even more pertinent.

Launched at the last ICCS, religious leaders pledged to be united in promoting the common good and to stand against division and discord. They undertook to build strong bonds across religious communities through interactions such as attending each other's festivals. More than 750 of Singapore's religious organisations have affirmed this Commitment. It is our hope that ICCS too provides a platform for people to learn from one another and be comfortable with differences.

Moving forward, how do we safeguard and promote social cohesion amidst these challenging times? How do we bridge divides and harness our diversity for the common good? These questions remind me of a quote I came across two months ago when Singapore celebrated our annual Racial Harmony Day. I quote, "Racial harmony means we can all be friends because we are all human beings." Unquote. These words were spoken by Gaia Amedi, a four-year-old pre-schooler. It is a moving reminder that despite all our differences and disagreements, we are human beings at the end of the day, equally fragile, yet equally resilient. We may come from different backgrounds, countries, cultures, and religions, but we share the same core values of kindness, compassion, and love. We are connected. And yes, Gaia, we can certainly all be friends.

The theme of ICCS 2022, 'Confident Identities, Connected Communities', echoes Gaia's words. Building on the foundations of ICCS 2019 where we discussed who we are, what we stand for, and how we can find common ground with one another, ICCS 2022 will explore the role of our identities, beliefs, and faiths in shaping social connections and cohesion.

I am glad to welcome over 800 participants from more than 40 countries. You come from different countries and disciplines. There are religious leaders, policymakers, academics, and civil society practitioners in your midst. With such a diverse group of speakers and delegates, I am confident that there will be a rich exchange of views and ideas over the next three days.

Building social cohesion is an experiential endeavour. This is why we have arranged visits to Singapore's multicultural communities as a way to spend your evenings. I encourage you to sign up for these community explorations if you have not done so. I wish to thank our community and religious leaders for opening up their community spaces and houses of worship to our ICCS participants.

We also need to develop our youth to take the lead in shaping their communities. I am glad that we have gathered 120 youth leaders for the second run of our Young Leaders Programme (YLP). They join the first cohort of YLP participants from 2019, many of whom have gone on to drive social cohesion initiatives in their communities. I cannot emphasise enough the importance of young people being involved in building cohesive communities. An article in *The Straits Times* today made the point that there are not many young people involved in interfaith activities. In the Harmony Circle, for instance, the average age is about 60. Young people need to be involved to ensure that the building of social cohesion continues to the next generation.

Two of these YLP alumni are Basil Kannangara and Nicholas Pang from Singapore. They met through YLP and share a passion for facilitating deep conversations about race, religion, nationality, and disability. Basil and Nick believe that it is possible to have fun while generating constructive dialogue. They developed a card game called Diversity by Default, which features diversity-related questions. Such initiatives help dispel misperceptions, build bonds, and create trust. The pair are among us today as mentors to the new batch of YLP delegates. Basil and Nick-thank you for returning to nurture fellow youth leaders.

This year's YLP will help our young leaders harness their energy and creativity to discuss common challenges, develop capabilities and form partnerships to advance their ideas. They will have an opportunity to pitch their proposals to a judging panel at the end of the YLP on Thursday. Singapore's Ministry of Culture, Community and Youth will provide funding to develop the selected projects.

We face common challenges globally as we emerge from the pandemic. We must continue to create and build safe and open platforms to discuss sensitive issues and work together to strengthen unity and resilience in our societies. I hope that the ICCS can be such a platform for you.

I thank RSIS for organising this Conference. The importance of its work cannot be overstated, and it can go further. RSIS can play a role in strengthening the body of research, studies and programmes in the region and globally to promote social cohesion. It can pilot and act as an incubator for innovative ideas for such work and enable useful experiences to be shared broadly, especially through harnessing the drive, talent and creativity of our young. RSIS can continue to groom local researchers to expand on the studies to help us identify the emerging threats and opportunities to promote social cohesion, supporting RSIS' mission of understanding traditional and non-traditional security challenges.

In closing, I encourage everyone to use this opportunity to speak our minds respectfully and without prejudice, and to keep our hearts open to learning from one another. In this way, we can improve the quality of our conversations, relationships and practice in forging social cohesion.

This is a time to come together as a family, to recognise the beauty in our diversity and use that to our advantage in tackling greater challenges to come, so that we can build brighter and more cohesive societies for all.

I wish you a fruitful Conference. Thank you.

https://doi.org/10.1142/9789811285387_0002

Chapter 1.2

SPECIAL ADDRESS

Cardinal Pietro Parolin

Secretary of State, Holy See

6 September 2022

I cordially greet all the speakers and delegates participating in the International Conference on Cohesive Societies; I greet and thank the Singaporean Authorities, especially Madam President Halimah Yacob (2017–2023) and the Minister of Culture, Community and Youth, Mr Edwin Tong, for organising this conference.

It gives me great pleasure to speak to you today, since the global context in which we find ourselves necessitates even greater introspection and action on our part if we are to foster harmonious communities. In light of this, I believe that the International Conference on Cohesive Communities 2022 is a sign and a signal to not lose hope and to continue with a strong sense of responsibility to establish communities based on fraternity and justice.

Introduction

From the dignity, unity and equality of all persons derives first of all the principle of the common good to which every aspect of social life must be related if it is to attain its fullest meaning. According to its primary and broadly accepted sense, the common good indicates "the sum total of social conditions which allow people, either as groups or as individuals, to achieve their fulfilment more fully and more easily" (Compendium of the Social Doctrine of the Church, 164).

I would like to carry out my contribution on this definition of the common good according to the Social Doctrine of the Catholic Church, highlighting the relationship between society, the individual person, and the pursuit of the common good. So, what do we mean by "cohesive societies"?

Undoubtedly, many partial or complete answers may be offered, but education for the common good and a sense of "humanity" are the first steps towards constructing cohesive societies. We do, in fact, belong to humanity, and the duty to develop and progress towards the total fulfilment of what is truly "human" rests with everyone, both the individual and society.

This awareness cannot be achieved solely through ideas, discourses, or the theoretical presentation of horizons; rather, it is necessary to promote a specific human willingness to enter into relationships with others through social behaviour, that is, intentionally tending to do good to others in everyday life, personally and responsibly committing oneself without expecting anything in return, with the goal of realising the full dignity of each person created in the image of God.

Societies consist of the networks of relationships that people are able to build with one another, but such encounters are not based on algebra and mathematics, but rather on cooperation, since if individual goods are put together, it is logical that a total good will be produced, but a common good will never be acquired in this manner. The objective of cohesive societies, on the other hand, is the formation of individuals capable of relationships, of inhabiting societies, and of transcending the individualism of "I" to embrace the diversity of "us." Indeed, it is the connection with the other, particularly the relationship of love, that enables us to grasp our dignity. But, as Martin Buber said, relationships are not produced; they "happen" and come to us. When we are loved, our genuine worth is revealed, when we get a gift, our highest dignity is shown; and when we are forgiven, we become fully conscious of our value. When we obtain what we are entitled to, we become aware of the other, but not of our inherent dignity. This is something we learn when we are appreciated, when we get a free gift that benefits us. To put it another way, modern man has lost sight of the value of human life because he ascribes it to his own efforts rather than acknowledging that he is a mere recipient of it.

Within this context, the idea of social cohesion has been central to the study of sociology and other social sciences from the very beginning and refers to the set of constituent factors of the relationship between the individual and society, and in particular to the dimensions of belonging, trust, and cooperation between individuals, social groups, and institutions.

Opening up the area of social cohesiveness through interventions that recognise the benefits of enlarged cohesion seems to be a worthwhile objective. Another of the tasks that should not be forgotten in order to construct cohesive societies is working on the connection between the efficiency and efficacy of social programmes, the engagement of people in the administration of public affairs, and the inclusion of peripheral realities, again in both geographic and social dimensions.

This introductory reflection confronts us with a problem: our contemporary society is characterised by new forms of individual insecurity and community fragmentation as a result of social, cultural, demographic, and economic transformations; a problem that has intensified during the COVID-19 pandemic. How can we restore cohesion?

To address this subject, I will make an effort to provide some directional guidance from a Christian viewpoint that I believe may aid in the planning and establishment of cohesive societies.

Individualism – Relationship – Fraternity

In 1936, de Lubac, a French Jesuit, theologian, and Cardinal whose works were significant in the formulation of the doctrine of the Second Vatican Council, took a stance against the individualistic and, by extension, self-centred inclinations of his own day by stating: "Catholicism is essentially social in the most profound meaning of the term: not merely because of its applications in the realm of natural institutions, but first and foremost in itself, at the very core of its essence" (H. De Lubac, Cattolicismo Aspetti sociali del dogma, trad. it. a cura di Elio Guerriero, Jaca Book, 1978, p. XXIII).

From this perspective, the believer is never alone; to begin to believe is to emerge from isolation and into the community of God's children. In fact, the deepest foundation of this Christian "we" is the fact that God is also a "we". The God professed by the Christian Creed is not a solitary, self-contained being but a relationship, just as Pope Francis reminds us, "every day we are offered a new opportunity, a new stage. We should not expect everything from those who govern us; that would be childish. We enjoy a space of co-responsibility capable of initiating and generating new processes and transformations. We must be active participants in the rehabilitation and support of wounded societies. Today, we are faced with the great opportunity to express our being brothers, to be other good Samaritans who take upon themselves the pain of failures, instead of fomenting hatred and resentment [...]. The word "neighbour" in the culture of Jesus' time usually indicated those who were closest, neighbours. It was understood that help should be directed first of all to those who belong to one's own group, one's own race. Jesus completely reverses this approach: he does not call us to wonder who are those who are close to us, but rather to make us neighbours, nearer" (Fratelli tutti, nos. 77,80).

Today, we are confronted with a situation in which fraternity and solidarity are widely acknowledged as values, but there is a major crisis of solidarity in our societies: never before has solidarity been more topical, and never before has it been so inactual, in other words, penalised in real experience. Our society is paying less and less attention to the dynamics of solidarity: we are seeing an ever-expanding growth of dependency, which even aspires to become universal, but which is characterised, particularly at the cultural level, by inclinations towards closure.

The subject's withdrawal within itself corresponds to a withdrawal into daily existence as an eternal present: contemporary man feels less and less of the interaction with the past, interpreted as creative memory, and less and less of the prospect of future openness. The quickening of time makes yesterday's events appear so remote that they have little bearing on what we feel today. The future is feared rather than expected; as a result, there is a retreat into the present, which is the source of our society's and the youth's reluctance to set ambitious goals.

In a post-globalisation society, the objective is to begin addressing the challenge of coexistence among many cultures while being proud of each culture's achievements and without expecting everyone to become like ourselves. Philosopher and theologian Ramon Panikkar distinguished between dialectical discourse and dialogical discourse in his thinking. The first type is that of talk shows, in which participants fight passionately and attempt to convince one another in a dialogue that radicalises perspectives. Dialogical discourse, on the other hand, is a trip in which both parties are confident of their own ideas but seek a third point that is not in the centre but entails a road of change in both parties.

In light of this, what does it mean to construct and create a cohesive community in the present day? In the Christian viewpoint, which is the biblical one, we must state that solidarity, prior to becoming an ethical example, is a theological value: the Christian is invited to practice solidarity in the first place because he encounters a God who has revealed himself to him as a God of solidarity. As Pope Francis has taught us from his first Encyclical: "Today, when the networks and means of human communication have made unprecedented advances, we sense the challenge of finding and sharing a "mystique" of living together, of mingling and encounter, of embracing and supporting one another, of stepping into this flood tide which, while chaotic, can become a genuine experience of fraternity, a caravan of solidarity, a sacred pilgrimage. Greater possibilities for communication thus turn into greater possibilities for encounter and solidarity for everyone. If we were able to take this route, it would be so good, so soothing, so liberating and hope-filled! To go out of ourselves and to join others is healthy for us. To be self-enclosed is to taste the bitter poison of immanence, and humanity will be worse for every selfish choice we make" (Evangelii gaudium, n.87).

Defending such an essential good as social cohesion, as was evident during the pandemic, where many played a secondary role of civil protection and supplemented state intervention in supporting people who were not left alone, made us realise that a different arrangement of welfare and social cohesion systems is possible and can therefore evolve into a welfare community in which the state, other structures, and individual contributions can coexist in a subsidiarity relationship.

What other alternative do we have to the pervasive individualism that seems to exist in every society of today? For the sake of simplicity, we call this the third method, which is a vision in which the person is central; the person is understood in the round, thus in terms of discernment, relationships, and motivations, and with all the repercussions this has for how society and everyday life are conceived. I will now attempt to construct this third approach through four paths:

1. Discernment as a compass,
2. Together as agents of hope,
3. For a welcoming city and world,
4. The value of friendship.

Discernment as a Compass

In realising one's existence, man is not called to rely on vague generic prescriptions, to dive headfirst into ideologies, or to graze on hypothetical visions of the future in which there is much heart and little intelligence; rather, man is called to patiently seek his way in today, enlightened by the great truths, which do not absolve him from the responsible, strenuous, and sometimes difficult search.

In this view, discernment is first and foremost an attitude of vigilance, assuming a critical posture, and refining one's vision in order to separate good components from those that are just seemingly such or not at all, recognising clearly and precisely the real issues and potential remedies. This entails, among other things, emancipating oneself from relativist examples, which tend to minimise distinctions and see all alternatives, proposals, and values as technically similar.

This task of differentiation contributes to the reconstruction of the horizon within which one is obligated to decide and act, since only a comprehensive perspective enables one to identify the spaces accessible for responsible initiative and to assess the actual opportunities for practical engagement, while also safeguarding unrealised potential. The effective completion of such a process, particularly when it involves a broad reality, cannot be left to the activity of a person or a group, but requires the conscientious and proactive participation of all interested parties.

It is not enough, then, to make a choice; one must also decide, that is, be conscious that the authenticity of a decision implies a dramatic placing of oneself on the line, shifting from the position of a neutral and external observer to that of a person who involves himself and commits himself in first person alongside others.

Together as Agents of Hope

A strong focus on decision-making projects us into the future and calls attention to the obligation of all those involved in discernment to act intentionally for the common good. In essence, discernment enables us to look around and uncover, in the experiences and occurrences of the human community, those seeds, energies, and reconciling forces that are already clearly at work on many societal levels. This occurs even at those levels and in those realities, such as megacities, where so many negative and disintegrating forces seem to act.

Even though we are living in a confusing historical moment owing to the uncertain transition that is happening throughout the world, the objective is to capture the inherent potential of society and activate its positive energies so that they may be put to work in the service of a better city, in which the dignity of each individual is respected and protected.

Our period seems to be characterised by a gradual rise in frustration and despair. Consequently, it is society's duty to give people hope, not only for the future but also for the present.

Even we, men of the third millennium, are challenged by the biblical imperative: Remember! Do not forget man, your brother, just as God never forgets you; and Hear! listen to his cry of pain. In the biblical perspective, the children of memory and of listening will be the generous fathers of a future of peace and concord.

The tragic sights of war reminded us once again of how precarious man's path in history is and of how much horror we may be responsible for or complicit in. As a result, the ethical dilemma of evil has been re-posed with renewed urgency to the consciences of individuals and nations.

But in the common responsibility to build a cohesive society, man is not alone, just as Prophet Isaiah describes in perhaps the most intimate text in the entire Bible, "Zion said, 'The Lord has forsaken me, the Lord has forgotten me.' Does a woman forget her child so that she is not moved by the child of her bowels? Though these women forget, yet I will never forget thee" (Isaiah 49:14–15); or as witnessed by the beautiful page in Luke's Gospel about the Merciful Father, who waits for his own son to return, and when the Father, who is the image of God, arrives, he runs to meet him moved: everything in this parable is surprising and never had God been depicted to men with these features, showing God's tenderness for every man.

Let me recall the universal witness of the peace prayer convened by Pope John Paul II in Assisi in 1986 when voices were raised in deep accordance with Isaiah and the Gospel. The Buddhist sage Shantideva (8th century) prayed thus, "May all who are exhausted by cold find warmth, and all who are oppressed by heat find refreshment [...]. May all animals be free of the fear of being devoured by one another; may the hungry spirits be content; may the blind see and the deaf hear [...]. May the naked find clothing, the hungry find food, [...]. May all who are frightened no longer be afraid, and those who are chained find freedom [...] and may all men show friendship among themselves."

Not different were the accents of Hindu prayer, taken from the Upanishads, the ancient meditations on the Vedas: "We confirm our commitment to the building of justice and peace through the efforts of all world religions [...]. May Almighty God, the friend of all, be conducive to our peace. May the Divine Judge be the Giver of peace for us."

We are also well-versed in the rich theological and human connotations of the term "peace," as expressed in the Muslim (salam) and Jewish (shalom) traditions, which equate peace with the presence of God's kingdom and the obedience of faith (Islam) and use the desire for peace as a standard form of greeting among believers. These accents of faith and profound humanity, prevalent throughout the sacred texts of the world's faiths, might remind us of the "book of the peoples" mentioned in the Bible (cf. Psalm 87:6): a celestial book in which God himself writes, but whose pages also appear in the sacred texts of the world's peoples.

From this brief introduction to the many religious traditions, we may derive an additional lesson for the topic we will be discussing today: to develop a cohesive community, we must labour in the world without losing sight of the hope that only heaven can provide.

For a Welcoming City and World

In the 4th century, Saint Ambrose wrote: "The guest does not want wealth, but rather a gracious welcome. Not a lavish banquet, but ordinary food. It is better to provide friendship and generosity with beans than to slaughter calves in the stable with hostility" (AMBROGIO, Opere morali, Tutte le opere di Ambrogio, vol. XIII, p. 303).

I decided to quote this passage from the early periods of the Catholic Church's existence because it concretely demonstrates the conviviality of disparities at the table of society, where new guests unanticipated by our calculations or plans always appear and swarm in.

Even today, building community with the "different" is not an easy process. On the contrary, it is a sort of misery that is always before our eyes. It is challenging to bring together "diverse" individuals from different ethnicities, beliefs, and backgrounds. Living together, coexisting, and building communities that share everything from labour to welfare, from basic amenities to security, demands a heavy burden that, if accepted, provides the advantage of paving the way for civilisation.

It requires fortitude to see beyond one's own self-interest ghetto or one's own culture and religion, which, if not open to acceptance, would become an absurd Berlin "Wall" blocking all kinds of human growth, of every man who now, more than ever, considers the whole planet to be his home.

For this reason, establishing a cohesive society also requires a moral commitment that must be maintained by the concerted efforts of several people acting at different levels. Starting at the educational level, efforts should be made to instill values of openness, diversity, autonomy, morality, and finally, respect for differences, fraternity, and solidarity, which may subsequently be reflected in public discourse and cultural life. We must begin in a practical manner with brief relationships, regulating our emotions of distrust and rejection of the unfamiliar. We must watch over future generations so that they learn to be welcoming and eliminate the seeds of xenophobia that history and tradition have planted in their hearts.

In addressing the topic of hospitality, we must first approach the situation with a prophetic mindset, ready to see in the daily journey a providential opportunity, a call for a more fraternal and supporting society, and evidence of God's presence among mankind. We have to make the transition from a homogeneous to a multicultural society, with all its attendant challenges and opportunities. This means that politics should evolve into a platform for the collective human advancement, a terrain for growth in which all individuals provide their different inherent contributions. Saint Paul VI remarked in Octogesima adveniens (no. 48) that it is not enough to recall principles, affirm aspirations, point out glaring injustices, and utter prophetic denunciations; these words will have no real weight unless they are followed by a heightened sense of responsibility and practical action on the part of each individual.

The Value of Friendship

We are aware that a city is the product of several historical, economic, commercial, political, and even competing circumstances. In the end, however, it is always the outcome of an act of harmony and cooperation: a collection of individuals who choose to live and work together for shared aims and advantages. The fundamental value upon which a city stands is not primarily the goodwill of its citizens, despite the fact that the book of Proverbs correctly states, "By the blessing of righteous men a city is raised" (Ps. 11:11); nor is it the fundamental value of good governance, despite Sirach's admonition that "a city prospers through the wisdom of its leaders" (Sir. 10:3). In actuality, the classical world attributes the term "friendship" to a considerably more meaningful value. Already, Plato created an equivalency between friendship and harmony that contributes to the prosperity of the community.

Furthermore, Aristotle dares to say that "the highest point of justice seems to belong to the nature of friendship (Ethics to Nicomachus, VIII) by describing friendship as that good without which no one would choose to live, even if he possessed all other goods; he gives this good a political significance by stating that all communities are manifestly parts of that politics, and the particular species of friendship correspond to the particular species of community.

Initial expressions of friendship are directed towards the city as a whole, which is compared to a living person. In a 1954 speech in Geneva, the saintly mayor of Florence, Giorgio La Pira, said, "Cities […] have their own face, they have, so to speak, their own soul and their own destiny: they are not random piles of stone; they are mysterious dwellings of men and, in a certain sense, mysterious dwellings of God: Gloria Domini in te videbitur" (Giorgio La Pira Sindaco, vol. I, p. 383). La Pira grasps the relationship between person and city with such clarity that he asserts that the crisis of our time may be described as the detachment of the individual from the organic setting of the city: "Is it not true that the human being is rooted in the city as a tree is rooted in the soil?" That it is anchored in the key parts of the city, namely the temple for its connection with God and prayer life, the home for its family life, the workshop for its work life, the school for its intellectual life, and the hospital for its physical life?" Moreover, he emphasises that "just because of this vital and permanent relationship between the city and man, the city is, in a sense, the appropriate instrument for overcoming all the possible crises to which human history and civilisation have been subjected throughout the centuries" (Address to the Conference of Mayors of Capital Cities, October 5, 1955, vol. II, p. 108).

The commitment to build connections between individuals and groups beyond each person's natural affinities is a second aspect of friendship that helps us better grasp the mission of a cohesive society. Too often, the city looks like a collection of distinct bodies, a succession of layers that do not connect with one another. These layers are comprised of social categories, classes, professions, labour interests, political interests, and diverse ethnic and subethnic groups. Occasionally, one has the sensation that the city is too large to feel like a community. In order to bridge these gaps, friendships must be formed between people of diverse backgrounds, cultures, and languages.

There is a need to forge the kinds of connections that crystallise into warm embraces and friendships and which, if genuine and profound, may extend to individuals of other backgrounds. In this framework, it is the responsibility of the Church and all religious groups, in particular, to forge friendships that transcend natural affinities, thus contributing to the civic and moral sense of a community. A broader dedication then follows: the dedication to opening lines of connection between workplaces and academic institutions; places of suffering and places of leisure, cultural institutions, and everyday citizens; the socially excluded and the socially connected. Only a strong communication effort can provide a foundation for the many public and private projects that are designed to give the city a new look — the face of a unified society.

The third quality of friendship is the will to foster not just the circumstances for living well, in the sense of being comfortable, but also the conditions for working for good, in the sense of fostering the social and civic conditions essential to the growth of virtue.

In his essay titled "The City of Man," Giuseppe Lazzati explains why he prefers the phrase "creating the city of man" as a metaphor for politics. By doing so, he hoped to restore politics to its rightful place as the pinnacle of human activity within the natural order, in which each individual being – in his or her particular set of social and religious relations – functions as a subject artefact and end that composes itself harmoniously for the common good (La città dell'uomo. Costruire, da cristiani, la città dell'uomo a misura d'uomo, Roma, AVE, 1984, pp. 11–17).

This harmonious ideal may be traced back to Plato and Aristotle through Jesus' Sermon on the Mount, specifically the Beatitudes, from which he extracts the characteristics of a cohesive community:

"Blessed are the poor in spirit, for theirs is the kingdom of heaven. Blessed are those who mourn, for they will be comforted. Blessed are the meek, for they will inherit the Earth. Blessed are those who hunger and thirst for righteousness, for they will be filled. Blessed are the merciful, for they will be shown mercy. Blessed are the pure in heart, for they will see God. Blessed are the peacemaker, for they will be called children of God. Blessed are those who are persecuted because of righteousness, for theirs is the kingdom of heaven." (Matthew 5:3–10)

For this reason, Saint Paul VI wrote in Octogesima adveniens (no. 8): To build the city as the place of existence of men and their enlarged communities, to create new forms of contact and relations, to glimpse an original application of social justice, and to assume responsibility for this difficult future is a task in which Christians must engage. Even today, the Church desires to contribute as a friend of the city by becoming nothing less than the voice of the Gospel in it and for it.

Conclusion

As I conclude my presentation, I think that a cohesive society necessitates rewriting the "grammar" of leadership and care for others, taking into account the life, history, and circumstances of each person. In this context, Pope Francis reminds us that "Upholding the dignity of the person means instead acknowledging the value of human life, which is freely given to us and hence cannot be an object of trade or commerce. We are all called to a great mission which may at times seem an impossible one: to tend to the needs, the needs of individuals and peoples. To tend to those in need takes strength and tenderness, effort and generosity in the midst of a functionalistic and privatised mindset, which inexorably leads to a "throwaway culture". To care for individuals and peoples in need means protecting memory and hope; it means taking responsibility for the present, with its situations of utter marginalisation and anguish, and being capable of bestowing dignity upon it" (Pope Francis, Address to the European Parliament and the Council of Europe, 25 November 2014).

Pope Francis identifies compassion as the most effective way to address a sick person. Because an observer without compassion is unaffected by what he observes and moves on; whereas a compassionate heart is touched and engaged, stops, and cares. This is the legacy entrusted to us by Mother Teresa of Calcutta, who lived a life of proximity and sharing, recognising and respecting human dignity till the very end and making death more dignified. Mother Teresa often reminded her sisters that their lives were not in vain if they had kindled even one candle in someone's darkest hour (Address to participants at the CDF Plenary Assembly, January 30, 2020).

Before concluding and thanking the Singaporean Authorities and the ICCS organisations once again, I would like to highlight six points that I think will help make the concept of a cohesive society more concrete:

1. Everyone, without exception, is a promoter of solidarity.
   To construct a fair and cohesive society, the commitment of all parties is necessary (Pope Francis, Angelus of January 1, 2014).

2. Building solidarity with youth leadership.

    To construct a better society based on justice, fraternity, and solidarity, the leadership of young people is crucial: they must help solve issues with bravery, optimism, and unity. The world needs young people who are daring and fearless, who come to the streets and refuse to remain inactive. The young people of today and tomorrow are entitled to a peaceful global order based on the unity of the human family, respect, collaboration, solidarity, and compassion (Pope Francis, Message at the Conference on the Humanitarian Impact of Nuclear Weapons, December 7, 2014).

3. Solidarity is a commitment to creating inviting cities.

    The cities in which we reside will have an attractive appearance if they are rich in humanity; hospitable; inviting; if we are all attentive and kind to those in need; and if we are able to engage constructively and cooperatively for the benefit of everyone.

4. Solidarity is assuming responsibility for the other person's problems.

    Solidarity is the disposition that enables individuals to approach one another and to base their relationships on a sense of brotherhood that transcends differences and limits and compels them to pursue the common good together. Solidarity means assuming responsibility for each other's problems. The mandate of love is to be carried out not from thoughts or notions but from true meeting with the other, from recognising oneself day after day in the face of the other with his sufferings and heroism. One does not love abstractions or ideas, but rather people in the flesh: men and women, children, and the elderly; faces and names that fill the heart and move us to the gut (Pope Francis, Address to Participants in the Second World Meeting of People's Movements, July 9, 2015).

5. Solidarity is defined by closeness and generosity.

    Not only does solidarity include contributing to those in need, but it also involves taking care of one another. When we see in one another the face of a brother or sister, there can be no more division or exclusion (Pope Francis, Address at the Meeting with Civil Society, Quito-Ecuador, July 7, 2015).

6.   Solidarity is a way to create history.
     Solidarity entails overcoming the damaging consequences of selfish-
     ness in order to make way for the bravery of listening gestures. In this
     sense, solidarity is thus a means of creating history (Pope Francis,
     address to participants at the World Meeting of Popular Movements,
     October 28, 2014).

All of this illustrates that the great religious traditions of mankind are
capable of motivating the quest for and creation of peace and coherence
among people even now, and it seems to me that the persistent and far-
sighted dedication of the present Conference fits well within this dynamic.

An appropriate description of this dedication is found in John Paul II's
closing remarks at the 1986 historic prayer for peace in Assisi: "We
attempt to find in it a foreshadowing of what God would want the historical evolution of mankind to be: a brotherly journey in which we accom-
pany one another towards the ultimate goal he creates for us."

Thank you.

Chapter 1.3

IN CONVERSATION WITH DEPUTY PRIME MINISTER

Mr Lawrence Wong

Deputy Prime Minister and Minister of Finance of the Republic of Singapore

8 September 2022

Minister for Culture, Community and Youth, Mr Edwin Tong

Chairman, Council of Presidential Advisers, Mr Eddie Teo, Parliamentary Colleagues

Distinguished Guests and Excellencies

Ladies and Gentlemen

I'm very happy to join you here today for your last day of the conference and to see such a large crowd here. To all our overseas guests, a warm welcome! I hope you have had a very fruitful event so far, interacting with one another and learning new insights about how we can build more cohesive societies. This event could not have come at a better time, because about a week ago we relaxed our COVID-19 measures further — we have said that masks are optional now indoors. Optional means that you can still wear if you want to. It is interesting that, in this room, everyone has decided not to. It is okay if you choose to wear a mask for personal reasons, please do not feel uneasy. That is fine. Of course, if you choose not to wear a mask, that is okay too.

It's no mean feat to gather so many of us from all over the world here in one room. I'm sure we all treasure such physical gatherings more than ever, especially after what we have been through these last two and a half years.

We've all had our own experience navigating the last two and a half years of COVID-19. It has been a difficult journey, full of ups and downs. We have our share of setbacks everywhere around the world, but I believe it has taught us some valuable lessons. Beyond a public health crisis, the pandemic was also a test of social cohesion. It demanded the best of everyone in society. From government to healthcare workers, from essential workers to ordinary citizens, everyone had to come together and do their part. Key to that collective action was trust — trust in the medical authorities and in one's government to manage the crisis; trust in one another to do the right thing. Under the pressing strain of a pandemic, the true texture of society shone through. Whether people would mask up and get themselves vaccinated. Whether they would exercise personal and social responsibilities and whether they would rally together to support one another. All these revealed the strength of trust and social cohesion of our societies, and indeed it turned out to be a key factor why some countries fared better than others in dealing with the pandemic.

An Oxford study, for example, found that high-trust countries had lower COVID-19 death rates.[1] They looked at all the different factors, whether it was a country's healthcare system, or medical advice, but in the end none of these things were the defining factors that resulted in lower death rates. The key factor was the level of trust in a society. So having a strong foundation of trust matters, and it matters greatly. When a crisis hits, if trust is high, half the battle is won.

Across many countries we are fortunately now in a better situation than before where COVID-19 is concerned, but the challenges never end.

---

[1] Thomas Hale, Noam Angrist, Rafel Goldszmidt, Beatriz Kira, Anna Petherick, Toby Phillips, Samuel Webster, Emily Cameron-Blake, Laura Hallas, Saptarshi Majumdar, and Helen Tatlow. (2021). "A global panel database of pandemic policies (Oxford COVID-19 Government Response Tracker)." *Nature Human Behaviour*, https://doi.org/10.1038/s41562-021-01079-8.

Supply chain disruptions have led to the rising costs of food, fuel, and electricity, straining social cohesion in many places. Geopolitical tensions have made the world even more dangerous, troubled, and volatile. In such a backdrop, peace and stability in Asia can no longer be taken for granted. Each of our societies will be tested, perhaps severely in the coming years. Therefore, the question for all of us is this: How can we deepen the reservoir of trust in our societies, to strengthen social cohesion in our societies as we enter a more volatile world?

Naturally, every society has its own circumstances, its unique cultural and historical context. While we can learn from one another's experiences, it is up to each society to negotiate and balance the competing interests among its people. Let me today share very briefly a few of my own reflections from Singapore's vantage point today. I hope these may resonate with you in your various fields of work.

If I were to distil Singapore's approach, it would be this: That social cohesion does not come about by chance, but it is achieved only through a deliberate and consistent effort to understand one another, to accommodate one another, and to flourish together. Let me touch on these three points briefly.

First, social cohesion begins with all of us working together sincerely to understand one another. Because we naturally gravitate towards those who look or sound like us, and away from those who appear different. That is just human tendency. If we let these instincts take charge and get in the way of mutual understanding, social cohesion will be doomed. So we must actively seek to overcome these basic human tendencies.

This starts with something very fundamental — the idea of contact and interaction between people of different backgrounds. In Singapore, again we do not leave this by chance, we do this very deliberately.

For example, our public housing policy ensures that people of different races live in the same block, in the same neighbourhood, so they have opportunities to interact with each other in their daily lives. Their children will play together in the same playground, and they grow up together, fostering that sense of common identity.

Our national schools as well as National Service in Singapore (or compulsory military service for males) are the common formative experiences for all young Singaporeans, regardless of their backgrounds. Whether it is playing together, eating at the same hawker centres, or going to the same schools, these shared experiences help our people see that they have more in common than they might have first imagined.

At the same time, we put much effort into promoting dialogue among community, religious, and Government leaders. One way we do this is through the multi-racial and multi-religious Harmony Circles. This brings together local leaders and their communities. They visit one another's places of worship, learn about other communities' histories and cultures, and even participate in each other's religious and ethnic celebrations. Through such platforms, Singaporeans of different faiths and different races interact with one another, understand one another's perspectives — and hopefully establish friendship and trust with each other.

But engendering social contact alone is not enough, because in diverse societies, and many of ours are diverse societies, there are bound to be issues where we will not see eye to eye. There may even be deeply held positions stemming from fundamentally different world views. Often, these are strong convictions that we cannot easily set aside. The question then is how do we resolve these fundamental disagreements — how do we strike a balance and not allow different views to tear a society apart?

Across the world, we've seen many instances of such disagreements leading to division. In the absence of dialogue and compromise, the issues turn into zero-sum battles — if I win, you lose; there is no other way. Groups start pitting themselves one against another. The texture of society changes, to one of suspicion and antagonism. Under such strain, it becomes difficult to even tackle existential issues where we all have stakes in, like climate change.

Singapore's own history in resolving such differences was instructive because we had experienced violent racial riots in the sixties, and after that lesson, we resolved to go down a different path.

This leads me to my second point, that we have decided to resolve differences through negotiation and compromise by fostering a culture of accommodation.

How have we done this? Our guiding principle is to preserve maximum space for each community to lead their lives. You do not have to assimilate to any common standard. Every community is given space to lead their lives freely. It does not mean giving each group everything they want, but rather we strive to arrive at a balance of interests that everyone can accept and live with. It also means rejecting calls for maximum entitlements by any single group and avoiding attempts to construe every compromise as an injustice. This is not easy to do, but, over time, it has become ingrained in our collective mindset, and when people see that this is not only possible but also valuable and precious, it spurs them on to engage with one another, build consensus, find ways to compromise different views, and deepen social cohesion in the process.

This is of course a never-ending journey. It is always a work in progress because society's norms and views will continue to evolve, and so too must our policies, and the balance we strike in our society. So, we continually review and update our policies not through forceful top-down decisions, but through negotiation and compromise.

Finally, to foster social cohesion and trust, societies must allow everyone to flourish together. At the end of the day, individuals in a society must feel that they are part of the society, where they can: benefit from the nation's progress, forge dignified and fulfilling lives for themselves and their families; and see their children doing better than they did. In short, they must see an arc of progress in their society, and not feel eclipsed by it. That is why it is important that we pursue inclusive growth, where a rising tide does lift all boats, where prosperity is shared widely by all segments of society.

Again, it is easier said than done as we all know. Across many places around the world, we have seen inequality stretch out the gap between the haves and the have-nots. In the developed world, stagnant wages have led the middle class in many places to lose hope for a better life. When people find themselves excluded from the nation's progress, they grow resentful. They feel that the system is not fair, and that the system is stacked against them.

All this unhappiness and frustration become fertile ground for exclusionary and xenophobic politics, which only exacerbates social divides. No society is immune from these forces — certainly not Singapore. That is why we continually review our policies to see how we can pursue inclusive growth and continue to narrow our income gaps. And that is why we have embarked recently on an exercise to refresh and strengthen our social compact. To ensure that we can pursue robust and inclusive growth, with opportunities for every citizen, and to provide assurance to our people that they will be supported if they fall on hard times. That they will not be left to fend for themselves in a dangerous and volatile world.

We have called this exercise Forward Singapore because we hope to build consensus on the way forward and, in so doing, deepen our social cohesion. Crucially, we want everyone in Singapore to have a part to play in shaping this new social compact because building a better, more inclusive Singapore is not just the government's responsibility but also that of every community and every citizen. So, for the Singaporeans here, I hope you will actively contribute your ideas and efforts to this exercise, as an extension of the conversations you've been having these past few days, and as we urge society to come together, to hear from one another, and examine what each of us can contribute, and what trade-offs we would be prepared to accept, I am confident that we can strengthen our social compact to arrive at the future we all want as Singaporeans.

Meanwhile, to our international friends, we are sharing what we have done in Singapore; we hope it will be useful for you and will provide food for thought as you go back to your respective countries and think about how you might chart your own way forward to build more cohesive societies.

To conclude, each of us is involved in the project of social cohesion in different ways, in our respective communities and societies. It is not easy, and it can often seem like an uphill battle. Sometimes, it seems like you take three steps forward, only to then take another two steps back. But I hope as a community of practitioners and leaders, we will encourage one another, and we will press on in our shared labours because the work is never finished, and it must carry on. For if we do, if we deepen, tighten, and strengthen the societies we belong to, we will also do our part to make this world better, and perhaps a little brighter and that is certainly a project well worth our while to pursue.

Thank you very much.

Chapter 1.4

CLOSING ADDRESS

Mr Edwin Tong

Minister for Culture, Community and Youth and
Second Minister for Law of the Republic of Singapore

8 September 2022

Distinguished guests

Ladies and gentlemen

Good Afternoon

All too soon, we have now reached the last few hours of the International Conference on Cohesive Societies (ICCS) 2022, 2nd edition.

Lovely to see everyone, but time has just flown by, hasn't it? It seemed only a moment ago that we had President Halimah (2017–2023) open ICCS, standing right here.

I must say that not long after the first ICCS which we hosted in 2019, the COVID-19 pandemic unfortunately hit us, and we were not sure whether or when we could host the second one. But we were determined to find a place to hold the second one. And looking back on those days and seeing you all the past couple of days, we are so glad we did. Thank you very much to all of you.

This event has been a tremendous opportunity for us to rekindle old friendships and make many new ones. After all, building cohesive societies starts with you and I. All of us, each of us, building strong friendships, fostering a deep sense of camaraderie, and lasting ties, among all of us. And what we build here, we can bring back to our own countries. And that can grow exponentially.

On this note, my colleagues and I in Singapore are very glad to have all of your support in making ICCS 2022 a very successful one.

We are so honoured to host more than 50 speakers and 800 delegates from about 40 countries, including 120 youth leaders. As I was saying, we have also been joined by 300 online participants over the past three days.

I hope that this has been a fruitful conversation, fruitful Conference, but more importantly, your presence, each of your presences from so many different parts of the world, is a reflection of the strong, deep interest, in the topic and the collective, shared sense of responsibility that we all have. We all see this as our mission to build a culture of cohesion in our own societies.

This also tells us that while we might live in different societies, different parts of the world, in different continents, with our own different nuances, cultures, practices, traditions, each with our own sets of different circumstances and challenges. I think our shared commonality is that we are bound by responsibility to make cohesion happen in our own societies. And we all see value in listening to, and learning from one another.

Overview of ICCS

So let me thank all the speakers that we've had past couple of days for your thoughtful and thought-provoking speeches, and for sharing your experiences so richly and so generously. It left us with a lot to think about.

I also want to thank our moderators for facilitating the discussions, and all our delegates for actively participating and lending a lot of vibrancy and vibe to ICCS 2022.

I hope you all found it to be also a very practical-driven session. We were very careful to try and plan this so that it was not just about the theory, but about exposing you to practices and reality.

Indeed, social cohesion is not just a theory, it must be a culture of practice, of lived experiences, powered by active and engaged citizenry, with open, frank, respect for each other.

To this end, at this year's ICCS, we've had many rich discussions over the course of three special addresses, three plenary sessions, nine breakout sessions, and one community dialogue.

What stood out to me were the nine community explorations, where many of you had a chance to visit a place of worship, met our multi-racial and multi-religious community leaders, and gained first-hand, our experience of multicultural living in Singapore.

And I am very glad to hear that the Community Experience in particular has allowed many of the participants to experience for yourself and also ask questions about a different faith you've not had a chance to experience before. You got to probe, ask questions, understand, and know. Because it is only with understanding and knowing can we foster acceptance and eventually, embracement of each other's beliefs, and different practices.

In addition, I'm also very glad to see that the discussions were grounded on the extensive use of data, including the Southeast Asian Social Cohesion Radar that RSIS just launched. It is important that it gives us a good grounding and good reality check at what we're doing, continue to cultivate and to look at the different needles that mark fault lines. And we learn better how to address it.

I am heartened to know, from the many discussions we have had, the experience shared by so many of you thought leaders out there tells me that we face many common challenges in building cohesive societies.

Some of the difficulties, after we speak about it, are not quite so different. And even though we come from different parts of the world with different contexts, I'm glad to see that this has become a platform for us to exchange ideas that we can bring back to our own countries, our own societies and perhaps with a little bit of nuancing and contextualising, we can use them to good effect.

This is why it is important to continue to have a platform like ICCS. To learn from one another, share insights and experience, and work together to develop solutions to address our common challenges.

As our President (2017–2023) said in her opening address, we have to understand the drivers and dimensions of social cohesion more deeply, so that we can bridge divides and harness our diversity for a common good.

All of your enthusiasm enriched the deeply robust interactions we've had, frank exchanges with our moderators and our speakers, and reflects our shared purpose and our urgency.

As Professor Katherine Marshall said, we are in a "Kairos" moment in history where we should go beyond talking and towards actively building a better future for all.

Professor Lily Kong also emphasised why building social cohesion and resilience is today more important than ever.

And all of these theories and themes exemplified our Conference theme of "Confident Identities, Connected Communities".

So, as we close, I thought I'd share my reflections from this Conference on what we've learnt over the past three days.

It is not possible to capture the breadth of wisdom that we've heard in all the sessions, but let me try to encapsulate the key points.

One common thread across our discussions that I've seen in our dialogues and practice sessions about Faith, Identity and Cohesion has been that mutual trust and shared experiences are critical in building cohesive societies. They're a fundamental building block.

Faith can bridge divides. Some of the deepest chasms in society are a result of differing ideological or religious beliefs. And in recent times, perhaps driven by the COVID-19 pandemic, we've become more insular as a people.

Fault lines, often around the lines of identity, have been deepened. What we can do more to foster peace and harmony is to appreciate the commonalities, rather than the differences, across different faiths. Look at what binds us, rather than what divides us.

Dr Sadhvi Bhagawati Saraswati, Lord John Alderdice, Venerable You Guang, and Imam Uzair Akbar all spoke about how our different beliefs could connect us through universal values that bind society together.

It is often in crises and times of insecurity where differing beliefs can widen divides. Therefore, dialogues and occasions like this are all the more important for us to generate greater understanding, and foster a sense of respect among different communities.

And it is in such times, that our respective beliefs can indeed guide us to be the best version of ourselves in engaging with and being open to people from different backgrounds and different faiths, people who are totally different, look different, from each of us.

Our diversity can also increase our resilience in the face of divisive narratives and global challenges. For example, Master Tan Zhixia shared how a Singapore community organisation Humanity Matters brought people of different faiths together to provide local and regional pandemic and disaster relief, working side by side.

Such efforts don't just tell us how compassion can go a long way in bridging our differences, but also that the challenges we face as a society, as humanity, they don't cut across different colours and different creeds. Everyone is affected by the pandemic and how we respond to it as a unified front makes us much stronger.

Second, our diversity can in fact be often harnessed for the common good. And central to harnessing this diversity is mutual trust and respect.

As Mr André Azoulay said, we must treat each other with the same dignity and freedom that we enjoy ourselves. What we want for ourselves, we do to other people. A very simple principle but perhaps not often used enough.

I was particularly captivated by Professor Ashiwa's suggestion of "finding the otherness in yourself". This was particularly poignant to me. And I believe that if we can do that, we can begin reaching out to those we see as "other" and in turn, we'll have more authentic shared experiences and foster a deeper sense of mutual trust and respect.

In the same vein, we can also do more to harness the strength of our diversity through dialogue, education, shared goals and action.

For example, Dr Iyad Abumoghli spoke about how faith and non-faith actors can come together, work together on our sustainable development goals, such as food security and climate change. These, as I said, are all universal issues, they cut across boundaries, and they are not particular to any race or religion.

Here in Singapore, we try to find strength in diversity. And most of you know we are one of the most religiously diverse societies in the world.

We ourselves are a small nation that sits in the middle of ASEAN in Southeast Asia (itself the most religiously diverse region in the world with more than a thousand dialects and languages).

But this diversity is fundamental to the fundamental aspect of our respective identities. Each of us as Singaporeans must have our own space and freedom to practice our own customs, traditions, and beliefs so that this uniqueness remains and we value this uniqueness. We find ways to assimilate and not force anyone to conform with another, or even to conform with the majority.

There is space for everyone. We may be of different ethnicities, or different colour, or creed, but we are bound by a singular national identity as Singaporeans.

I believe this approach truly makes us stronger than the sum of our parts as Singaporeans.

Third, we spoke a lot about technology and how it can be used to lever and build mutual trust and a stronger sense of respect for one another.

Over the past three years with the COVID-19 pandemic, we have experienced the power of technology. After all, everyone knows what Zoom is, everyone knows what Skype is, though we're a little sick of it now, staring at our screens and at a small little box.

In the context of social cohesion, however, I must say that we've seen the best and possibly also the worst of technology.

Technology can bring people together across vast distances. President Halimah (2017–2023) spoke about a project that Basil was involved in, he set up something using virtual reality, allowing people to connect with one another and learn something different sitting in the comfort of your own home without having to travel. A lot of information can go across in a positive way.

But at the same time, technology can also widen divides, especially through the spread of misinformation and hate speech. We have seen the strife and tension that's been caused by such uncalled for and callous behaviour. Some were accidental but many were not; many of them were deliberate.

The question then is "what can we do?" We can't rewind the advancements that we've made in technology.

But I will say that technology itself is value-neutral: it is neither good nor bad. It is completely neutral in the sense that much depends on the user and how that user marshals the use of technology.

With mutual trust, we can use technology as a truly powerful and positive enabler for social change. And with the right approach, we can transform the digital space into a catalyst for building cohesive societies.

On that score, I agree with Dr Shashi Jayakumar on the potential dangers of social media, and also with Dr Patrice Brodeur and Mr Jasvir Singh that we should collectively tap into the power of digital platforms to strengthen outreach and understanding, thereby foster a greater sense of unity, trust, and respect between communities.

And in my view, with the quick advancement of technology, we must urgently take steps to move ahead of the curve, move faster than technology to mitigate technology's most adverse and hateful effects, and stamp out hate, violent extremism, and misinformation.

Our Young Leaders have discussed how they could use social media to promote the good to promote positive communities and counter negative portrayals of their respective faiths by bringing depth and authenticity to their social media content and interactions. We need to put this into practice and into motion.

Investing in Our Youth

Finally, on that note, let me speak about investing in our youths.

On this note, I really agree wholeheartedly with Cardinal Parolin, who spoke on the first day, that youth leadership is crucial in building a better society based on justice, fraternity, and solidarity.

And that is why we are investing heavily in our next generation of community leaders through efforts such as the Young Leaders Programme (YLP) here in ICCS.

I hope our young leaders out there (and those young at heart out here), have had an exciting and impactful programme over the last three days. You've all had opportunities to make new friendships from around the world, and I believe that these types of networking and building social relations are ever so critical in this fast-paced world.

And I bet our youth leaders have also picked up new skills through a Faith in Leadership workshop and were inspired by youth speakers to be fellow changemakers through community projects and social media. And our youth leaders also came together to develop projects.

I am also glad to see some of the YLP alumni from 2019, three years ago, have become invested in our outcomes here and are now coming back to give back to the programme. Some of them have been part of the design team while others have served as peer facilitators.

Some YLP alumni like Venerable You Guang and Farahnaz Ali Ghodsinia have also "graduated" (though you never fully graduate from this; you're always a part of this programme), but you return as speakers for the main conference. I think all of this, coming back, serving, and lending experiences, have been one highlight for me at this ICCS.

Going Beyond ICCS 2022

Finally, before I finish off with this speech, let me do a little bit of a look-ahead.

After we've had three good days of discussion, thought-provoking, deep, sustainable conversations, and building networks and making friends from across the globe, how do we keep this going? How do we build on this?

And I will say that we must leave today with the clear notion that ICCS does not end here. It does not end in ICCS 2022.

We want the conversations that we started here, and the relationships we have forged, to continue to grow and spur collective action, not just in Singapore, but also in the region and well beyond.

So let me offer what I think we can do to build on what we've discussed the past few days, to deepen the conversations and indeed, more importantly, like many of our speakers have said, how to put our ideas and suggestions into action.

Research stream – First, this year's regional survey is just a first step. Lots of research went into it, lots of data. The study creates an awareness of the factors that contribute towards social cohesion in Southeast Asia. These insights help us to more deeply understand the challenges faced by our respective communities. With this knowledge, we are much better equipped to seek meaningful solutions to strengthen cohesion. We should have this study continued and conducted regularly so that we can track how social cohesion trends evolve in the region, and our actions can then be powered by these data.

YLP–Second, let me talk to the YLP and the young leaders here. We will continue to support the young leaders in developing their projects and continue to build a strong community of young social cohesion champions.

The YLP, after this afternoon, will make a pitch of their projects this evening. After that, MCCY will provide funding and support for your respective ideas to be scaled up, implemented, and put into practice and used to foster a stronger sense of social cohesion in our communities.

We will also continue to build up our YLP alumni. The youthful thought leaders of today will become the experienced thought leaders of tomorrow. And we must continue to create a path for the alumni to pay it forward. Just as the 2019 alumni have done.

We will also support YLP projects, through our Harmony Fund, and perhaps also the Youth Action Challenge, to turn proposals, ideas, and aspirations into reality.

Virtual Partners' Showcase — Finally, the virtual Partners' Showcase will remain online as a resource for all of you. I hope that this will help build our collective knowledge and showcase the work so many of the organisations here are doing to support social cohesion-building. So, it becomes a repository of good ideas, of exchange of information and a place we can all turn to for resources.

Conclusion

As I conclude, on behalf of MCCY and RSIS, I would like to thank all of you, our speakers, our delegates, our youth leaders, everyone for your active participation over the last three days.

My colleagues and I really cherish this time spent with all of you and we hope to be able to keep in touch.

To all our overseas participants, in particular, I hope that you have enjoyed your stay in Singapore, that it was eye-opening, and that you had a chance to be exposed to some differences you have not seen in your own countries. And that you will bring back special memories, not just of Singapore but also of the networks and friendships you've made here in Singapore, and that we can continue to serve, because it starts with each of us here in this room. And if we can go back to our home countries and home societies to multiply that, that would be a great market for ICCS.

To our organising partners, I thank you for your support. It's not been an easy task to manage such a large conference in these times, but you pulled it off successfully.

I want to thank you for all the work we see and also the work we often don't see, often behind the scenes at very late hours of the evening as well.

I thank you for all this and to all our friends from overseas, I hope we've left you with some good memories to want to come back the next time we hold ICCS again.

Finally, I must say that the friendships we've made at this conference have been the highlights. To be able to see many of you, to chat with many of you, to build relationships have been the true highlights.

So on that note, as I leave, I will leave you with a video that captures the highlights of the last few days, you'll see many of you there, and I hope that this little memento will remind you of ICCS 2022, of the hospitality of Singapore and will remind you that even as you go back to your home countries that ICCS 2022 does not end here.

Till the next time, thank you very much.

Chapter 1.5

VISUALS

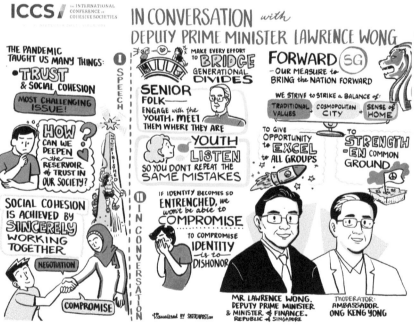

Part 2

ESSAYS AND SPECIAL PRESENTATIONS

https://doi.org/10.1142/9789811285387_0005

Chapter 2.1

THE NORMALITY OF UNCERTAINTY AND COMPLEXITY

Professor Farish A. Noor

The world that we live in today is in need of serious and sustained attempts for genuine and meaningful dialogues between communities. But it is also a world that seems to be set apart and one that appears to be teetering on the edge of crisis.

Past Optimism and Current Pessimism

That we live in a complex age of uncertainty is a fact that we are constantly reminded of today. A cursory look at the state of popular and social media would present us with a plethora of apocalyptic visions of the impending future, with images of a world torn apart by civil conflict and social strife, pandemics and nightmarish renditions of a near future populated by undead zombies, criminal networks, terrorists, and a host of other evils. The common lament that the world is on the brink of disaster and that humanity is about to meet its end is heard often enough. A historian might interject at this point and note that human beings the world over have been talking about the end of the world for as long as recorded history can recount, all the way back to the demise of the Roman Empire. And yet humanity stubbornly persists. This begs the question: Why is our vision of the world so bleak today and why is it so hard for many to live in this complex and uncertain world?

The historian with an abiding interest in political economy will note that our collective sense of optimism and pessimism can be positively dated and located at specific points in history. For those of us of the so-called 'boomer generation', there remains the memory of a better world where people believed in the idea of progress and who were persuaded by the idea that scientific innovation, capital development, and rational governance could bring us to greener pastures. One only has to compare the television programmes and movies of today with those that were made in the 1950s and 1960s: TV series such as *Star Trek* presented audiences the world over with a vision of a future guided by science and logic and where the idea of progress was intimately linked to the ideas of discovery and learning. It seems as if those who lived in the 1950s and 1960s believed that the world could be made into a better place, that the universe was benign, and that we were still capable of genuine discovery.

Fast-forward to the present and we can see that much of this optimism has waned. In today's world, the media presents us with an endless stream of apocalyptic stories about nuclear destruction, rampant diseases, zombie invasions, and so on. What has happened to us, and where has our collective self-confidence (and resilience) gone?

Perils of Unsustainable Development — 'Solo-Darity'

The historical factors that contributed to this decline in faith in the future and social resilience can be identified clearly by now. Decades of rampant capital-driven development have contributed to the destruction of the climate and global ecosystems, forcing humanity to confront the fact that development alone cannot solve all our problems or be sustained indefinitely without the enormous social-environmental cost that comes with it. Technological advances have given us a wired-up world with a communication infrastructure that now connects all of humanity, but it has also opened up new pathways for groupthink, ethno-nationalistic parochialism, hate speech, and disinformation as never before. Even the ordinary layman or laywoman can see that we cannot continue along this path of development or at least continue without paying the price sooner or later.

It is not surprising, therefore, to see how and why there seems to be a decline in human solidarity and societal resilience the world over. This is particularly true for the younger generation, who were born into a world where the optimism of the 1950s and 1960s has long since faded and passed away. The younger generation today was born into a world where terrorism, climate change, ecological collapse, social division, decline of living standards, etc. were household words bandied about at the dinner table. They were born into a world where wars, acts of terror, social collapse, and public anger were fed to them via the television or their smartphones as they sat for dinner every evening. Should we even wonder why so many among the young today have lost faith in political systems and social contracts and, by extension, in humanity itself?

What we are seeing today is the coming together of a range of variable factors — the relative weakness/withdrawal of the state, the rise of communitarian identity politics, and the dominance of 'me-first' possessive individualism valorised by a market system that sees human beings as either units of production or units of consumption — that has created an almost ideal setting for a politics of disenchantment and widespread pessimism. The grand narratives of the past — of enlightened modernity, of scientific progress, and of rational governance — have been eclipsed by a myriad of narrower narratives that target and prioritise the atomistic individual as the only unit that matters.

And yet, the individual today is weaker and more vulnerable than in the past. Bereft of a social system that nurtures and protects, and buffeted by incessant reminders to promote themselves, think of themselves, and value themselves above all, people today feel the need to be recognised for who they are but at the same time feel that their personal or collective identities are constantly being threatened. Against such a backdrop, it is hardly surprising that we see around us the rise of demagogic parties and organisations that appeal to the identity of their members, and that constantly harp on and on about 'external threats' to their well-being and very existence.

Embracing Complexity and Uncertainty

One observation that can be made about the state of popular politics today is how so many movements across the world — regardless of their ethnic, linguistic, and religious identities — seem to yearn for a world that is simple and easy. This search for simplicity is often linked to a sense of vulnerable identity that is brittle and easily challenged. This has now become the common critique of the so-called 'strawberry generation' that seems unable to deal with contingency, crisis, complexity, and difference, though it should be remembered that such insecurities are not generation-specific and that older people are just as susceptible to the appeal of narrow communitarian politics. One look at the language utilised by such exclusive communitarian movements would show that more often than not, complexity and uncertainty are seen as existential threats to be avoided at all costs. The ideal they seek points to the opposite: A search for a simple world where identities are also simplified and reductive, where social roles are never challenged, and where meanings are set in stone.

Yet once again, a historian may interject at this point and ask the obvious question: *When* has life ever been simple? Was there *ever* a time when human existence was not complex and uncertain?

Permit me to give a simple example to illustrate this point: As I type these words, I am conscious of the fact that I happen to be a Professor of History. Yet, at the back of my mind, I am also aware of the fact that I happen to be a husband, a son, a father, and a brother, all at the same time. It is not as if I need to mentally juggle and balance all these identities simultaneously, all the time, to the point of exhaustion and collapse. These differences exist within me, as they do with every other person on the planet, and they can co-exist with no difficulty whatsoever.

In the course of dealing with the crises of our times, we need to constantly bear in mind the fact that many of these crises were themselves engineered and manufactured to serve politically instrumental ends. Diversity and complexity — be it at the individual level or that of society — have never been a problem or threat *per se*. For complexity and uncertainty to be deemed threatening, there has to be human agency and human decisions that go into the process of crisis-making, and a deliberate effort to present complexity and uncertainty as problematic in the first place. We *never* encounter 'problems' as if they were stones on the pavement. Something has to be *deemed* a problem for it to become a problem.

Dialogue

Related to the broad theme of this conference, that is, how can societies deal with complexity in their midst and how can we forge genuine, meaningful dialogues between different faith communities in our complex world today, we ought to begin with the working premise that any attempt at dialogue has to start with an awareness of the complexity inherent in such attempts at meaningful communication. This entails the need to be aware of the fact that when we engage with the Other — be it a cultural, ethnic, linguistic, religious, or gendered Other — the Other we are talking to happens to be a complex thing. *Awareness of the complexity of the Other means also having to accept and appreciate the complexity within ourselves.*

Dialogue is always a complicated and uncertain venture. Indeed, it can only be a complicated and uncertain venture, for there is no way that we can literally get 'into the mind' of the Other to ensure that we are understood. Linguists in general understand this, for they know that miscommunication is the condition of possibility for communication to get off the ground in the first place and so are not so naive as to believe that there can ever be perfect, seamless, and unmediated communication at any time, all the time.

In practical terms, this means that as we engage in a dialogue, we also need to be aware of the pitfalls of groupthink, the echo chambers we may create and eventually inhabit, our propensity to judge and assume things about the Other, etc.

Meaningful dialogue, I would argue, only begins with genuine acceptance and the ability to recognise that in some instances, the total agreement will not be possible, and it is acceptable not to agree all the time. In other related practical terms, it also means that attempts at dialogue should not assume that identities (be it religious, ethnic, cultural or gender identities) are already predefined, fully constituted, and/or compartmentalised, like specific items found on a supermarket shelf. Religious, ethnic and gender identities are not readily constituted fixed identities that are frozen in time. In fact, they are organic and dynamic and they constantly evolve over time, according to contexts that change.

To be aware of how complexity and uncertainty are real, and how they have always accompanied the train of human development, is a step forward in the march to enhance and improve human understanding in the world today. It signals the willingness for us to embrace the cultural-ethnic-religious Other as an Other that is complex and sometimes even confusing and confounding. And despite this, to persevere in the face of such complexity also signals our willingness to think outside the box and to realise that our own identities are never fixed, reductive, and static.

If we can take this first step by embracing complexity and uncertainty as mere facts of life, as things that are in fact normal, and thus to be expected, we may be able to discard the tendency to over-protect our own identities and to assume the worst about the Other we dialogue with. It marks the moment when dialogue becomes human and humane — because human beings are naturally complex, rich, and also flawed — and it takes us beyond the simplistic format of 'us versus them' encounters, where the Other is often presented as the opposite of everything that we are and stand for.

Recognising the *normality* of complexity and uncertainty as facts of life brings us back to *this* real world, populated as it is by communities that are internally varied, complex, and dynamic. And though such a recognition of the normality of complexity may not be a miracle cure for all that ails the world today, it would at least take us away from the trap of narrow reductionism, exclusive groupthink, and communitarian identity politics that seems to be tearing the world apart all around us today.

Chapter 2.2

SOCIAL COHESION IN SINGAPORE: CONSIDERING MULTIPLICITIES AND THEIR MANAGEMENT

Professor Lily Kong

This chapter addresses the important topic of social cohesion in Singapore. It begins with recognising the conceptual range and complexity associated with the idea and then highlights the multiple factors and conditions in Singapore that give rise to potential or real fault lines which stand in the way of a cohesive society if not appropriately managed. While race and religion have traditionally constituted the official focus in the effort to build a socially cohesive society, this chapter broadens the discussion to other conditions that could potentially fracture Singapore society. The topic of social cohesion is particularly significant for the island city-state, which, like other societies, relies on a cohesive society for political stability, economic competitiveness, and growth but which, unlike other societies, is particularly vulnerable given its compact size, the coincidence of city with island with state, and its lack of hinterland and natural resources. Over the years, social cohesion has been carefully tended, led by political leaders, with contributions by community leaders, embedded in the efforts of educational and other public institutions. As global, regional, and local conditions evolve, these efforts will need to keep pace with changing circumstances in order to remain effective in fostering the social cohesion needed. These efforts require long-term investment, given that social cohesion is built over years.

Social Cohesion: A Multiplicitous Concept

Social cohesion is a multiplicitous concept. The academic literature is not short of discussions about what the concept means, and it is not uncommon to find discussions suggesting that, as a concept, it has been too vague, or too slippery, or that it encompasses too much.

In much of the literature, significant attention centres on the following ideas. Social cohesion entails an enduring sense of trust, a strong sense of community, a sense of shared loyalty, and a sense of solidarity. Some of these ideas have a long provenance. The concept of "solidarity", for example, goes back to sociologist Emile Durkheim who developed the distinction between mechanical solidarity and organic solidarity. Each of the other concepts, of trust, community, and so forth, has similarly deep theoretical roots and is laden with nuance and interpretation, but this is not a theoretical exegesis and I do not intend to go into a parsing of what these concepts mean. For current purposes, we can take it that a sense of social cohesion encompasses these various connotations.

Besides the range of conceptual ideas underpinning social cohesion, multiple frameworks also exist to give coherence to the analyses of the phenomenon. A study undertaken by the S. Rajaratnam School of International Studies on social cohesion in Southeast Asia based its entire approach on Bertelsmann Stiftung's Social Cohesion Framework. This framework identifies three dimensions of social cohesion: (1) social relations which underpin cohesion through a network of relationships — horizontal relationships between people and individuals, and between groups of different kinds, (2) connectedness that promotes cohesion through positive identification with the country, high level of confidence in the institutions, and a perception that social conditions are fair, and (3) a focus on the common good. I present this as but one example of a range of efforts at framing the study of social cohesion; it is by no means the only one.

Social Cohesion in This Historical Era

Is social cohesion more important now than in the past, and if so, why? When viewed through the lenses of a historian, social cohesion and fault lines in society have always characterised societies through the centuries. Yet, it is perhaps more important now than in the past because of the conditions that the world faces today. The historical moment is such that with globalisation, and increased mobility and migration, there are more fault lines that have emerged. And in the face of globalisation are pressures for de-globalisation, and so those forces are pressing on one another. The result is that we have more diverse societies because travel and movement and mobility are much more accessible and intensive today than in the past (COVID-19 notwithstanding, which hopefully is a blip in human history). The complexity of challenges is perhaps unprecedented, including the crisis of a generation: COVID-19 with the economic crises that have ensued, the geopolitical complexities, and so on. Thus, more than ever, there is a critical need to build social cohesion and the resilience that accompanies it. That resilience is so important because as societies confront the challenges that we all face today, we need to learn to cope with the stresses and of disturbances that arise from social, political, economic, and environmental challenges. Not only must we be able to cope with them, but it is also critically important to be able to recover from adversities without societies splintering.

Singapore is not immune to any of these forces at play. In fact, some might suggest that, as a small nation-state and city-state, Singapore is still somewhat more vulnerable than others might be. For a very long time, Singapore has focused its attention on race and religion as key fault lines. Indeed, the very focus of this conference is very much on religion, suggesting this continued sense of urgency around bringing religious groups together in a cohesive society. There is no question that addressing these fault lines remains of utmost importance: inter-religious relations are very important in the making of a cohesive society and, indeed, so too are intrareligious relations. But in "zooming in" on religion as a potential or real source of challenge to social cohesion, it is as important that we "zoom out" and remind ourselves that religion and race are in complex ways interweaved with other social conditions and social factors. Growing migration complicates the multiculturalism that was there already but is now still more variegated. Social class, economic class, and the attendant inequalities and inequities may intersect with race and religion in some societies and put further stressors on social cohesion. The bifurcations for those who are digitally savvy and live in a technological world, and those who do not, suggest that fractures to cohesion stem from bifurcations between the virtual and the physical worlds, and for those who dwell very much in a virtual world, divisions are present too. Further, as societies age, intergenerational relationships have an impact on the building of cohesive societies. Intergenerational inclusiveness, or the lack thereof, deserves attention too, as a potential source of societal fracture.

Considering Multiplicities and Their Management: Social Cohesion in Singapore

In the context of a city-state that is small, open to the world, and therefore vulnerable to myriad external influences, social cohesion has not been left to fate and chance. Significant effort has been put into building a socially cohesive society, and much of it has been state-led. The key instruments that have been induced include legal instruments, policy instruments, and regulatory instruments. In addition, a very important additional "tool" has been the use of discursive instruments: public suasion. Besides state-led efforts, there are also community-led efforts, and increasingly, this could become more important. In what follows, I will elaborate on each of the potential (or real) sources of social tension and how they threaten cohesion, as well as highlight key ways in which these multiplicities have been managed.

Singapore is not only a multiracial and multireligious society but also a secular state. For race, Singapore has long used a CMIO categorisation to characterise the population, inherited from colonial times: Chinese, Malay Indian, or Others. There is, however, increasing complexity and superdiversity. Thus, even within the Chinese population, there are new diversities. Whereas the Chinese population used to be characterised along dialect lines in colonial and early pre-independence years, such as Cantonese, Teochews, and Hokkiens, this has been somewhat moderated through the intentional use of Mandarin as the lingua franca. However, today, there are many Chinese migrants from elsewhere — clearly, from China and also Taiwan, and from within China, migrants from different regions have different cultural norms and mores. Thus, while these migrants may be Chinese ethnically, they have come from different contexts, backgrounds, and historical conditions and add layers of complexity and diversity, even within the Chinese population. The same is true for the Indian population, as well as other ethnicities and nationalities that are not reflected in Singapore's ethnic mix. The increasing superdiversity has led to new racial as well as religious pluralisms.

These new pluralisms have led to the contestation of pre-existing categories and drawn attention to how interest in inter-racial and inter-religious relations must be expanded to include greater understanding and management of intraracial and intrareligious diversities. As part of a research project on new religious pluralisms, Woods and Kong[1] have examined if religion is serving as a force for building a cohesive society through both intra and intergroup dynamics.

In managing inter-religious relations, a range of instruments are well in use. There are legal instruments like the Maintenance of Religious Harmony Act, clearly targeted at inter-religious and secular-religious relations. The Broadcast Act, which one may not ordinarily think of as impinging on or influencing inter-religious or inter-racial relations, is another instrument, with detailed codes of conduct, spelling out what is acceptable or not in the public domain through radio, television, and other traditional forms of media. These circumscribe what can or cannot be said, or how things can be said, in order not to cause offence. There are policy instruments: the ethnic housing policy is a key one where there is an attempt to ensure that different racial or ethnic groups are mixed together. There is public suasion: religion in public discourse, led by political leaders, is articulated as an agent of progress and development for the country, and as a promoter of communitarian values. These represent the myriad ways in which efforts are made to build a more

---

[1] https://www.asianscientist.com/2019/06/academia/smu-grant-religious-diversity-orlando-woods/.

cohesive society in Singapore based on inter-racial and inter-religious religious harmony.

Intraracial and intrareligious relations are much more taken for granted but are in fact much more subtle and complex. There are no state-led frameworks and guidelines to influence and shape intragroup relations in the same way that there are for inter-religious and inter-racial relations. However, the gap needs to be acknowledged and addressed. To cite one example of where attention is needed, in some religious institutions, the segregation is practised intentionally as a way to bring new groups into the religious institutions and the religion. The best way to have them — often migrant communities — feel comfortable is to keep them in communities that they are comfortable with, that is, with other migrants. Integration is not intentionally on the agenda: converting rather than converging is the primary focus.

Migration and the new social groups that it brings are evident in Singapore society in other ways beyond the religious context. Migration brings in about one-third of Singapore's resident population. One in three marriages registered in Singapore is cross-national and may also be cross-ethnic; one in five Singapore households depends on a live-in foreign domestic worker. There is clearly a highly diverse society and economy at all levels. At the same time, about six in every hundred Singaporeans reside abroad. These figures demonstrate the potential challenges to social cohesion: xenophobia can emerge, NIMBYISM (Not in my back yard-ism) and the "us" versus "them" mentality can arise, which may stem from perceptions of greater crowding, greater job competition, greater competition for opportunities like education, and the formation of enclaves: physical enclaves, residential enclaves, language, and cultural differences.

Singapore has sought to address some of these issues, not necessarily by addressing these relationships themselves but by addressing the larger societal, infrastructural, and economic conditions because when there are improved infrastructures and facilities, people feel that access to transport is easy; they do not feel crowded; when there is a vibrant economy with a healthy employment rate, and opportunities for Singaporeans exist in schools and jobs, then there is much less of a likelihood to feel like somebody else is taking away my rice bowl and my comfort.

The third area that can threaten social cohesion is inequality and inequity. Income inequality, wealth inequality, and reduced social mobility impact social cohesion when a stratum in society feels like they are constantly the 'have not', and no matter how hard they work, and how much they choose to do, they are unable to bridge that divide. And that has been exacerbated by the pandemic when the bottom 20% of households have experienced the steepest wage decline. So, an increasing stratification along class lines is something that we need to pay very careful attention to. In a study by the Institute of Policy Studies (IPS) in 2017, they suggested, from their empirical evidence, that the stratification along class lines might be more pronounced than along race and religion. To address these issues, it is important to create more diverse networks through schools, workplaces, national service, and common interest associations whether based on sports, arts, culture, heritage, or something else. All of these help build social capital, foster trust, strengthen social cohesion, and create opportunities for upward mobility.

The fourth challenge to social cohesion centres on the existence of the virtual alongside the physical. The digital divides between the seniors and the younger generations, between the poor with little or no access to digital technologies and those who are better endowed and better educated, create what we might call the "digital left-behinds". Even within the group that is digitally engaged, there could be digital tribes and echo chambers that reflect upon their own views and reinforce them all the time, shutting out/down other perspectives; this can be extremely divisive. Such "digital tribes" can get into their comfort zones and reduce common spaces. There is a great opportunity for that divide to sink in, but there is also a great opportunity for us to address that as a society because the digital penetration rate is extremely high. Fifty percent of Singaporeans use social media to expand their social networks: How can that be leveraged to create a digital common space for respectful dialogue, cultural understanding, and community support? How might virtual communities around common causes be developed? These may be organic, sometimes organised efforts from the community, and sometimes efforts led by government agencies.

A fifth and final disconnect could be intergenerational, and this can impact social cohesion. With an ageing population in Singapore, an increase in single-elder households and an increase in working adults working overseas (many of the six in one hundred Singaporeans who are overseas are working adults), intergenerational divisions can develop, and ageism can creep in as a societal attitude. So, a constant effort in promoting intergenerational interactions and an age-integrated society is important. Here again, there are different instruments in use: legal (Maintenance of Parents Act) and policy instruments that have been introduced over time (for example, public housing designs for three-generation living and public housing allocation priority when proximate to parents). These seek to build intergenerational relationships and support networks.

Concluding Remarks

For a long time, Singapore has paid careful attention to race and religion as fault lines that could have an impact on building a socially cohesive society. The complexity of Singapore society today is such that there are many more conditions and circumstances that impact social cohesion. The five areas that I briefly discussed above are complex in their own rights, but they are further complicated by the fact that they are not discrete but cross-cutting. They interweave and therefore make for much more complex conversations and management.

https://doi.org/10.1142/9789811285387_0007

Chapter 2.3

DIVERSITY AND COHESION: NAVIGATING CHALLENGES AND OPPORTUNITIES

Professor Katherine Marshall

The 2022 Polycrisis: Diverse Challenges

The multiple challenges that societies face in late 2022 are aptly termed a "polycrisis". They come from many directions and, like a ferocious, unpredictable storm, touch different places in different ways at different moments, but with an eerie global reach. And the different types of crises — economic, social, religious, political, ecological, and psychological — all seem far more interconnected today than ever before.

A central theme for the ICCS conference is to look to the lessons leaders are learning and, at this moment of extraordinary crisis, reflect on how they (and we) might change and act so that this time will mark a "Kairos moment," that is, a time that we can see now and in the future as a turning point, a pivot to action, and a moment of grace and opportunity. A Kairos moment could serve, as writer Arundhati Roy urged near the COVID-19 pandemic's start, as a portal forcing humans to imagine the world anew.[2] This pandemic, she argues, is "a gateway between one world and the next.

---

[2] Roy, Arundhati. (2020). "The Pandemic is a Portal." *Financial Times*, April 3, 2020. https://www.ft.com/content/10d8f5e8-74eb-11ea-95fe-fcd274e920ca.

We can choose to walk through it, dragging the carcasses of our prejudice and hatred, our avarice, our data banks and dead ideas, our dead rivers and smoky skies behind us." We hope, instead, that we can walk through the portal ready to imagine another world.

My comments focus on the challenges of diversity, intricately linked to the focal point of this ICCS: cohesive societies. Like the polycrisis, diversity can and should be a social and economic gift, but it demands great wisdom and care in management. Beyond the remarkable Singapore approach that Lily Kong has outlined in the previous presentation, global experience offers both sobering lessons, where diversity drives conflict and disarray, and inspirational examples of what can be achieved.

In this reflection, I focus on five interconnected topics: diversity as a distinctive feature of modern and modernising societies, distinctive features of religious diversity and its links to other forms, some positives and negatives of diversity from a political and communications perspective, the potential contrasting impact of gaps between ideal and actual, and continuing demands that diversity places on leadership, with some emerging lessons from recent global experience.

Diversity as a Facet and Face of Modernity

"The most certain prediction that we can make about almost any modern society is that it will be more diverse a generation from now than it is today."[3] (Robert Putnam)

Diversity is a central feature of contemporary societies, and its contemporary character and differences from earlier historical periods are worth exploring. There are obviously many different forms of diversity, but a distinctive feature of modern societies is their dynamism, propelled above all by rapid urbanisation and migratory flows (voluntary and involuntary), as well as social and economic change. Today, across nations and regions, "living together" differs markedly from the past. In much of the world over the centuries, most people lived not more than 10 kilometres

---

[3] Putnam, R. (2007). E pluribus unum: Diversity and community in the twenty-first century ... Available at: https://puttingourdifferencestowork.com/pdf/j.1467-9477.2007.00176%20 Putnam%20Diversity.pdf. (Accessed: December 14, 2022).

from where they were born. Most people were materially poor, poorly nourished, and faced a constant barrage of illnesses. Rural people were generally healthier than those living in cities but laboured long and lived short lives. But romanticised views of an idyllic past that are quite common obscure the cruel realities of life and the absence of choice. A feature of most traditional societies was that identities were generally given (religious affiliation and subject to others authority, for example), as were expected life trajectories (status in life and jobs). A gift of our times, something with an aura of miracle, is today's global goal of ending abject poverty but still more offering to each human being a range of options that were unimaginable for most in the past. These hopes are reflected in the sustainable development goals approved by member countries of the United Nations in 2015. In short, the multiple forms that modernity can take in the current era, for all the realities of suffering, pain, and uncertainties, are very different from the past. They are diverse and also full of possibilities.[4]

The context for contemporary diversity is both the close proximity of diverse communities and continual interaction and, in many situations, considerable fluidity in identities. For many people, identities are still acquired with birth and are quite immutable; religious affiliation, ethnicity, and nationality are examples. But for growing numbers of people, identities are dynamic, often subject to change, with multiple identities that often overlap. This contributes to the dynamic demographics and constant innovation that contribute to the characteristic diversity of many modern societies. And as Robert Putnam predicts, diversity is likely to increase.[5] Contributing factors include human migration propelled by a positive search for opportunities and less positive drivers like conflict and pressures linked to climate change.

In the past, social peace was seen as depending on social homogeneity, including religious practice. A response to diversity was and sometimes is to coerce conformity, on values and behaviours in particular. Today, diversity is more often seen as a social and economic asset, even

---

[4] https://www.globalgoals.org/.
[5] Putnam, Robert D., and David E. Campbell. (2010). *American Grace: How Religion Divides and Unites Us.* Simon and Schuster.

(as with the United States and Indonesia) a feature of national identity. Acceptance of diverse identities is fundamental to understandings of human rights. But there is an irony: many studies demonstrate that diversity is positive over the long term for society, economics, culture, etc. However, the social strains of diversity and associated dynamics can be testing and complex to manage in the here and now.

Where Does Religion Come in for Policy, Practice?

Religious affiliation is an important facet of diversity and one that is especially dynamic because, in many situations, it can change. With an estimated 84% of the world's population affiliated with a religious tradition, religious communities are characteristics of most communities worldwide.[6] Whereas in the past it was more common to see communities sharing a single often imposed religious tradition, today religious diversity is growing as a characteristic of most societies. This is linked to rapid urbanisation and, in many regions of the world, to the predominant mode of secular national approaches where religious freedom and tolerance are explicit national values, within a framework of diverse affiliations. It is somewhat puzzling, therefore, that religious identity tends to be less studied than, notably, ethnicity (though religious and ethnic affiliations often overlap or are intertwined). Class, caste, gender, and nationality are the subject of intensive study as to their interrelationships and contributions to social order and progress. Religious roles in diversity are less so.

Why? Religion can be a sensitive or uneasy subject, its role in societies coloured by historic conflicts and discrimination. There are especially complex issues that cut to the heart of family dynamics and openness to change. Where some religious communities are far wealthier than others, or far poorer, specific tensions may arise. Also important is the phenomenon of grinding resentments that persist, often below the surface, but can explode in moments of crisis into violence. The influx of refugees with different religious affiliations from national communities can be disruptive to societies, but there are other kinds of disruption. The large shift from Catholic Church dominance to charismatic Protestantism in parts of

---

[6] https://www.pewresearch.org/religion/2012/12/18/global-religious-landscape-exec/.

Latin America is an example. In some societies, specific tensions are associated with minority groups, some with ancient roots and some far more contemporary.

An interesting project led by the Institute of Development Studies at the University of Sussex (CREID) aims to reframe or refocus discussion about religion away from a focus on violations of religious freedom and specific harms to explore the issues in terms of inequalities, thus highlighting ways in which different features of religious affiliation affect social, economic, and political treatment within society, positive and negative.[7] While there are clear examples of distinctively unequal treatment that can be traced primarily to religious affiliation, more often an analysis of context highlights the diverse factors at work. That said, the roles that religious affiliations play in social harmony, conflict, and mobility have been a significant blind spot in much analysis of development.

The ideals behind the shared goal and human right of freedom of religion or belief are indeed equality of treatment among religious communities and those following specific practices. A more recent phenomenon linked to the growth of inter-religious approaches, from education through community and global action, is to highlight the benefits of religious diversity, how communities can benefit both from shared common values and from the rich differences that different traditions bring.[8] Inter-religious initiatives can take many different forms, spanning a range from theological and intellectual to eminently practical and from global (Religions for Peace,[9] for example) to very local and even to families.

Despite the commonly shared desire for peace and harmony, tensions in religiously diverse societies are not uncommon. They range from unequal treatment by states to societal prejudice and discrimination. Such tensions can result in violence and, at the very worst extreme, genocide. An effort to move towards and articulate a constructive framing and direction of such tensions and competition among communities is covenantal pluralism, an approach that looks to "loving competition", based on

---

[7] https://www.ids.ac.uk/programme-and-centre/creid/.

[8] https://berkleycenter.georgetown.edu/publications/interfaith-journeys-an-exploration-of-history-ideas-and-future-directions.

[9] https://www.rfp.org/.

knowledge of one's own and other religious traditions and a clear and informed mutual respect.[10]

The goal is to move beyond "tolerance", where communities coexist side by side with little interaction, to a more dynamic approach to religious diversity that seeks to benefit from it.

National and multilateral approaches to religious matters differ widely. One debate in various countries (the United States among them[11]) contrasts religious engagement and religious freedom as the central organising principle. The focus on religious freedom aims, often negatively, to address tensions and discrimination, thus violations of religious freedom, and, more positively, to highlight the benefits to society of religious freedom, seen to unleash dynamism and promote harmony. Religious engagement, in contrast, aims at a broader and more positive approach, starting with knowledge of the religious landscape and the multiple roles of religious communities in health, education, family dynamics, entrepreneurship attitudes, and land tenure, for example, and in promoting active dialogue and partnerships. Ideally, a combination of the two should be feasible.

Historic blindness or gaps in religious engagement by different organisations, national and multilateral, are less prominent today, and there is rising interest in understanding religious dynamics as they apply to different sectors of activity. The focus on religious roles in health but also social safety nets and addressing cases of discrimination during the COVID-19 pandemic is an example, though too often the attention has been sporadic and short-lived. For some, different manifestations of religious beliefs and practices remain an elephant in the room, discussed in broad generalities or deliberately ignored until tensions or conflicts flare up. In today's diverse societies, the elephant needs to be named, studied, and engaged.

---

[10] https://www.fpri.org/article/2018/11/the-call-of-covenantal-pluralism-defeating-religious-nationalism-with-faithful-patriotism/.

Seiple, Chris. (2018). "The Call of Covenantal Pluralism: Defeating Religious Nationalism with Faithful Patriotism". https://www.fpri.org/article/2018/11/the-call-of-covenantal-pluralism-defeating-religious-nationalism-with-faithful-patriotism/.

[11] https://www.usip.org/publications/2021/11/advancing-global-peace-and-security-through-religious-engagement-lessons.

Religious affiliations are a complex and intertwined part of social, economic, and, yes, political diversity and need to be taken into account.

Ironies: Long-Term Benefits versus Short-Term Challenges

Diversity can and should be a blessing: the "spice of life". The critical role of biodiversity is well understood, and those passionate about the arts also appreciate the beauties of difference. Competition is often a spur to excellence. Research and lived experience attest to the benefits of diversity for creativity and innovation in human society, as well as for maintaining different forms of social balance. But these are benefits that are most readily appreciated in the long term. Especially when there are significant changes (as when new communities enter), religious as well as ethnic, the disruptions involved can result in or aggravate tensions. In the long run, immigration and shifts towards more diverse and dynamic societies are likely to have important cultural, economic, fiscal, and developmental benefits. In the short run, however, immigration and ethnic diversity can reduce social solidarity and social capital because of friction among groups and especially inequalities, real or perceived.[12] A further irony is that the impact may be felt very differently by different groups; diaspora communities, for example, may gain strength through their distinctive community identities even as other groups perceive the difference as undermining their core sense of community and identity. This points to the need for open-eyed and purposeful approaches to religious diversity.

---

[12] J. Dinesen, Peter Thisted, Merlin Schaeffer, and Kim Mannemar Sønderskov. (2020). "Ethnic diversity and social trust: A narrative and meta-analytical review," *Annual Review of Political Science* 23: 441–465. https://www.hoplofobia.info/wp-content/uploads/2022/05/2020-Ethnic-Diversity-and-Social-Trust-A-Narrative-and-Meta-Analytical-Review.pdf; Kirk, Tom, Danielle Stein, and Annette Fisher. (2018). *The Relationship between Ethnic Diversity & Development: A Diversity Dividend?* London: Konung International, May, pp. 1–3, 41–54. https://assets.publishing.service.gov.uk/media/5b507c88e5274a73380f7b3e/The_Relationship_between_Ethnic_Diversity___Development-_A_Diversity_Dividend_Kirk__Stein___Fisher_21.6.18.pdf.

Religious diversity in modern societies takes many different forms. In some homogenous societies, the arrival of refugee communities can be welcomed or can be met with hostility. The growing roles of "nones" (groups with no specific religious affiliation) can present new obstacles for practising religious communities if either group is perceived to challenge emerging or shifting social norms. Some situations are easier to manage than others: economic and social inequalities, for example, can put pressure on welfare and education systems, especially if there are large population shifts. Crisis situations can bring different communities together if they perceive a common interest or, conversely, it can tear them apart.

The dynamics of diversity call for leadership in different sectors of society at various levels (transnational, national, and local). Leaders in different sectors play important roles in shaping narratives that include the roles that different communities play in a nation or a city, for example. Responses to incidents, positive or negative, can play outsize roles in shaping perceptions and understandings of relationships among different communities. There are many examples of religious leaders standing together after violent incidents as a visible symbol of their shared commitment to peace. Certain responses can shape perceptions that one community gains at another's expense, while others can underscore the benefits to the whole. A striking example is the positive roles that city leaders can play. In contrast, the challenges of situations where religious nationalism is a rising force present large challenges, casting some communities as minorities or, worse, outsiders who do not belong to or in society.

Building consensus around accepting diversity and equality is tough but feasible. Narratives about marginalisation are tactically useful up to a point, but hopefulness and a conscious celebration of the virtues of diversity can be a powerful motivator.

Ideals and Actual Practice

A common pitfall applies, with particular force, to the challenges of diversity, when ideal and actual practice diverge. Diversity is a common ideal, even, as in the United States, presented as a central feature of national identity. There, it is part of civic education, speeches, heartening stories, films, and patriotic songs. But wide gaps often separate the ideal, including how people think their society should be, how it actually is, and what takes place on the ground. The gaps here can be significant if they obscure tensions that are acknowledged only reluctantly. In the United States, the deep fears articulated as "the Great Replacement" and the realities of day-to-day racism and persistent anti-Semitism and Islamophobia are searing examples both of how far the ideal is from lived reality and also how fragile is its grip. There are important lessons here for all societies.[13]

What is the message as we look at cohesive societies? Diversity demands dynamic, constant attention, and effort. While some nations and societies adjust readily to changing patterns and religious dynamics, experience shows that rapid changes can happen, with resulting tensions and violence. Lingering tensions in societies that pride themselves as tolerant and open can erupt unexpectedly and upend social peace.[14] The COVID-19 pandemic has highlighted the fragility of some intergroup relationships and the propensity for people and communities to fasten to a hostile vision of a specific community as they search for explanations or someone to blame for ills.[15] There are far too many examples here, but they include religious and ethnic groups: anti-Asian prejudice, rising anti-Semitism, islamophobia, blame directed at Christians or specific denominations, and generalised xenophobia have appeared in many societies.

Trust is the most critical factor here, and as we know all too well, it can only be built over time and with performance, but it is all too easily eroded or destroyed.

Leaders at all levels need to focus on the practical aspects of bridging and bonding capital.[16] Bridging capital works to establish and enrich

---

[13] https://www.adl.org/resources/backgrounders/the-great-replacement-an-explainer?gclid=Cj0KCQjwhsmaBhCvARIsAIbEbH4hWRmLnc8z418CcrwXqZUz9FEjncCVsa1LzTXCK_7Eh0Axv_lhuU4aAtg5EALw_wcB.

[14] Mandaville, Peter and Chris Seiple. (2021). *Advancing Global Peace and Security through Religious Engagement: Lessons to Improve U.S. Policy.* https://www.usip.org/publications/2021/11/advancing-global-peace-and-security-through-religious-engagement-lessons.

[15] Tropp, Linda R., and Ludwin E. Molina, "Intergroup Processes: From Prejudice to Positive Relations Between Groups." University of Kansas.

[16] https://www.wzb.eu/system/files/docs/sine/nvsq_36_1.pdf.

relationships among communities. And bonding capital is about building trust within and among them. Most important of all are well-functioning government institutions that earn the trust of citizens and establish skills and capacity in responding to changing circumstances.

Promising Areas for Action

I began by posing the challenge of looking to this time of crisis as a Kairos moment, where we would see vision, action, and renewal, worthy of the emergence from the global trauma and disruptions of the COVID-19 pandemic. A part of the demands involved is the ICCS's focus on cohesive societies. How can modern and changing societies better act to benefit from the rich diversity and dynamism of modern times? Religious diversity is a critical but also deeply intertwined part of broader social, economic, and political diversity, a complex mix of practical community, deeply held beliefs, and attention to spiritual needs and gifts. It cannot and should not be taken or seen in isolation but as an inseparable part of the whole. But, given the long history of different approaches and special sensitivities around religious engagement, a common response to a call for action is as follows: "What am I supposed to do with that insight?"

The first logical step is to look for promising examples of positive management of diversity. Here, the Singapore example offers impressive approaches, and there are others, some national (for example, welcoming refugees in constructive ways) and others more local. A critical area where there are numerous scattered examples is education, where building diversity into national curricula as well as specific programmes is an effective starting point. Inter-religious work in different settings can set a broad climate celebrating diversity and, like the Document in Human Fraternity for World Peace and Living Together, signed in February 2019 by Pope Francis and the Sheikh of Al-Azhar to symbolise the shared approach and commitment of the leaders of the world's two largest religious communities, with a long history of enmity and mutual suspicion.[17]

---

[17] *The Document on Human Fraternity on World Peace and Living Together*. (2019). https://www.vatican.va/content/francesco/en/travels/2019/outside/documents/papa-francesco_20190204_documento-fratellanza-umana.html.

Religious engagement as a central part of efforts to build social cohesion is rarely simple or easy and many complexities and uncertainties are involved. An illustration is an attitude not far off schizophrenia where conflict and religion are concerned. When and how are religious factors involved? Looking at the same conflict, some will argue that religion is entirely responsible, while another wise voice may assert that the sole cause is political manipulation. For some, religious differences are deep and non-negotiable and lead to intractable conflicts that have littered the pages of history. Others see primarily political manipulation, acting on grievances or a simple quest for power. And the realities are always complex, with multiple factors and identities involved in any conflict, religiously fueled or not. A simplistic but vital counsel is to focus on context, as it always matters.

Looking ahead and hoping for the inspiration and leadership needed to see a Kairos moment take form, actions on promising and central topics need to be identified, set in the broad context of today's polycrisis, but not neglecting, as happens so often, the positive religious dimensions. These include education and social protection (which focuses on the most vulnerable) and addressing wide inequalities. Other promising areas are media, arts, and sports. Actions here can inspire and look beyond material gain to areas that can bring joy as well as unity. Leaders need to combine the essential need for data and knowledge with the capacity to move beyond data to a story and an appeal to the heart. Framing objectives in terms of common values, including human rights, compassion, and empathy, can help, point to and celebrate differences. The goal is to focus on creating and nurturing belief in different forms of diversity, and tools to advance it, as a pillar of social, cultural, economic, intellectual, and political cohesion in the dynamic, varied, and too polarised societies of today.

Chapter 2.4

VISUAL

Part 3

HOW FAITH CAN BRIDGE DIVIDES

Chapter 3.1

RECONSTRUCTING THE QUESTION TO IDENTIFY THE CALL OF ACTION

Ms Nazhath Faheema

How can faith bridge divides? This question typically comes from an old-age notion that religions can collectively create a world order because they direct a way of life for humans. Yet, it would be an injustice to explore this question without reflecting on what the terms 'faith' or 'religion' mean. Understanding these elusive concepts is critical before examining their power to affect society. How can we determine the ability of faith or religion to affect society without acknowledgement or agreement on the meaning? Therefore, defining this idea seems to be the logical first step in addressing the topic.

However, drawing a standard definition for this term is nearly impossible. Faith is a term that is often interchangeably used with religion and belief. Though the World Religion Paradigm offers some framework to define a category and dominates how religion is studied, it is criticised by many scholars.[1] There is no consensus within academic scholarship for a

---

[1] Christopher R. Cotter and David G. Robertson, "Introduction: The World Religions Paradigm in Contemporary Religious Studies", in *After World Religions: Reconstructing Religious Studies*, ed. Christopher R. Cotter; David G. Robertson (London: Routledge, 2016), 1–20.

definition of religion.[2] Any attempts to academically explain and theoretically explore these terminologies will not be sufficient, as the identities, experiences, and emotions associated with them will always be unique to each individual and community. Therefore, the fundamental understanding has to be that it is problematic to have a premise that faith or religion is a singular and homogenous idea.

Now that we have settled the conundrum over the definitions of faith and religion, we can dive deeper into understanding the effect religion has on society. A religious ideology, good or bad, cannot act on its own by its very virtual existence in a society of varied beliefs. It requires an active agent through which it needs to be conducted before it can cause any effect. For example, secularism as a political ideology, operates on the premise that religion and state must be separated. However, this idea does not come into effect until these are put into practice through policies and the behaviour of politicians. At the same time, different governments can also practice secularism differently. Along these lines, it can be argued that faith or religion cannot cause or solve problems in the real world. It must be integrated into a set of actions that may have impact on society.

What, then, is the purpose of this chapter? It is not to explore, theoretically, if faith can unite people. Instead, it is to identify a faith-based call to action to develop and maintain peaceful coexistence. If so, the question initially posed about how faiths can bridge divides needs to be clarified and reconstructed into a practical query that will facilitate a more beneficial discussion. Perhaps, asking how leaders and followers of different faiths can bridge divides in plural societies like religiously diverse Singapore is more valuable. Such a topic enables a focused examination of what people with varied and sometimes conflicting beliefs can do to prevent and repair polarisation that may lead to hostility and threatening social cohesion. Moreover, this question identifies a collective duty among specific groups of actors. These are the essential factors when we seek to prevent and resolve damaging segregation within a multicultural country.

---

[2] Arthur L. Greil, "Art: Defining religion." in *The World's Religions*, eds. Clarke, Peter B. & Peter Beyer (London: Routledge, 2009, 135–149 quoted in Michael Bergunder. "What Is Religion?: The Unexplained Subject Matter of Religious Studies," *Method & Theory in the Study of Religion* 26, no. 3 (2014): 246–286.

The above discussion highlights two key points. First, it surfaces the challenge of diversity in comprehending and experiencing the idea of faith which is the central problem of societal divides when it concerns religions. Second, it proposes that when seeking a solution for peacekeeping, it is crucial to construct a straightforward question that identifies actors and actions. Reflection on these observations, this article will deliberate on the following:

(a) factors related to faith or religion that may lead to the development of social polarisation in countries like Singapore,
(b) the role of local religious leaders in reducing and removing communal divides,
(c) interfaith dialogues that facilitate a cohesive community of diverse beliefs

Identifying Faith-based Problems Contributing to Social Polarisation

In countries like Singapore, where people of different beliefs co-exist together, religious exclusivism and faith-based extremism can and do cause social polarisation. The first refers to the mindset of a person who believes their religion is the only true truth while all other religions are false. The latter arises from political motives based on extreme religious dogma. Therefore, the awareness of how these two phenomena manifest in multireligious societies is critical to identifying, preventing, and countering divides among the citizens and residents.

Behaviours of religious exclusivism in Singapore can be classified into three categories: "those involving religious leaders, those involving foreign preachers, and those involving lay persons."[3] Religious exclusivism

---

[3] Lily Kong, Orlando Woods, and Acmal Zuheyr Idefan bin Abdul Wahid, "Countering Exclusivism, Promoting Inclusivism: The Way Forward for Singapore ," Interreligious Relations (IRR), no. 19 (August 4, 2020), https://www.rsis.edu.sg/rsis-publication/srp/interreligious-relations-irr-issue-19-countering-exclusivism-promoting-inclusivism-the-way-forward-for-singapore-by-lily-kong-orlando-woods-and-acmal-zuheyr-idefan-bin-abdul-wahid/#.Y8PgQOxBwqu, 4.

cannot be construed as a negative behaviour. It can and should be regarded as a choice of belief. However, religious exclusivism that may induce religious intolerance and segregationist mentality is problematic. There are notable cases of such religious exclusivist behaviours that have raised national-level discussions. An article by Dr Lily Kong, Dr Orlando Woods and Acmal Zuheyr amply discusses these.[4] The first category includes religious leaders in Singapore making negative or mocking remarks towards members of other religions. The second category concerns foreign preaches whose teachings would influence divisive and intolerant mindsets. The third category, similar to the first, refers to the general public or 'lay persons' who engage other religions in an insensitive way through words or actions. The common characteristics of these types of religious exclusivism are prejudice and disrespect towards another faith.

Two examples concerning religious leaders are worth further discussion. In 2010, the Internal Security Department investigated Pastor Rony Tan from Lighthouse Evangelism for remarks about Buddhist and Taoist beliefs that were considered offensive.[5] He apologised, and the material concerned was taken down. The case of Pastor Mark Ng from New Creation Church in the same year was similar. Pastor Ng ridiculed the Taoist beliefs. He, too, made a public apology to the Taoist community. This ridiculing of other faiths stems from the misconstrued thought that one belief is more sacred than another.

The other example is Imam Nalla Mohamed Abdul Jameel Abdul Malik from Jamae Chulia Mosque, who was investigated in 2017.[6] Imam Nalla had recited a verse that was perceived as promoting the idea that Muslims must be saved from Christians and Jews. He was fined and repatriated to India. Unlike the earlier example, this was not a case of disregarding equality in another religion. Instead, it shows the faith-based hostility between different religious groups. It was clarified that this verse

---

[4] *Ibid.*

[5] "Singapore Denounces Pastor for Ridiculing Buddhists," *Reuters*, February 9, 2010, https://www.reuters.com/article/idINIndia-46014320100206.

[6] Hermes Auto, "Imam Who Made Offensive Remarks about Jews and Christians Will Be Asked to Leave Singapore," *The Straits Times* (Singapore Press Holdings, April 3, 2017), https://www.straitstimes.com/singapore/imam-who-made-offensive-remarks-against-christians-and-jews-charged-in-court.

was not from Quran and that Imam Nalla had cited it from material from India. However, it may be the case that the content question was inspired from verses in *Quran* such as: "And never will the Jews and the Christians approve of you until you follow their religion. Say, 'Indeed, the guidance of Allāh is the [only] guidance.' If you were to follow their desires after what has come to you of knowledge, you would have against Allāh no protector or helper".[7] Of course, these and many other verses in the Islamic holy text and traditions are contextual. However, there can be no denying that these have been exploited to spread inaccurate beliefs.

The above-discussed cases are particularly concerning to our topic because they involve locally based religious leaders with access to large congregations of followers. They highlight the production, consumption, and spread of material that promotes prejudicial and hostile sentiments towards other religions. A young person listening to a pastor, imam, or monk who makes fun of another religion will think it is okay to speak like that and that he, too, should pursue similar narratives. Since religious leaders are held in high regard among their followers, they have the power to influence. This creates the inflammatory nature of religious leaders' speeches, which can build negative prejudice among diverse religions. Their beliefs and positions spread widely and deeply into the religious community. Over the years, such occurrences have been observed in different parts of the world. This probably explains the amendments to the Maintenance of Religious Harmony Act in Singapore, which provide stronger regulations on religious leaders compared to ordinary people.[8]

While a regulatory framework can somewhat prevent religious leaders from making inconsiderable comments that will rock social harmony in Singapore, it does not solve the problem. The fact that the above-mentioned incidents happen regardless of a strongly governed religious diversity highlights a challenge. The source of these problems is the lack

---

[7] Quran, verse 2:120 (English translation).

[8] "Second Reading of the Maintenance of Religious Harmony Amendment Bill 2019 — Wrap-up Speech by Mr K Shanmugam, Minister for Home Affairs and Minister for Law," Ministry of Home Affairs, October 7, 2019, https://www.mha.gov.sg/mediaroom/parliamentary/second-reading-of-the-maintenance-of-religious-harmony-amendment-bill-2019---wrap-up-speech-by-mr-k-shanmugam-minister-for-home-affairs-and-minister-for-law/.

of appreciation of religious diversity, the othering of people whose beliefs are different, and the non-acceptance of them as equally faithful. When religious leaders carry such worldviews, it breeds a community that develops an "us vs them" mindset. This is just one part of the problem.

The other problem raised earlier is faith-based extremism, which is becoming concerning. In this regard, two recent cases of youth radicalisation need to be examined. The first is a 16-year-old Singaporean boy detained in December 2020 for plotting attacks on two local mosques. According to the report, this teenager was "self-radicalised, motivated by a strong antipathy towards Islam".[9] He came to believe the terrorist group Islamic State in Iraq and Syria (ISIS) represented Islam and that "Islam called on its followers to kill non-believers," such as Christians.[10] This youth, a Protestant Christian of Indian ethnicity,[11] was inspired by Brenton Tarrant, a right-wing terrorist who mass murdered Muslim worshippers in a mosque in Christchurch, New Zealand, in August 2019. This was Singapore's first case of violent right-wing extremism.

The second similar case involves a 20-year-old Muslim youth detained in February 2021 for planning an attack on Jewish people after their Saturday prayers at the Maghain Aboth Synagogue in Waterloo Street.[12] Amirull was "enraged by the Israel-Palestine conflict" after watching[13] online videos of Palestinians suffering from the bombs thrown

---

[9] Aqil Haziq Mahmud, "16-Year-Old Singaporean Detained under Isa after Planning to Attack Muslims at 2 Mosques," *CNA*, January 27, 2021, https://www.channelnewsasia.com/singapore/16-year-old-singaporean-detained-isa-planned-attack-2-mosques-435241?fbclid=IwAR0AXus2J_ugWmXWC8qSoJbycVunrREo0z0vtt_jdozthMjl1f-PHLsi8VZg.

[10] *Ibid.*

[11] Hermes Auto, "Teen Detained for Planning Mosque Attacks: Rise of Right-Wing Extremism in Singapore Worrying, Says Shanmugam," *The Straits Times*, January 27, 2021, https://www.straitstimes.com/singapore/rise-of-right-wing-extremism-in-singapore-a-worrying-development-shanmugam.

[12] Hermes Auto, "Singaporean Youth Detained under ISA for Planning Knife Attack on Jews Leaving Synagogue," *The Straits Times*, March 11, 2021, https://www.straitstimes.com/singapore/singaporean-youth-detained-under-isa-for-planning-knife-attack-on-jews-leaving-synagogue.

[13] It must be noted that to the perpetrators it was a matter of religion, which most scholars and people from the religion will disagree with.

by Israeli fighter jets. As a result, he "developed a hatred for Israel" and wanted to travel to Gaza to join Hamas, a Palestinian Sunni-Islamic fundamentalist, militant, and nationalist organisation, to fight Israel. Almirall believed that this would earn him martyrdom.[14] Then in 2019, he decided to attack the Jews in a local synagogue after watching a documentary about the Jewish community in Singapore. Singapore's Minister for Home Affairs and Law, Mr K. Shanmugam, said that had Amirull successfully carried out his plans to attack the Jews, it would "probably incite greater animosity, distrust, between races and religions in Singapore."

While these cases of radicalisation that lead to the pursuit of violent extremism are not directly religious, they contain faith-based elements. Though motivated by political views, such incidents of extremist thinking or behaviour with religious aspects can stir a sense of fear among people of different beliefs and, eventually, inter-religious hate. For example, a report published by the Institute of Policy Studies (IPS) in Singapore presented findings from a survey that "some 15 per cent find Muslims threatening".[15] Dr Mathew Mathews, a principal researcher at IPS, cited the global terror and its association with Muslims as contributing to such a feeling among a small group of Singaporeans.[16]

These cases provide a brief overview of issues and incidents connected with religious people in Singapore that may contribute to the polarisation of society. While this essay has spotlighted the faith-based elements, it is essential to note that such cases may also involve extremist narratives on social media and the influence of foreign identity politics. The toxic mix of these various parts creates divides; therefore, it is hard to argue that religious views alone should be blamed. Nonetheless, the intention behind the focus on religion in this chapter is to argue for a

---

[14] Tan, Bridget. "S'pore Youth Isa Detention: How a Former NSF Was Radicalised, Planned to Attack Jews." *The Straits Times*, March 13, 2021. https://www.straitstimes.com/singapore/how-a-former-nsf-became-radicalised-and-planned-to-attack-jews-outside-a-synagogue.

[15] Rashith, Rahimah. "15% Of Respondents Find Muslims Threatening: IPS Report." *The Straits Times*, March 29, 2019. https://www.straitstimes.com/singapore/15-of-respondents-find-muslims-threatening?utm_campaign=STFB&utm_medium=Social&utm_source=Facebook&fbclid=IwAR1UaB6xcHCDuohTABpmNny09oUPaE9kLEJxZVZgXD7Mw5LrPKtix9JZpjA.

[16] *Ibid.*

collective duty from religious leaders and communities. Their role becomes crucial if faith is used or exploited to divide people.

Establishing a Collective Duty That Begins with Religious Leaders

A common undertaking in Singapore following an incident that can cause inter-religious strife is the public display of reconciliation and affirmation of solidarity among religious leaders. This can be observed in all of the cases cited earlier. In the case of Pastor Rony Tan, the then President of the National Council of Churches of Singapore (NCCS) issued a statement to affirm that some of Pastor Rony Tan's statements were "insensitive and offensive to followers of Buddhist and Taoist faiths".[17] This statement also informed that the Council of NCCS was "committed to continuing its efforts in promoting religious understanding and respect". In 2008, the Council of NCCS issued a guide on inter-religious relations, which advised Christians not to denounce other religions and show respect for different beliefs while carrying out evangelism.

In the case of Imam Nalla, an inter-religious gathering with 30 religious leaders from the Christian, Sikh, Taoist, Buddhist, and Hindu faiths was organised.[18] During this session, Imam Nalla extended his apologies. A similar meet-up was organised at the Maghain Aboth Synagogue, where he apologised to the Jewish community's, where he apologised to the Jewish community. News articles of these meetings carried photos that showed the presence of inter-religious solidarity during these occasions.

Similar interfaith meetings were also held after reporting the news about the detaining of the Amirull, who planned to attack Jews in Singapore, and the 16-year-old Christian youth who wanted to attack the

---

[17] Rev Dr John Chew and Lim K. Tham, "In Response to Comments by Pastor Rony Tan, 9 February 2010," Home — (National Council of Churches Singapore, February 9, 2010), https://nccs.org.sg/2010/02/in-response-to-comments-by-pastor-rony-tan-9-february-2010/.

[18] Today, "Imam Has Shown Sincere Remorse, Regret: Shanmugam," *Today*, April 5, 2017, https://www.todayonline.com/singapore/shanmugam-meets-imam-who-made-offensive-remarks-against-jews-christians.

two mosques. Dr Naziruddin Mohd Nasir, the Mufti of Singapore, said in a statement that the acts of self-radicalised individuals, such as Amirull, dishonour and desecrate the faith they claim to defend. He emphasised that they are against the Islamic religion, which upholds the sanctity of places of worship like the synagogue.[19] During a meeting between Jewish and Muslim leaders at the Jacob Ballas Centre on 10 March 2021, Mr Esa Masood, the Chief Executive of the Islamic Religious Council of Singapore, was quoted as "Jews and Muslims are proud to share a common Abrahamic heritage."

What would be the purpose behind these media-centric inter-religious events? First, the coming together of different religious leaders to proclaim trust, respect, and friendship among themselves is a public declaration of tolerance and acceptance of religious diversity. These offer an immediate counter-narrative to the behaviours of religious exclusivism or extremism. Besides that, it also shows religious leaders' role in undoing a faith-based problem. This can be observed in the leaders' statements, who condemn behaviours that hurt other religions. In doing so, they fronted a mindset that all faiths, regardless of differences, must be equally respected. On the other hand, silence from religious leaders would have been construed as condoning the behaviour of the exclusivists and radicals whose actions are harmful to peace and harmony.

If the negative words of influential religious leaders would cause divisions among people of different religions, then positive words and actions can also lead to resolving divisions. But, of course, it will be unwise to think that the cause-effect is as simple as that. Nonetheless, this method provides for a collective duty towards developing interfaith understanding and friendship, which should begin with religious leaders. This is because they are perceived as having the knowledge, experience and, most importantly, the authority to speak about and for religion. Such power of religious leaders has to be harnessed to reduce and remove divisive opinions in society.

---

[19] Hariz Baharudin, "S'pore Youth Isa Detention: Harmonious Ties Won't Be Affected by Thwarted Attack, Say Faith Leaders," *The Straits Times*, March 11, 2021, https://www.straitstimes.com/singapore/jewish-and-muslim-community-leaders-in-spore-say-close-harmonious-ties-wont-be-affected-by.

Within the Singapore context, beyond the circumstances, such as the cases highlighted earlier, there has to be a concentrated effort to transform exclusivist thinking and proactively counter religious extremism. This has to go beyond the mere inter-religious gathering of leaders to affirm and reaffirm common values. Instead, local religious leaders and scholars have to be responsible for having constructive discussions about individual religious principles and teachings that may be exploited to spread hate among people. There are existing examples of this approach within some religions. For example, the Religious Rehabilitation Group in Singapore has a resource centre where Islamic concepts and doctrines such as *Al-Wala' wal Bara'* used by religious fundamentalists are clarified.[20,21] However, this is an effort by some within the Singapore Muslim community. What may be worth exploring is an interfaith model of such. How this will work requires careful planning, but this will be the start of moving from religious tolerance towards effective inter-religious dialogues that strengthen social relationships.

Enabling Interfaith Dialogues for Better Appreciation of 'Others'

Moving beyond religious leadership, there is a collective duty of society to eliminate faith-based and other factors that divide followers of religions. This may seem like an unfair onus on religions people when other factors such as social media and identity politics, may also cause the polarisation of societies. However, the proximity of religious communities to faith-based problems presents a strategic opportunity to engage them more closely to counter them. Awareness, education, and dialogue about religious diversity may more effectively negate the power of radical and insensitive religious leaders and individuals. Interfaith dialogue, which is "an intentional encounter and interaction" among the members

---

[20] "About RRG," Religious Rehabilitation Group, May 26, 2016, https://www.rrg.sg/about-rrg.

[21] "Al Wala Wal Bara," Religious Rehabilitation Group, May 26, 2016, https://www.rrg.sg/al-wala-wal-bara/.

of different faith traditions as members of diverse beliefs, is one way to approach this.[22]

Interfaith dialogues are not new and have been happening worldwide for centuries. The 1893 World Parliament Religions is said to be the beginning of an organised inter-religious dialogue. Since then, interfaith dialogues have become a core agenda of public and international policies. Within Singapore, interfaith dialogues have been a significant part of religious harmony efforts since 1949, when the Inter-Religious Organisation, Singapore, was established.

How do organised interfaith dialogues help towards a better appreciation of religious diversity? First, it provides a space for people with different beliefs and world views to meet so that they may know one another. This leads towards familiarising people with different and conflicting views about religious principles, such as God, messengers, and the way of life. Such acquaintances ease discomforts in a multireligious setting. At the basic, interfaith dialogues are like school orientation camps, where they establish connections and develop relations. The direction and depth of the dialogues after the meeting point depend on the participants and the facilitators. These can be as simple as getting to know each other's religion or a mutual change and transformation.[23]

The usefulness of interfaith dialogue to promote social cohesion has been much discussed for years, though there is little empirical evidence of its efficacy. In countries like Singapore, where the state manages religious diversity through regulations, policies, and community efforts, it is hard to assess the impact of inter-religious engagement on the relationship between citizens and residents. Perhaps, the lack of a focused study on interfaith dialogue in Singapore needs to be given attention by the academic, government, and religious networks.

If faith-based issues that create misunderstanding between people are of growing concern, then exploring faith-based approaches is pertinent. Integrating interfaith dialogues into the social harmony agenda must

---

[22] Sallie B. King, "Interreligious Dialogue," Oxford Handbooks Online, March 2010, https://doi.org/10.1093/oxfordhb/9780195340136.003.0008, 1.

[23] Oddbjrn Leirvik, *Interreligious Studies: A Relational Approach to Religious Activism and the Study of Religion* (S.L.: Bloomsbury, 2015), 33.

become a serious undertaking on all levels of society, rather than an after-thought. The recent case of a teacher in Singapore arrested for terrorism offences is evidence of interfaith dialogue being needed at workplaces, schools, and other public spaces.[24]

Moving Forward with Commitment to Shift the Needle

This article highlighted the need to move away from vague and idealistic aspirations on how faith can help safeguard us from emerging problems given the rise of global religious consciousness. Instead, preventing the use of religion to spread hate among people must be recognised as a collective duty with specific calls to action from different stakeholders. The absence of such clarity is the roadblock to identifying solutions for social polarisation.

Then, there must be a good understanding of religiously motivated or affiliated issues contributing to this problem. Some examples within the Singapore context were discussed in the earlier paragraphs, following which two suggestions have been put forth. The first is to introduce a collective effort by religious leaders to seek a faith-based approach to clarify and correct the wrong understanding of religious diversity within Singapore. The second is a concentrated effort to study the effective use of interfaith dialogue as a mainstream effort to strengthen social cohesion. These broad-stroke ideas need further consideration, but they help move the commitment to make a society friendlier rather than merely being tolerant of diversity.

---

[24] Louisa Tang, "Moe Teacher Becomes First Public Servant in Singapore to Be Arrested under Isa for Terrorism Offences," *CNA*, January 11, 2023, https://www.channelnewsasia.com/singapore/internal-security-act-moe-teacher-public-servant-intention-armed-violence-palestine-israel-conflict-3197866.

Chapter 3.2

FOSTERING PEACE BY ALLEVIATING SCARCITY: CASE STUDY OF GLOBAL INTERFAITH WASH ALLIANCE (GIWA)

Dr Sadhvi Bhagawati Saraswati

I want to begin in the forest. A lot of religious traditions have stories of their sages, their saints, their mystics, and their prophets spending time dwelling in the forest and connecting with the Divine. But I want to start today by talking about a specific forest, the redwood forest, which is indigenous to California where I am originally from before I moved to India 26 years ago.

The redwood trees are the world's tallest trees growing to hundreds and hundreds of feet tall and they're also some of the world's oldest trees living for many hundreds and even more than a thousand years through earthquakes and fires among other kinds of changes in nature. Now, one would think in order to live so long and be so strong their roots must be really deep in the ground. In actuality, the secret of the redwood forest is that their roots, rather than being individually deep, are interconnected. The roots of every redwood tree are connected to the roots of every other redwood tree and that interconnection is what nourishes and nurtures their strength.

Religion: Basis of Connection, Not Contradiction

And that is the message for us today, it is a message of connection. And religion ultimately is that which is supposed to connect us, to connect us to God, or the Divine, or however we conceive of that supreme reality. To connect us to our true self, which is not separate from the Divine. To connect us to each other, to our communities, to connect us to a system, an order of understanding, and to our values, morals and ethical principles, individually and for our communities.

But tragically, as Professor Katherine Marshall spoke so beautifully about this distinction between the ideal and the real, in the reality, we are seeing that religion which is supposed to connect us is actually also leading to disconnection, to polarisation, and to othering. And human psychology teaches us that in times of stress, in times of fear, and in times of threat, real or imagined, we contract. Fear makes us contract. The lines between us and them get thicker and thicker. The circle of us gets smaller and smaller.

We saw this recently very tragically during the COVID-19 pandemic. Fear of illness and death led to so many instances of finger-pointing, vilification, and scapegoating of who was responsible for super-spreader events and who was not following safe COVID-19 protocol. It got so bad that there were times when groups of different religions would not even buy fruits and vegetables from each other's carts.

Another major source of fear and stress, of the 'us versus them' mentality, and therefore a source of contraction, is scarcity of resources: scarcity of water and scarcity of food, and this scarcity is increasing day by day.

Fostering Peace by Alleviating Scarcity: Case Study of Global Interfaith WASH Alliance (GIWA)

And that's why we launched our Global Interfaith WASH Alliance or GIWA. And it's a beautiful acronym as well because in the Sanskrit language, GIWA means life. We launched our Global Interfaith WASH Alliance with UNICEF, with the government of the United States, and with the government of the Netherlands to bring about a revolution in

WASH — Water, Sanitation, and Hygiene — to bring about a water safe world in which everyone has access to clean water, to sanitation, and to hygiene. And we do this work because we are committed to alleviating suffering, today and tomorrow. We also do this work to confront the impending scarcity of resources, and that directly works to prevent the violent conflict that we see when there is scarcity.

Our work begins with an extended definition of peace — that it is not enough to just refrain from killing each other with guns and missiles and bombs but that peace must include prevention of that which leads to suffering, conflict, and strife. It is predicted that by 2040, the world is only going to have half the drinking water it needs. India is on track to be there by 2030 and we're told that up to hundreds of millions of people will become refugees, having to leave their homes due to issues directly related to this water crisis.

At the time that we launched GIWA, over 600 million people in India were defecating in the open every day and about sixteen hundred children under the age of five were dying every day due to the ramifications of this open defecation, specifically the lack of clean water, sanitation, and hygiene. And since our launch just under a decade ago, we've been able to trigger mass mobilisations of hundreds of millions of people in India and across the world. And over the years, we have also expanded our focus to include widespread work for gender equality, ending gender-based violence, ending child marriage, and bringing about a revolution in menstruation so that our girls do not have to drop out of school when they hit puberty.

It is said that faith can move mountains. We are very happy for the mountains to be where they are, but we have been harnessing the power of faith to move the minds, and therefore, the behaviours, of communities towards healthier and sustainable societies for all.

But the power of these relationships between the religious leaders and the power of friendships transcends a revolution towards clean water sanitation and hygiene. These connections and these friendships have enabled us to help bring people together to dissolve borders between 'us and them', to end scapegoating, to end polarisation, and to end the vilification. There is no time to share all of it, but just in COVID-19, for example, even during the time of lockdowns, we were able to bring so many leaders together in webinars, through public service announcements in that time of crisis. We were able to do so because we had the foundation of friendship and relationships that had been built up over the years.

Lessons Learnt: Sow Seeds of Interconnectedness Now

There are so many lessons. Number one: Do not wait until there is violence. We must plant the seeds now — those seeds of interconnectedness. And this can be done by uniting together against a common enemy: fighting against climate change, against environmental destruction, against water scarcity, and against gender-based violence — this serves as an invaluable tool to prevent polarisation and violence.

Second, and lastly, and which makes me so happy to be here, is the work that we do with the youths. We have had great success in bringing students from *madrasas* together with Hindu students from *gurukuls* to spend days together, living together, learning from each other, and learning how similar we are in so many core ways. And those lessons have formed the foundation for peace in their minds and, therefore, in their actions.

Religion should give us the courage to resist that which must be resisted. It needs to give us the courage to say no just as much as the courage to say yes. And today, we have the power to say no to the polarisation, to the vilification, to the othering, and to all of those aspects of society that are creating, strengthening, and exacerbating that division. And we have the power to say yes to working together before we hit crises. We have the power to not only put out fires of violence but actually successfully fireproof our communities.

And it is such an honour to be here and I have deep gratitude to the organisers for giving us this opportunity.

Thank you so much.

Chapter 3.3

RELATEDNESS AS THE ESSENCE OF COHESION: BRIDGING THE DIVIDE BETWEEN US AND THE 'OTHER'

Lord John Alderdice

Bridging divides should come naturally. From the start, there is in us an impulse to engage with, to relate with, the wider universe of being — not just people and other living beings but our environs. As babies and young children, we relate with what is close by and later we engage with people and places as widely as it is possible for us. We explore and engage to understand and find meaning but also to experience a sense of relatedness that moves us and takes us beyond the boundaries of ourselves. We search not only for those engagements that will satisfy the basic requirements of survival — water, food, warmth, and shelter — but more importantly, we seek the relatedness that makes these things possible and gives us an experience of relationship — of not being alone.

But if we want to relate with others, why do we get into conflict? As René Girard has shown, when I relate with you, I will often imitate you.[25] We can see this most easily in children, but it is true of all of us. When I imitate your desire, I start to want what you want, or who you want, and

---

[25] Girard René. (1972). *Violence and the Sacred*. Baltimore: The Johns Hopkins University Press.

so I come into rivalry with you for the attention of the person we both now want. That rivalry for attention creates conflict and we create boundaries of law, culture, and religion to contain that rivalry and prevent it from becoming violent.

I just engaged in asking and answering the question 'Why?' As soon as we are able to do so, we ask that question, 'Why?' — sometimes with infuriating frequency as any parent or child-care worker knows. We want to understand how things relate and connect, not only so that we can appreciate how to ensure our basic needs are met but also to understand how to relate to the people and the places where we find ourselves. We want to protect ourselves from harm, but we also want to ensure and repeat those experiences that give us satisfaction. So, we try to understand how the world works. This is not merely intellectual curiosity. It is part of how we try to relate better with our surroundings, at first, our close sur-roundings, and later, our universe relationships — however small or large we construe that universe to be. As we get much older, and we begin to lose some of our faculties, we slip back into simply trying to maintain the knowledge, understanding, and relationships we already have. However, relatedness — bridging the divide between us and the 'Other' — remains a fundamental driver of our existence.

Speaking of that relatedness, 20th-century Irish theologian J. Ernest Davey defined religion as *"...the most ultimate, the most real and the most compelling form in which we conceive the social or universe rela-tionships and obligations of our lives"* and he went on to point out that this was also the case for those who may think of themselves as non-religious *"the most ultimate, real and compelling form in which they conceive their social or universe relationships and obligations is their true religion"* whether or not they describe it as such.[26]

While many, especially since that time of intellectual upheaval that we call the Enlightenment, would like to believe that the intellectual com-ponent of our being should be regarded as the primary and dependable mode of engagement with the world, in reality, this does not really apply to us. Our drive to understand is important, but, as a great English football

---

[26] Davey J. Ernest. (2021). *Religious Experience: Its Nature, Validity, Forms, and Problems*. Glenariff, Northern Ireland: ARTIS (Europe) Ltd.

manager once said, *"Football is not a matter of life and death, it is much more important than that!"* For him and for many people, mostly men, football is their religion. That is not a rational choice but an emotional one. The dependence on rationality does not apply in our personal relationships either.

When as a boy at school, I started to make a relationship with the girl who became and still is my wife. It was not merely an intellectual calculus of benefit or suitability but powerful feelings of attraction, excitement, and attachment. That is why Davey went on to speak not just of religion as a cognitive conception but of an experience of all the ways, especially the emotional ways, that are involved in the process of engaging in and maintaining such ultimate relationships. And in the realisation of the principles and values, ideals and aspirations, which are bound up with this, the deepest life of humankind can be experienced. Humanity has long, perhaps always, had a conscious relation to something greater than ourselves. That realisation and relationship have their own peculiar satisfactions and discomforts and for many, their own relatively ultimate demands and purposes. However, this highest and best and most ultimate experience, especially when it transcends our immediate social and personal experience, also contains an element of mystery — that which goes beyond our intellectual understanding. We must recognise that, as brilliant 19th-century English theologian James Martineau pointed out, "All our intellectual propositions are provisional."[27] Science at its best maintains this provisional nature of our understanding, though some scientists seem to speak as though they had reached the end of understanding. When they do that, they are as mistaken as Francis Fukuyama was when he proclaimed the 'end of history' in the field of social science we call political science.[28]

Just as the building of relationships with other people involves taking a risk and venturing out beyond what we know, so a life of faith requires us to venture out beyond what we think we know of our universe of Other and others. This is not so much a theology, but a way of life, a way of being-in-the-world. And faith, understood in this way, is rather different

---

[27] Martineau James. (1890). *The Seat of Authority in Religion*. London: Longmans Green & Co.

[28] Fukuyama Francis. (1992). *The End of History and the Last Man*. New York: Free Press.

from belief, especially that belief that is held with a degree of certitude. As we try to understand our world of living beings and things, we inevitably search for meaning. That child-like question 'Why?' goes beyond the who, what, and where. We want to understand why. When we have had an experience of pleasure, satisfaction, or even exhilaration, we try to hold on to it by seizing on such understandings as we think we have, provisional as they are. We make them into doctrines and dogma, rules, and regulations. Such understandings, invocations, and the places that we associate with them become rituals and liturgies, professions of faith, and places of pilgrimage. They are attempts to express, hold on to, and re-experience the sense of transcendence that is relating beyond the boundaries of our individual selves.

In this, we have a struggle, especially those of us from later Western traditions that are based on the Enlightenment. We want to believe that, to understand rationally is to fully and deeply appreciate something. This is why many of my liberal colleagues focus so much on constitutions, the regularising of social relationships, and decision-making in voting and elections and on the law. However, while the law is a good servant, it is a bad master in relationships.

The Irish Peace Process led to the end of the period of political violence that we call 'the Troubles' and this was achieved through the negotiation of the 1998 Belfast-Good Friday Agreement. In it, we came to realise that our problems were not simply disputes about laws, borders, political systems, policing, and the administration of justice or even social and economic disparities but about disturbed, historic relations between the people that lived on the island of Ireland and their neighbours on the other island. We had to venture into the dangerous territory of building relationships with those who had done violence to us and our people. We had to step out, not just as individuals but as political leaders and party leaderships who could take their cohort of society with them. Trust, which is the way of peace, was not a pre-requisite of such a venturing out, a taking of risks, but rather an outcome of steps of faith which were rewarded by a positive response, not always and certainly not inevitably but sufficiently often to enable the relationships to develop.

As my Oxford colleague, Dominic Johnston, has pointed out in a more general historical survey, those who operate contrary to the laws of rational and responsible behaviour often do better than those who stick with those respected rules.[29] In more recent times, this has contributed to a profound polarisation in geo-politics. This has left those who regard themselves as rational, reasonable, and progressive in their politics deeply opposed to those who are driven by a more emotional response, informed by deep anxieties that the world and those with whom they have to share it are not dependable — that our relationships are not reassuring but threatening. The recent pandemic has been deeply unsettling, but we have had pandemics before and survived. However, unlike previous wars from which humanity and our world have recovered, since 1945, we have had the capacity not only to destroy each other in a nuclear war but to destroy human civilisation entirely and permanently. Through the climate change that comes from our lack of concern and proper stewardship of our environment, we have also been producing what could amount to a long, slow, suicide of humankind.

It is vital at this time of great danger that we recognise that an attempt to relate to each other as living beings, to our world and our universe as an organism of inconceivable complexity, and to the 'Other' that transcends all requires a humility and an appreciation of all aspects of our individual and social humanity: intellectually, emotionally, and spiritually. All these elements represented by our fractured humanity need each other. We are not just a great complicated machine with a part that has broken and needs to be fixed or replaced. We are participants in complex adaptive systems that can repair themselves if they are given the chance to rejuvenate.

We must listen to those of a conservative disposition who do not want things to change because they want to retain some understandings that we may have forgotten. We should not simply dismiss those who are fundamentalists because they want to change the future to conform to an idealised past that never existed and to force others to live with their fantasies. They may be profoundly mistaken about many things, but in their profound fear of what is threatening that which they hold dear, they may be 'the canary in the mine' that warns us of things that we should also be

---

[29] Johnson Dominic D. P. (2020). *Strategic Instincts: The Adaptive Advantages of Cognitive Biases in International Politics*. Princeton University Press.

more anxious about than we are. Those who we find to be too free, too liberal, and too excited to change everything should be listened to because they are calling upon us to build a better world and not be satisfied to be less than we can be. As my good friend Ed Shapiro often says, "When I meet someone with whom I profoundly disagree, I should not just address what they are wrong about, but ask myself the question, 'What are they right about?'"[30]

In Singapore, you have a particular opportunity, but that also means a profound responsibility, to address differences and your holding of this conference recognises this. You have grasped the opportunity to develop information, science, and technology to a high degree. Many of your citizens welcome these exciting developments, but as in all our societies, some are frightened by the consequences. You have the experience of different cultures, languages, ethnic groups, religions, and ways of 'being-in-the-world' that come from the people with whom you live in Singapore and the neighbourhood in which you are placed. You have a complex history and geography that means that you cannot comfortably ignore those with whom you have disagreed in the past or with whom you have uncomfortable relationships in the present.

Just as we in Ireland came to realise that while neither side could be defeated, neither could anyone win through physical force, or driving the other out. We had to find another way of relating with each other. It required us to take risks to reach out to those with whom we disagreed and find new ways of structuring our society that respects those different ways of being. It was not about finding an agreement that overcame our different perceptions of what was 'the good' but about finding ways of disagreeing and not killing each other. As Isaiah Berlin has taught us, there is not, and will not be, agreement on the good, and that fact requires us to develop a pluralism in our society — we ought all to try to find ways of agreeing, but more importantly of disagreeing, without damaging or destroying each other.[31] This is a transcending of our current ways of engaging.

---

[30] Shapiro Edward. (2019). *Finding a Place to Stand: Developing Self-Reflective Institutions, Leaders and Citizens*. Bicester, UK: Phoenix Publishing House.
[31] Berlin Isaiah. (2017). *Liberty*. Oxford University Press.

Around the world, people are coming to realise that our current ways of relating with each other are not working and we will destroy ourselves through war, climate change, famine, or disease. So, we must make the effort, and we may be able to find new ways of relating by transcending our current understandings.[32] This will require us to approach these challenges with a child-like naiveté — not childish but child-like — for we are all little, weak infants in the face of the immensity of time, space, and that which goes beyond time and space. We will need an openness to engage with each other and with mystery. It is not the certainty of our beliefs but the mystery of faith that will enable us to bridge the divide between a world in danger where we split apart and a doorway of hope through which we can pass together.

---

[32] Alderdice John Lord. "Conflict, complexity, and cooperation," *New England Journal of Public Policy* 33, Issue 1, Article 9. https://scholarworks.umb.edu/nejpp/vol33/iss1/9.

Chapter 3.4

THE SIMPLICITY OF PEACE: MAKING SPACE, HOLDING SPACE

Imam Uzair Akbar

Peace be upon each and every one. First of all, I would like to say thank you very much to all who organised this beautiful programme. We pray to the Creator who is the absolute guide, that He guides us, especially guide me right now, to say that which will be productive, which can be used by myself and by all those that are witnessing to leave this world as a better world. There have been beautiful minds before me and beautiful speakers before me and I believe there are going to be beautiful speakers, excellent speakers, after me that are going to speak about social cohesion.

I am going to start off by reciting a verse from the holy scripture, from the holy Quran, in which God Almighty takes us back to where we started:

يَـٰٓأَيُّهَا ٱلنَّاسُ إِنَّا خَلَقْنَـٰكُم مِّن ذَكَرٍ وَأُنثَىٰ وَجَعَلْنَـٰكُمْ شُعُوبًا وَقَبَآئِلَ لِتَعَارَفُوٓا۟ ۚ إِنَّ أَكْرَمَكُمْ عِندَ ٱللَّهِ أَتْقَىٰكُمْ ۚ إِنَّ ٱللَّهَ عَلِيمٌ خَبِيرٌ ١٣

The translation more or less is as follows: "O mankind, we have created you from a male and a female; then we made you into nations and into tribes; so you could recognise one another; verily in the best amongst you is that person who is god-fearing; verily, Allah, the Creator, he knows everything and he is all-aware; he has spoken the truth."

I would like to mention a few fine points pertaining to this verse. Indeed, we are divided from day one but God Almighty has given us a platform. Now, that platform can accommodate everyone. It is up to us how we manage that platform. As we see many a time that there are many, many people in a bus and from the outside, you see that there is no room. Yet, the doors open somehow. The people outside make it inside through some adjustments made by the people inside.

A better example for the women that are sitting here: when the women say that there are groceries, can you put them into the fridge? And I open the door, or we open the door, and we say that there is no room in the fridge. So, she says that is what you say all the time. So, we go and sit on the couch to watch something. After five minutes, when we return, there is nothing on the ground, it is all in the fridge. How did they do that? They moved a few things from here to the right, to the left, and they managed to squeeze the groceries into the fridge.

Indeed, we are going to be tested as human beings. Sometimes it will seem like that platform has no room or accommodation for anyone else. But if we are sensible and we are compassionate, and if we have empathy, we will find room. The question is, in terms of social cohesion: Are we ready to make sacrifice? That is the question because relationships — maybe relationship with the Creator or relationship with people around you that form communities and nations — demand sacrifice. No relationship can blossom and flourish and grow from strength to strength without sacrifice. How much are we ready to sacrifice to bring on people that are not on that platform? The religions, and as I am a Muslim, I am representing Islam. The religion of Islam speaks about internal purity.

When we head to the driving range for golf, there is a board and it says, "Let your demons out". So, the aim is to hit the ball as hard as you can. It does not matter if you shank it, you slice it, or you draw it; hit as hard as you can. So, everyone has demons inside. Faith comes to harness those demons, to control those demons. Wherever we see that the fabric of humanity has been disturbed, it is because of greed. It is because a person has not controlled his internal demon. The internal sicknesses are still present; we need to remove that. This body is a double-edged sword: with this hand, I can give and bring a smile on the face of a person. With the same hand, I can take and give grief to a person. With this articulator, I can say a word that will melt the heart. I can say to a person, "I love you." That person will fall fond of me. I can say something very, very aggressive, and it will burn the heart. Faith, and all faiths I will say, they speak about using this machine productively.

I have many, many experiences in this field and most of us have our own experiences. I am going to mention one experience. One day I was with my wife at the store and I was paying for my groceries. And I saw a person with tattoos staring me down. And I was wearing this. So, the person is staring at me and the first thing that came to my mind is that once I pay, I am going to have to pay for the hospital bill because he is going to knock me. So, I looked at him, he looked at me and then he disappeared. Then, I was pushing the trolley and I saw him at the exit door. So, think about what is going through my mind. And I am walking with my trolley, and I see him at the exit door. And he says, "Excuse me." And I am getting ready. He said, "Excuse me." I said, "Yes?" He said, "Are you a Muslim?" I said, "Yes, I'm a Muslim." He said, "You're the first Muslim that smiled at me. For many, many years, I've been looking to speak to a Muslim but I'm hesitant, I have reservations. And whenever I look at a Muslim, I don't find a smile."

I was smiling because I was scared; that was why I was smiling. But it worked in my favour and we sat down. And he said, "Look, I'm a Christian brother. I've been working in this sector, and I wanted to speak to a Muslim brother, but I haven't found a Muslim brother that I feel comfortable with." Indeed, all these brilliant minds will speak about things that we need to do on a government level and media level, but if we can go from here with one thing, let us walk away from this conference with a smile on our face, a permanent smile. Whoever we come across, it might be someone from a different faith, someone who looks different from us, but we can smile. This will go miles towards bringing social cohesion.

This smile is amazing. In our culture, Pakistan, India, and Bangladesh, they say "zaban ka barakarava dil kabaracha". They say that this person is very bitter with his tongue but very good with his heart. I do not agree with that. I will never know what is in his heart. I will only see what is on the face. The first thing that you will come across, if you are looking at me, visiting me, is the face. Similarly, the first thing that I will see of you is your face. That face has to have that radiant smile that makes people around you feel comfortable. And that is the first ingredient towards cooking the pot of social cohesion. I can have all the ingredients and I can put the pot on the stove, but if I do not have the match, I am not going to cook anything.

If our body language does not give comfort to people around us, and my face does not give comfort, then I am not going to succeed. I would like to conclude on the statement of Prophet Muhammad, peace be upon him, he says the entire creation is the family of God and if we are in our own capacity trying to please God. But if we're not pleasing the family of God, we cannot please God.

Thank you very much.

Chapter 3.5

PERSPECTIVES FROM A BUDDHIST INTERFAITH PRACTITIONER

Venerable You Guang (Shifu)

As a Young Leaders Programme (YLP) alumnus, I am humbled to have the opportunity to share how faith can bridge divide between people. My journey in exploring the meaning of happiness, faith, and well-being started with learning to bridge the best of two worlds, growing up in Singapore.

Interconnectedness of Economic Welfare and Spiritual Welfare

Before that, let us step back 2,500 years to the time of the historical Buddha, who once gave practical advice in a market town to a merchant in ancient India. The merchant Dīghajāṇu[33] asked, "What are the conditions for happiness and well-being in this life and beyond?" The Buddha

---

[33] "Dīghajāṇu" is the householder's given name and literally translates as "Long Knee." His family name, "Vyagghapajja" (sometimes Romanised as "Byagghapajja," as in Bodhi, 2005, and Nyanaponika & Bodhi, 1999), can be translated as "Tiger Paw" or "Tiger Path." Thanissaro Bhikkhu (trans.) (1995). Dighajanu (Vyagghapajja) Sutta: To Dighajanu (AN 8.54). Available online at http://www.accesstoinsight.org/tipitaka/an/an08/an08.054.than.html.

identifies four traits conducive to happiness (or '*sukha*' in the original Pali language) in this life:

1. diligence (*uṭṭhāna-sampadā*) — being skilled and hardworking in one's livelihood,
2. vigilance (*ārakkha-sampadā*) — protecting one's wealth from theft and disaster,
3. virtuous friendship (*kalyāṇa-mittatā*) — associating with and emulating those embodying faith, virtue, generosity, and wisdom,
4. balanced living (*sama-jīvikatā*) — abstaining from promiscuity, drunkenness, gambling, and unwholesome friendships.

Skilfully maintaining one's livelihood and cultivating diligence, the wise balance their finances and preserve their wealth with balanced living. The Buddha further identifies accomplishments (*sampadā*) that lead to a layperson's happiness:

1. faith (*saddhā*), or confidence in the teachings of the Buddha and other enlightened beings,
2. virtue (*sīla*), as exemplified by the Five Precepts,
3. generosity (*cāga*), giving charity and alms,
4. wisdom (*paññā*), having insight into the arising and passing of things.

The path to balancing economic welfare and spiritual welfare comes when one is faithful in loving, displays kindness and insight, is accomplished in ethics, and is bountiful and not miserly in his generosity.

Journeying on the Bridge

Back to modern Singapore, I was born to a family that held ancestral Chinese cultural beliefs, and at the same time, I was a student in a mission school. Navigating differences between these two worlds as a teenager, I learned to respect, observe, and practise the values evident in different systems of faith.

i.   Respect as the cornerstone of virtuous friendships

As my interest in interfaith dialogue grew, in 2006, I was introduced to the Braddell Heights Inter-Racial and Religious Confidence Circle (IRCC). IRCC, founded four years before that (in 2002) by then Prime Minister Goh Chok Tong, comprising leaders from racial, religious, social, educational, and business groups and other organisations. This is a closely-knit group of religious leaders and community leaders under the leadership of then chairman Mr Bernard Chiang. I appreciated how we bridged different backgrounds through the generous sharing of lived experiences. The recent renaming of IRCCs to "Racial and Religious Harmony Circles" signalled a progressive shift from building confidence among communities to creating harmonious understanding.

When we look into a running stream, it is not easy to see our reflection clearly. Only on still water can we see our own reflection clearly, and we may even see what is gathered at the bottom of the water. The same principle applies to our minds — we need to cultivate greater mindfulness in our lives to discern new ideas and perspectives with greater clarity.

The point of dialogue is not just about making one's point. It is also about clearly seeing different perspectives. There are always "two sides to a coin", and it is essential to understand different points of view. For example, forcing one's religious ideology on others, especially to those already practising their own religion (or own faith), can provoke tensions within the family and sow discord among friends. If our friends who profess another religion are already happily practising their faith, undermining their beliefs by foisting our own views on them not only disrupts their way of life but such attempts threaten our social fabric. Instead, we can share about our faiths with a pure intention to share our views, debunking any misinformation and being non-intrusive. Such an attitude would mean we do not insist that others live according to our beliefs but respect the space of others.

ii.   Bridging diversity in inclusive environments

In 2014, I represented the Singapore Buddhist Federation in the first Association of Southeast Asian Nations (ASEAN) Interfaith Dialogue for Religious Leaders for Peace at Chulalongkorn Rajavidyalaya University,

Thailand. In discussing interfaith and intrafaith issues, we made a joint declaration[34] in Ayutthaya to promote religious tolerance and peace. Representatives from other countries requested to take photos of the Singaporeans of diverse faith groups at breakfast, as they were curious to see us sitting together and eating comfortably despite adopting different dietary preferences. A sight that most in Singapore may take for granted reminds me of the inclusive environment I grew up in; and how precious it is that our society encourages the deepening of friendships in diverse communities.

On hindsight, interfaith dialogue can be likened to a buffet. Just because someone enjoys rice does not mean that everybody else should be forced to have it and that we need to throw the noodles out. Instead, we need to learn to respect everyone's preferences and offer a wide variety of options, like in a buffet. In this way, not only enjoy the food that we like but also sit together for a shared meal. This buffet becomes an eye-opening experience, where we can sample new cuisines that we would otherwise never have encountered. Similarly, we can view dialogues as a valuable platform at which we can gain opportunities to learn new insights and develop new ways of practising our values.

As one listens with an open heart and receptive mind, one would be able to find common agreements that everyone can act on. What we may not agree on, we can respect one another and let it be. We may not endorse some ideas or teachings, but we do not need to be trapped in a state of internal conflict in our minds.

With the IRCCs as a springboard, I gained a deeper understanding of inclusive spiritual leadership. I participated in the Inter-Religious Organisation (IRO) and was recently appointed to the IRO Executive Council. In the IRO, as part of the 'Prayers and Blessing group', representatives from 10 different faiths stand united side by side to offer prayers in their respective religious traditions. Interfaith prayers by the IRO have been commonplace at national ceremonies and private events in Singapore since the founding of IRO in 1949. Such practices truly exemplify Singapore's religious harmony.

On age inclusiveness, the IRO Youth Wing facilitates sharing of multigenerational faith and practices through regular catch-up '*kopi*' or

---

[34]Ayutthaya Declaration 2014. The First Interfaith Dialogue of Religious Leaders for Peace in ASEAN Community: Religious Tolerance (24–28 September 2014).

'coffee/tea' sessions. In these dialogues, members across larger age groups learned about one another's beliefs in an open and safe environment.

The intersection between gender and spirituality is also explored in the 'Women of Faith', formed by women of different faiths. Members share their lived experiences and spirituality so that people across both genders can gain a deeper understanding of issues, such as the stereotyping of women. Other issues that are commonly discussed include how women can be empowered and gender equality can be upheld, especially in the religious spaces where women play an important role in the nurturing of young people through different stages of life.

iii. Observing common values (cultivating wisdom)

For the Buddhists, faith serves as a guide for individuals to nurture their spirituality and practise a wholesome lifestyle that is skilful, blameless, and praiseworthy, just as Dīghajāṇu was taught. In the context of a multi-religious society, it is healthy to communicate one's faith with the intention of offering clarity about one's religious beliefs to others. It should not be based on a desire to convert or win others over to one's point of view nor should it be about pressuring others to accept one's line of thought or beliefs. Nor should the process of interfaith dialogue culminate in undermining one's own beliefs or shoehorning others' beliefs into our mental constructs.

In my journey of faith, contributing to dialogues and panel discussions has helped in deepening my faith and in cultivating wisdom and compassion. Being mindful of diverse views and being grounded in everyday lived experience give rise to the opportunities of observing impermanence and suffering which in turn induce compassion, and selflessness. Some of these precious opportunities are programmes like the Common Senses for Common Spaces (CSCS) and Ask Me Anything (AMA) that are organised by community partners like Rose of Peace, hash.peace, IRO, IRCC, OnePeople.Sg, Humanity Matters, and Harmony Centre. These programmes and platforms unite us in the practice of selfless humility. In addition, each year, the Harmony Games hosted by different religious groups bring children and youth together through sports and games.

One of the popular metaphors among dialogue participants is that of the bamboo plant. The hollowness of bamboo reminds us to empty our minds of preconceptions so that we can learn, unlearn or relearn as the case may be.

We can acknowledge that we may not know or have the answers to everything because we are not perfect. In this way, we can unlearn misinformation, relearn new knowledge and skills, and perfect our practice of values we hold dear to enable clarity in our lives.

We can learn to live like the bamboo: the higher we grow, the deeper we bow. The bamboo's foundation is solid, yet it moves harmoniously with the wind. It bends gracefully in a storm but does not break at the core.

"Majority or Minority"?

As we respect and protect the dignity of all, regardless of race, language, or religion, words like 'majority' or 'minority' may limit our perceptions. In fact, whether we are part of a majority or minority depends on how we draw our circles of context.

Another example, I may belong to a Chinese majority in terms of race. But in the context of lived practices of faith, I represent a minority in terms of being a Buddhist monastic among Singaporeans.

For example, as a Mahayana Buddhist monastic, I am also vegetarian. When attending events, if the organiser forgets to order a vegetarian meal for me, very often my reply would be, "Don't worry, I'm here for the purpose of the coming together, not for the food."

I would not see it as my right for the host to make special arrangements to serve me because of my specific dietary requirements, and I would certainly not make a big fuss. Instead, I would take the opportunity to share why I am a vegetarian. As a 'minority' in this case, I do not feel slighted but rather regard the occasion as a chance for the 'majority' to understand the needs of the group I represent. This way, both the 'majority' and 'minority' can interact harmoniously, with an enhanced understanding of each other's needs.

Compassion as Our Common Bridge

Harmony arises when our faith and practice are aligned in terms of what we envision and what is reflected through our actions, speech, and mind.

As Karen Armstrong, the last ICCS speaker and founder of the International Charter of Compassion, shared in her book "Twelve Steps to a Compassionate Life", *"Compassion is the test of true spirituality in all faiths, brings us into relation with the transcendence ... Further, they all insists that we cannot confine our benevolence to our own group; we must have concern for everybody — even who we consider enemies."*[35]

With such efforts, we can foster deeper connections in our diverse communities. With humility and integrity, we can dig deep and weave deeper connections in the social fabric with wisdom and compassion, regardless of race, language, religion, ideology, gender, or age.

Bridging Compassion in the Closure of Human Lives

Spiritual support is vital at all stages of life, from the cradle to the grave. I have journeyed with people at different stages in life, and palliative care is close to my heart.

One experience is with a cancer patient with a six-months prognosis. His nieces requested my visit. During the visit, we could only communicate through writing due to the advanced cancer, which impacted his speech and hearing. After doing Buddhist chants and blessings, I continued to assist him and his family to have a proper closure. With my prayers, and with the visits of his family members, he got good closure to his life. He passed on peacefully on the third day after my visit. The family members were glad I had assisted their uncle with relational closure and spiritual blessings, thus, shortening the physical suffering from the disease.

I have come across many patients. For non-Buddhists, I will encourage them to pray in their own faith. If they need to connect with their faith representatives, we will make this spiritual connection for them. To bring closure and offer spiritual edification for our devotees, clients, or patients when they transition to death, I have aimed to dispel their stress and unease by focusing on shared universal values and providing uplifting support. I would take time to find out what faith means to them, how they

---

[35] https://charterforcompassion.org/share-the-charter/compassion-and-the-real-meaning-of-the-golden-rule

practise, and how I can support them with my network of interfaith friends if they do not identify with Buddhist teachings.

In the spirit of compassion, avoiding death-side or bedside faith conversion practices is beneficial. Faith conversion at the end of life can bring confusion and tension. In the spirit of respect, it is vital to speak to the dying in terms of the faith they have practised most of their life and find ways to support them so they can take their last breaths peacefully.

Wise Leadership Builds Compassion

So, what is stopping us from understanding the benefit of others' views? Is it our personal ego that we find hard to overcome? For example, let's think about an apple now. What do you have in mind? A red apple? What about a green one? Or even a purple apple? An apple pie may even arise in one of your minds. You may even recall its taste, scent, or texture in your hand.

From this thought experiment, we clearly observe a multitude of causes that can lead to a mental formation: perceptions, assumptions, stereotyping, or prejudices that can be as diverse as all the images that an apple can conjure.

While we broaden our common ground of virtues that we stand upon, we may find that compassion is one value that causes our lenses to expand beyond prejudices or stereotypes to regenerate positively charged perceptions. As negatively-charged perceptions arise from greed, hatred, delusion, and ignorance of the mind, we can observe differences or opposing ideologies that we may not endorse or agree with. Understanding that different beliefs may depend on different sets of causes and conditions, we can come to this calm acceptance of dependent arising, such as respecting another's right to choose another system of beliefs. I have practised the Buddha's teachings from a young age while respecting my family's traditional Chinese cultural beliefs. By understanding the above principle of interdependence of causation, I have found it easier to bring life, loving-kindness, and equanimity to our relationships.

With this as foundation, we can practice active listening which opens more communication channels, allowing us to establish more common ground regarding values. Listening does not mean looking for opportunities to debate or voice my view actively. Instead, when I listen during any interfaith discussion, the emphasis is aligning the values of my faith with the circle I am in.

Ground sensing is essential to effective leadership so that we can understand the voices of everyday people. A leader needs to have a keen awareness of public concerns or topics that may be sensitive, and know the proper contexts to raise these concerns. Sometimes this calls for seeking permission from stakeholders to raise these concerns for deeper understanding. No matter what the answer to a sensitive question may be, we can be grateful for the opportunity to have indicated a desire to learn more about others' beliefs and perspectives. Respect, trust, and virtuous friendship are crucial to achieving this sense beyond labels and stereotypes.

Faith serves as a guide for individuals to nurture their spirituality and practise a wholesome lifestyle that is skilful, blameless, and praiseworthy. When we create the causes for spiritual welfare with faith, we can experience wellness and happiness beyond our imagination.

Closing Prayer and Dedication

If my speech or action has unknowingly caused offence, or if I am unclear in my points, I seek your understanding and forgiveness.

May there be peace in the heart and harmony in mind for all sentient beings. May you and your loved ones be well and happy. Thank you for listening to my journey.

Annex

We, the 53 participants representing the different religions from nine out of the ten countries of the ASEAN Community, namely Cambodia, Indonesia, Laos, Malaysia, Myanmar, Philippines, Singapore, Thailand, and Vietnam, came together from 24–28 September 2014 for The First Interfaith Dialogue of Religious Leaders for Peace in ASEAN Community: Religious Tolerance. We met at Mahachulalongkornrajavidyalaya University, Wang Noi, Ayutthaya and at the Classic Kameo Hotel, Ayutthaya, Thailand. The event was hosted and organised by Mahachulalongkornrajavidyalaya University of Thailand and supported by the Office of National Buddhism.

The primary objective of this conference was to gather religious leaders from the ASEAN Community to discuss religious tolerance and peace in light of the impending creation of the ASEAN Economic Community (AEC) in 2015. This gathering made it possible to strengthen a network of relationships among religious leaders so as to promote interfaith dialogue for the purpose of peace and harmony in ASEAN Community.

We, the participants, hereby declare to commit ourselves

1. to promote and advocate the concept of religious tolerance meaning respect, acceptance, and appreciation as found in the Declaration of Principles on Tolerance adopted by the General Conference of UNESCO 1995,
2. to continue to promote interfaith relations in our respective countries and enhance a network of dialogue among religious leaders within the ASEAN community in order to support one another in our efforts towards tolerance and peace,
3. to educate our faith communities that they will be knowledgeable of their own religion and the religions of others,
4. to work tirelessly at the grassroots level to promote interfaith dialogue, to build bridges among the various religious communities, and to find ways to work together for common good and human dignity,
5. to continue to build familiarity and strengthen relationships by promoting mutual understanding, appreciation, and unity among religious leaders and their communities,
6. to promote cooperation and collaboration among religions at all levels so that our religions will not be instrumentalised by political systems, ideologies, vested interests, or the media.

Ayutthaya, Thailand
28 September 2014

Chapter 3.6

RESILIENCE AND COHESIVENESS IN SOCIETY: PERSPECTIVES FROM THE RAMAKRISHNA ORDER

Swami Samachittananda

Thank you for inviting all of us to share our views on religion, resilience, and a cohesive society. As introduced, I am a Hindu monk, belonging to the Ramakrishna Order of monks. So obviously my perspective will be from the Hindu point of view and from the monastic or monk's point of view.

The resilience and cohesiveness in society do not come by themselves. Collectively, both the people and the government must put in the effort. All individuals have a responsibility to see that he or she maintains and contributes to peacebuilding and creating cohesiveness in society. Here, in Singapore, we have a strong political will to establish harmony and cohesiveness. That does not happen everywhere. I will be speaking today from a universal perspective.

As I said, I belong to the Ramakrishna Order. Many of you could be familiar with the name Ramakrishna. He was a saint born in 1836. His speciality was that though he hardly received any education, he could read and write. It was his sheer thirst for knowledge that led him to think that if there is a Truth, he must realise it; if there is God, he must have a vision or he must have an experience of Him or Her or It. With that sheer thirst, he went on practising not only the denominations of the Hindu religion but also, in his own way, other religions such as Christianity, Islam, Sikhism, and Buddhism. At the end of his spiritual practices, he proclaimed — *As many faiths, that many paths.*

Many Paths, One Destination

Let us understand this concept. All of us came here in different ways. We followed different paths to reach here. None of us followed the same path. But eventually, we all came here. Though our routes were different, we reached the same destination. This was Ramakrishna's idea — religion is nothing but a path to realising the Truth. Truth cannot be two, God cannot be two. Sun is the same, which gives light and life to us. Water is the same that we all consume. God is the same, we call Him by different names. This truth was declared in the Vedas, the Hindu scriptures more than 5,000 years ago, which says "Ekam Sat Vipra bahudha Vadanti" which means that the Truth is one which is called differently by different sages who realised it in different ways.

Religious harmony has many aspects. One aspect is the philosophical perspective of harmony. We are different in many ways, different cultures, different languages, different clothes, different foods, etc. But there is something which is common. We must find a common basis for all religions. We may have apparent differences, but we must find the common ground where all religions meet. Religion is a path for the seekers of Truth. For those who are not seekers, it is difficult for them to find the common ground among all religions. Seeking Truth in my way is my Religion. The other person may seek the Truth in his way, but the Truth remains the same. The paths could be different. We may call water by different names, but quenching thirst is the purpose of drinking water. For example, a person believes in the existence of water but imagine the conviction of that person who does not need to *believe* because he has consumed water and quenched his thirst. Realised souls are those individuals who were not only believers but they experienced God or Truth. They started their journey as seekers of Truth. Unless we all touch that common basis of religion, we may not be able to realise the true meaning of the harmony of religions.

Religion Is for Peace

Swami Vivekananda, the chief disciple of Sri Ramakrishna came to Singapore on his way to America in 1893. In Chicago, they had organised a meeting of all different faiths and religions. They called it "The Parliament of Religions". It was for the first time on an international platform that the harmony of religions was discussed. Swami Vivekananda spoke with all his convictions that all religions are but different paths leading towards the same goal, and this goal is named differently in different religions. He said that the temple, the books, and the rituals are the secondary details of religion. The primary idea is the divinity within us which must be realised. If there is no goal of realising this divinity, religions will remain as a bunch of beliefs only. Every religion, in a way, speaks the same. The realisation of the innate Divinity in us is the goal. Eternal witness in the hearts of all, as Hindu scriptures put it, is the same as 'The Kingdom of Heaven' within all of us, as the Bible says. There was no prophet or incarnation who was incorrect. All of them were correct. Only the followers either do not understand the teachings of their prophets or misunderstand them. Religion was always for peace. Our less understanding or misunderstandings have made religion a source of disruptiveness.

Religions originate in different places by different incarnations or prophets. The languages, the similes, and the examples given in the scriptures must be different because they originated in different places. However, the main tune of realising the truth, realising God, and realising the divine is the same. Until that is accepted, we cannot go very far towards true harmony. Unless and until all of us accept that God is one and we are children of the same God, true sustainable peace and harmony would be difficult to achieve. As the water is called by different names like jal, pani, aqua, H_2O, etc., so God also is called by different names like Father in Heaven, Allah, Bhagavan, etc.

For any religious problems in society, we should not blame religion. Religion was never at fault. Let us understand and accept this first. If there is a fault, it is in the followers because we have no capacity to understand what the prophets and incarnations have said. So, if we do not understand, or we misunderstand, then we misrepresent the religion.

Important Role of Religious Leaders

Whenever you see any kind of radicalisation, it does not come by itself. It is preceded by fundamentalism, which precedes exclusivism. No religion preaches exclusivism, radicalisation, or fundamentalism. To prevent this here is the key: Leaders who are true seekers of Truth in that religion must come out with a solution and teach the people of their own faith.

Once an incident happened in India. There was a big clash between followers of the two religions. Afterwards, there was a meeting to establish harmony among the followers of those two religions. One of our Swamis was also invited to speak at that gathering. He told a very simple but important and meaningful idea. Those who fought in the name of religion, do you think they were the representative of your religion? He asked. No, the answer came. They were self-appointed, and they did something wrong that their religion does not profess or condone. When this type of incident happens, religion should not be blamed. We need to understand this. We have to correct the understanding of the people.

Spirituality Rather than Religion

The eternal truth, which is in the heart of all of us, must be realised. If the realisation of Truth is not the goal, then religion becomes a socio-cultural activity, a socio-cultural get-together. Let us try to understand our own scriptures, our own prophets, and incarnations. No religion was ever illogical. Misinterpreted teachings become illogical and thereby become a source of all trouble. Respecting prophets and the scriptures of other religions will increase our tolerance and slowly we will accept all religions as true. It is the same God who establishes different religions in different places and at different times for the benefit of humankind.

So, to create a cohesive society, we should put more stress on spirituality than religion. Religion can be many, but spirituality is one and universal. Love, kindness, compassion, and above all love for God and His children are common in all religions. No religion can possibly oppose this idea. These universal values would make us more spiritual, and they will bring us a step closer to God. This is the only religion, everything else is secondary.

Thank you.

https://doi.org/10.1142/9789811285387_0014

Chapter 3.7

THE SINGAPORE STORY AND THE ROLE OF TAOISM

Master Benjamin Tan

Singapore is a sunny, tropical island in Southeast Asia, off the southern tip of the Malay Peninsula. The city-state is 710 square kilometres and inhabited by five million people from four major ethnic communities: Chinese, Malay, Indian, and Eurasian. Accordingly, Singapore has a diverse religious demographic with the most common being Buddhism, Christianity, Islam, Taoism, and Hinduism. Since its independence on 9 August 1965, the country has adopted a parliamentary democracy system and holds racial and religious harmony to a high standard. Over the years, Singapore has become a highly developed metropolis which is viewed as a role model by many nations. Singapore has accumulated numerous accolades, such as being the business hub of Asia, the top maritime city in the world and clinching the title of world's best airport for eight years in a row. This chapter aims to explain how Taoism as a religion contributes to the Singapore story, in particular, the maintenance of racial, and religious harmony.

Trials and Tribulations

While Singapore may enjoy high levels of peace and security today, this was not always the case. It is necessary for us to look back on the turmoil which the nation has conquered and to learn from them. Only by holding our past dear to us can we truly appreciate what we have today. At the same time, it reminds us not to be complacent as threats are omnipresent, and ignorance of such threats could bring catastrophic consequences. In reminiscence of Singapore's tumultuous past, several prominent racial and religious conflicts stand out: the Maria Hertogh riots and the communal riots. In recent times, several concerning incidents have also occurred.

Maria Hertogh Riots

Seventy-one years ago, riots broke out in Singapore over the custody battle of a 13-year-old girl, Maria Hertogh. Maria was born to a Dutch-Eurasian Roman Catholic family and put in the care of a family friend, Che Aminah, during World War II. Maria was raised by Aminah as a Muslim and renamed Nadra binte Ma'arof. After the war, Maria and Aminah lived in Aminah's hometown in Terengganu, Malaya. At this time, the Hertoghs returned to the Netherlands and decided to search for Maria. Upon locating her, they launched a legal effort to reclaim her through the Dutch authorities. Eventually, the courts awarded custody of Maria to her birth parents, and Aminah applied to appeal against the decision. There was contention over whether Maria was given to Aminah for adoption or just to be looked after temporarily.

The case was covered extensively by local and international newspapers. However, some newspapers sensationalised their coverage and others used the custody battle to push their own agendas or those of their backers. Their articles deliberately presented a biased selection of facts and information to sway the opinion of their readers and to divide the public. They portrayed the case as a religious issue between Christianity and Islam.

This built-up tension exploded when the colonial court swiftly dismissed Aminah's appeal on 11 December 1950. Demonstrations outside the Supreme Court building grew hostile and turned into a riot, which spread outwards across the island. The three days of violence that followed left 18 dead and 173 injured with widespread destruction of property. During this period, Maria left Singapore with her birth mother to the Netherlands. Singapore was put under lockdown until law and order were restored by noon on 13 December 1950.

The riots reveal the potential harm that can come from sensationalised and distorted information. Today, with the speed at which social media spreads news, hostile entities may use it as a rapid means to sow discord within and between communities. Now, we need to be extra critical of what we see, read, and hear. More importantly, we must strive to understand and communicate with one another better. This is especially so when dealing with hyper-sensitive issues, such as race and religion. In malicious hands, the strength of people's faiths can be weaponised against their own communities. Such incidents remind us of the fragility of social construct and to be ever vigilant of devious schemes.

Communal Riots

On 21 July 1964, some 20,000 Malays gathered at the Padang for a procession to celebrate Prophet Muhammad's birthday. Amidst the celebrations, a glass bottle was hurled into the crowd, hitting someone on the head. Angry exchanges between the marching Malays and the Chinese bystanders ensued, escalating into widespread violence. As word of the riot spread, more joined in, resulting in fights breaking out across the island. The entire police force was activated, and the armed forces mobilised. Tear gas was used to break up fights and an island-wide curfew was imposed.

The person who threw the bottle was later traced back to Malay UMNO activists led by then UMNO secretary-general Ja'afar Albar. Prior to the riots, Ja'afar Albar started a campaign accusing the People's Action Party (PAP) government of depriving the Malays in Singapore of the special rights given to their Malaysian counterparts.

It took 17 days for the situation to stabilise, during which Goodwill Committees were set up across all 51 constituencies at the time, consisting of community leaders of all races. They were tasked to restore harmony among the races by listening to and addressing the concerns of residents. Peace Committees were also formed in the areas hardest hit by the riots to counter rumours. In total, 23 people died while 454 were injured.

However, peace was short-lived. Widespread communal riots broke out between the Malays and Chinese a month later, after the mysterious killing of a Malay trishaw rider in Geylang Serai. Curfews were imposed again, with the police and military mobilised. On 14 September, 12 days later, calm was established. However, 13 people had already died and another 106 were injured.

In 1969, riots between Malays and Chinese erupted again, spilling over to Singapore from Kuala Lumpur where fighting had broken out because of unhappiness surrounding the general elections results and rumours pertaining to the Chinese and Malays.

The election was preceded by outbreaks of racial incidents that created a tense atmosphere. A Malay political worker had been killed by a Chinese gang in Penang, while a Chinese youth was shot and killed by police in Kuala Lumpur (KL). While election day passed without incident, the parade by winning opposition parties Democratic Action Party (DAP) and Gerakan in Malaysia was alleged to be highly provocative with non-Malays taunting the Malays. They were seen as an attack on Malay supremacy, though the overall election results still favoured the Malay.

On 13 May, just before UMNO's procession, fist fights broke out in Setapak, KL, between a group of Malays and Chinese bystanders who taunted them, which escalated into bottle and stone throwing. Violence soon spread across the city and across the border into Singapore.

On 31 May, fuelled by rumours of the clash, Malay mobs and Chinese triads in Singapore began attacking one another. The seven-day clashes left four people dead and some eighty injured. However, the government was quick to contain the riots before they could spread. The Internal Security Department (ISD) stepped in with the police to suppress the conflict.

Recent Times

While the Maria Hertogh and communal riots occurred many years ago, Singapore must remain alert of any racial or religious discord festering below the surface. Even today, race and religion remain a contentious topic for many, potentially fuelling hatred and anger. In 2021 alone, several incidents remind us of this.

First, a Singaporean man was caught giving money to a Malaysian man to join Islamic State in Syria. Second, a 20-year-old was detained under ISA after planning to attack Jews at a Waterloo Street synagogue. Third, a 16-year-old Singaporean was detained under ISA after planning to attack Muslims at 2 mosques. Lastly, a 29-year-old Singaporean man was detained under the Internal Security Act after he became self-radicalised and made plans to travel to overseas conflict zones to undertake armed violence.

Evidently, race and religion can still be a source of conflict today due to the agenda of malicious individuals. If taken for granted, the peace and security which Singaporeans enjoy today could be lost in a blink of an eye.

Progress/Efforts

Moving forward from its tempestuous past, Singaporeans have grasped the importance of racial and religious harmony. Over the years, the government has taken active steps to inculcate appreciation and tolerance between the various racial and religious groups in Singapore.

Every year on July 21, Singapore celebrates Racial Harmony Day to remind ourselves not to let racial or religious differences divide us. On the contrary, we should transmute diversity into strength. It reiterates that no one race or religion owns Singapore. Rather, everybody will have his place in our democratic and meritocratic society, regardless of language, race, culture, or religion.

The Housing Development Board (HDB) introduced the Ethnic Integration Policy (EIP) in 1989 to ensure a balanced mix of ethnic groups in HDB estates and to prevent the formation of racial enclaves. It seeks to promote racial integration in Singapore by allowing residents of different ethnicities to live together and interact on a regular basis in public housing, where 80% of the population lives. The EIP has helped maintain racial and social harmony in Singapore by providing opportunities for social mixing among Singaporeans of different races. Consequently, there is a healthy mix of racial and religious population in all estates of the nation. As they live, work, and play together, people of different races and faith learn to be more accepting of one another.

Strict laws have also been imposed against perpetrators who harm racial or religious sentiments in the community. By severely punishing these individuals, Singapore firmly establishes its zero-tolerance position on the matter. Individuals are thus strongly discouraged from engaging in acts or speech which could incite animosity between different groups in our community.

Pillars of Support

In hopes of continually fostering greater understanding and tolerance between varying religions, several interfaith organisations have been set up. They aim to build stronger bonds between different religious groups, encouraging them to coexist harmoniously among one another.

Roses of Peace is a youth-driven, ground-up movement that aims to promote the interfaith messages of peace, love, and harmony. Roses of Peace envisions a Singapore in which youth from diverse faith back-grounds live harmoniously and cooperate with each other to serve the local community, thereby strengthening our social fabric and promoting common good.

Hash.peace is a youth-led advocacy group committed to catalysing conversations and developing programmes that contribute towards sus-tainable social harmony. It hopes to advocate racial and religious unity, build friendships that transcend differences, counter exclusivist and extremist mindsets in the community, develop cultural intelligence and critical thinking programmes, and establish a support network of peace leaders in Singapore and worldwide.

The Inter-Religious Organisation (IRO) Youth Wing serves youths and young adults aged 18–40 from different religions: Hindu, Jew, Zoroastrian, Buddhist, Taoist, Jain, Christian, Islam, Sikh, and Baha'i. The IRO legacy of religious harmony and its continuing activities steward an essential way of life in Singapore and an indelible part of Singaporean national culture and social inheritance.

The Racial and Religious Harmony Circles (Harmony Circle) is a platform to promote racial and religious harmony in Singapore, with a presence in every constituency. It sees itself as a bridge between religious, ethnic, and community groups. By being part of the Harmony Circle network, leaders from these various groups can come together to build friendship and trust. Harmony Circles also seek to deepen Singaporeans' understanding of various faiths, beliefs, and practices.

Interfaith Youth Circle is a ground-up initiative aimed at planting seeds that foster discourse around faith and beliefs. It explores high-quality engagements and creates a safe space for challenging potentially controversial intra and interfaith issues. In doing so, it makes religion a bridge and not a barrier. Also, it transforms public consciousness and promotes a deeper understanding of the role that faith groups can play in our complexly religious yet secular world.

In addition to operating within Singapore, these initiatives have extended beyond our borders. They work together with regional partners to encourage religious understanding and tolerance within and between nations. As such, these organisations foster greater cohesion not only within Singapore but also between our neighbouring countries. In turn, we may expect greater social stability in the region.

Background of Taoism and Its Role in Contributing to Peace

In Singapore, Taoism is widely practised among the majority Chinese population. As per the census conducted in 2020, approximately 8.8% of Singaporeans are Taoists. It is thus appropriate for us to explore the essence of Taoism and appreciate its significance in contributing to peace and harmony in Singapore.

Origins

Taoism is both a philosophy and religion indigenous to ancient China. It is often linked back to the philosopher Lao Tzu. Throughout history, Taoism has exerted a powerful influence over Chinese culture. Historical evidence indicates that the superior traditions of Taoism philosophies, with widespread and enduring influence, have long been nurturing and soaking the spiritual world amidst the human world. As an intrinsic force to promote social harmony and human development, Taoism has been playing a positive role in aspiring social progress and encouraging national advance.

Tracing back to 500 B.C.E., Lao Tzu is traditionally credited for being the author for the main book of Taoism, the *Tao Te Ching*. The *Tao Te Ching*, also known as "The Way and Its Power," is a collection of poetry and sayings. It provides Taoists with guidance regarding their thoughts and actions. Alongside the writings of Zhuangzi, *Tao Te Ching* serves as the fundamental text for both philosophical and religious Taoism. It also holds significant influence over other Chinese religions and philosophies, such as Chinese Buddhism, Confucianism, and Legalism. As the keystone text of Taoism, it shares ideas of Chinese origin and emphasises living in harmony with the Tao.

Reach

Spearheaded by the emigration of the Chinese population to all corners of the world, Taoism's influence has gradually spread far beyond the borders of China. Taoism is a major religion in Taiwan and many Southeast Asian countries, such as Malaysia, Singapore, and Vietnam. In its birthplace, Taoism is one of the five religious doctrines accepted by the People's Republic of China, including its special administrative regions of Hong Kong and Macau.

Adaptability

Through the sands of time, change is inexorable. When the winds of change blow, some people build walls, while others build windmills. In this respect, Taoism has proved itself to be adaptable. Over time, Taoism has evolved accordingly with constant revision and refinement of its practices and doctrines. This high degree of adaptability and flexibility has allowed Taoism to stay pertinent over its centuries of existence. By maintaining perpetual relevance, Taoism has cemented its role as a prominent faith in modern society.

At the same time, Taoism is seen as a vessel to preserve traditional national culture. With the advent of technology, our daily lives are moving at a faster pace than ever before. Coupled with the spill-over effects of global political strife while recovering from a pandemic, we seem to be in an era of great uncertainty. Cultures and societies are faced with profound changes, some of which erode the fabric of cultural identity and faith. As Chinese society has not been spared, the Taoist community is widely interested in exploring how it may adapt its beliefs to accommodate such profound changes.

In a time where religious affairs easily ignite controversy in public domains, Taoists must tread cautiously. Taoists should practice their beliefs in appropriate and transparent ways that seek to unify people, not divide them. In the current era of globalisation, cities are melting pots of cultures and religions. When advocating one's faith, individuals should do so tactfully and be considerate of the impacts on the community. Being cognisant of the cultural and religious sensitivities of the communities where they reside, Taoism can coexist harmoniously among other faiths and religions.

Concept

In general, Taoism holds that humans and animals should live in balance with the *Tao*. While the *Tao* can be difficult to define, it is understood as the way of the universe. Taoism teaches that all living creatures ought to live in a state of harmony with the universe and the energy found in it. Chi, or Qi, is the energy present in the universe and guides everything in it. The *Tao Te Ching* and other Taoist books serve as guides for the behavioural and spiritual methodology of living in harmony with this energy. However, Taoists do not believe in this energy as a god. Rather, there are gods as part of the Taoist beliefs, often introduced from the various cultures found in the region known now as China. These gods are part of the *Tao*, like all living things. Taoism has temples, monasteries, and priests who make offerings, meditate, and perform other rituals for their communities.

In understanding the *Tao*, philosophers believe that everything can only be understood by comparing it to its opposite. Just as day is only day in relation to night, coldness is relative to heat, and softness is relative to hardness. Looking deeper still, we observe that relationships are in a constant state of flux: Day flows gradually into night and back again. This forms the cornerstone of Taoist philosophy.

Yin-Yang

One of the main ideas of Taoism is the belief in balancing forces or Yin and Yang. These ideas represent matching pairs, such as light and dark, hot and cold, and action and inaction, which work together towards a universal whole. Yin and Yang show that everything in the universe is connected and that nothing makes sense by itself. Human beings are but a mere microcosm of the universe. Consequently, it is believed that one can understand the universe better by first understanding oneself.

Taoist cosmology is cyclic. The universe is viewed as being in a constant process of re-creation. Taoist cosmology shares similar views with the School of Naturalists (Yin-Yang) which was headed by Zou Yan (305–240 BCE). The school's tenets harmonised the concepts of the Wu Xing (Five Elements) and Yin and Yang. In this vein, the universe is seen as being in a constant process of re-creating itself with everything that exists being a mere aspect of Chi. Chi, when condensed, becomes life; when diluted, has indefinite potential. Chi is in a perpetual transformation between its condensed and diluted state. These two different states of Chi are embodiments of the abstract entities of Yin and Yang, two complementary extremes that constantly play with and against each other. Yin cannot exist without Yang and vice versa.

The Tai Ji Tu commonly known as the "Yin and Yang symbol" possesses great importance in Taoist symbolism. In cosmology, the universe creates itself out of a primary chaos of material energy, organised into the cycles of Yin and Yang and formed into objects and lives. Yin is the receptive and Yang is the active principle, seen in all forms of change and difference such as the annual season cycles, the natural landscape, the formation of both men and women as characters, and socio-political history. Beyond Taoist organisations, its principles have influenced Confucian, Neo-Confucian, and pan-Chinese theory. This symbol is extensively used as a decorative element on Taoist organization flags and logos, temple floors, or stitched into clerical robes. According to Song dynasty sources, it originated around the 10th century CE.

The Tai Ji Tu consists of two (one black and one white) swirling teardrop shapes that fit within each other to form a perfect circle. Each figure contains a part of the other such that there is a black dot in the white half of the circle and a white dot in the black half. These seemingly opposing but complementary halves make a whole and are thus incomplete without each other.

The black side represents Yin, while the white side represents Yang. Yin is associated with femininity, Earth, water, moon, and night time. It is considered passive, cold, soft, yielding, and wet. Meanwhile, Yang is associated with masculinity, sin, fire, sky, and daytime. It is considered aggressive, hot, hard, and dry. The white symbolises delusion and the black represents enlightenment. The idea conveyed by the Tai Ji Tu symbol is that everything exists in duality, which is the foundational aspect of nature. The concept of good cannot be present without the corresponding concept of bad. Men and women, right and wrong, light and darkness, positive and negative, hot and cold, day and night, and all the other contrasting elements are interdependent and cannot exist in isolation. Meanwhile, the swirling wave motion describes the flow of energy within the divine circle of life. The world changes constantly and moves forward in distinct cycles, where the day turns into night and the night leads on to another day, every birth ends in death and death leads to rebirth.

Beliefs (Three Treasures)

The Three Treasures are the core virtues of Taoism. It comprises compassion, humility, and frugality.

Compassion

Compassion is a central principle of Taoism that is discussed extensively in the *Tao Te Ching*. The principle of compassion lies at the heart of all religious, ethical, and spiritual traditions, calling us always to treat all others as we wish to be treated ourselves. Compassion impels us to work tirelessly to alleviate the suffering of our fellow creatures, to dethrone ourselves from the centre of our world and put another there, and to honour the inviolable sanctity of every single human being, treating everybody, without exception, with absolute justice, equity, and respect.

The compassion called for by Taoists is impartial, expects nothing in return, and is not possessive. According to Lao-Tzu, compassion leads to courage. When we see living beings suffering, we are naturally motivated to help. Compassion flows from an understanding that all things are one and interconnected. Once we comprehend that we are of the same substance as all things, our sense of identity naturally begins to expand, encapsulating all beings around us.

Tao Te Ching Chapter 49 states the following:

> "The Sage has no decided opinions and feelings,
> But regards the people's opinions and feelings as his own.
> The good ones I declare good;
> The bad ones I also declare good.
> That is the goodness of Virtue.
> The honest ones I believe;
> The liars I also believe;
> That is the faith of Virtue.

The Sage dwells in the world peacefully, harmoniously.
The people of the world are brought into a community of heart,
And the Sage regards them all as his own children."

Here, the sages advise people against being closed-minded or dogmatic. They should not be inflexible, having fixed ideas that resist change. Also, they cannot assume that they are always right. When personal opinions differ from that of others, they must examine alternative perspectives carefully. The compassion of the sages is truly universal. As they do not prejudge others, the sages treat people well, regardless of whether they are deserving of such kindness. They also have enduring faith in the basic decency of humanity. They trust everyone, regardless of whether the person is trustworthy. In short, the sages expect goodness from people and get it because people cannot help but raise their own standards to live up to the goodness that the sages see in them.

Humility

Humility is another essential ethical concept in Taoism with far-reaching influence on humanity. Though there were plenty of words that described "humility" in ancient China, Taoism elaborates on the concept in a profound way, adding to the theoretical depth and scope of humility. The understanding of humility in Taoism is systematic instead of random or fragmented. In Taoism, humility is considered a virtue. It is neither limited to interpersonal relationships nor is it simply considered a moral characteristic. Viewed broadly, humility is placed within a holistic context and considered the quintessential manifestation of the role of the *Tao*.

Tao Te Ching Chapter 54 states the following:

"See others as yourself.
See families as your family.
See towns as your town.
See countries as your country.
See worlds as your world.
How do I know that the world is such?
By this."

This verse teaches us to view everything as equal and to treat everything in this world as the same. While possible, it does not necessarily mean that one must treat strangers with the same care that one shows their near and dear ones. It simply means that the needs and actions of others can be understood by simply comparing to oneself. If one wishes to understand others, one must first understand oneself.

Frugality

Frugality is about using less resources for the purpose of giving more to others. The foundation for frugality is compassion. Compassionate people use little for themselves but are happy to spend lots on others. On the other hand, stingy people save money for selfish reasons and are unwilling to spend money for the sake of others.

Frugality counters greed and unhappiness. Often, the root of unhappiness is greed: We want something, and we cannot get it, hence we become unhappy. When we become unhappy, we treat others and ourselves badly. Frugality is a useful medicine for this problem. In all situations, we should aim to follow the Middle Path, which means not lacking but not excessive. Frugality follows the Middle Way: not too little, not too much.

Rituals

Taoist rituals involve purification, meditation, and offerings to deities. The details of Taoist rituals are often highly complex and technical and therefore left to the priests, with the congregation playing little part. The rituals involve the priest and assistants chanting and playing instruments, particularly wind and percussion. Dancing could also be involved.

With roots in Chinese ancestral worship, the burning of joss paper or hell money is also a common Taoist practice. This practice serves as a form of sacrifice to the spirits of the deceased or to the gods. It is assumed that the images consumed by fire will reappear in the spirit world, making them available for revered ancestors and departed loved ones.

Additionally, some would also partake in fortune-telling, including astrology, I-Ching, and other forms of divination. Mediumship is also a common practice in certain sects. There are academic and social distinctions between martial forms of mediumship, such as Tong Ji, and the spirit-writing that is typically practised through planchette writing.

Taoism Promotes Peace

All in all, the *Tao* aims to equip its practitioners with the tools by which to live their lives. The core of Taoism is to reject hatred and intolerance of human differences and live with balance, harmony, perspective, and compassion. While violence is not precluded in Taoism, it is a last resort. By increasing self-awareness and reducing the influence of ego, which is often at the heart of conflict, Taoism promotes peace within and without. Many studies have emphasised that without peace among religions, there could be no peace and harmony among nations and communities. Therefore, it is important for all religious personages to achieve a consensus by following the teachings of the founders and the classics of their religions.

Conclusion

Looking back, Singaporeans must be grateful for how far our tiny island nation has come. From being an underdeveloped third-world country just half a century ago, we have progressed rapidly to become a bustling metropolis revered by many. All these have only been made possible through the stable foundation laid out by our forefathers. Racial and religious harmony is a key component of this foundational network which we cannot afford to take for granted. It is a fundamental part of Singapore's social fabric and a main driving force for Singapore's success. After all, we are all in the same boat, either we sink or we float. So long as we continue to respect and appreciate the diversity we enjoy, Singapore would be on the right track towards continued prosperity.

Chapter 3.8

ROOM AT THE TABLE: HEALTHY RELIGIOUS IDENTITY FOR THE SAKE OF THE OTHER

Sister Julia Walsh FSPA

Let our hearts not be hardened to those living on the margins
There is room at the table for everyone.

The first lines of US American singer-songwriter Carrie Newcomer's song "Room at the Table" offer a joyful response to challenges of division: racial, religious, and economic division.[36]

I suspect most of us here would agree: diversity can enrich and strengthen us. Yet, when we feel our limited capacities and resources — when we are operating from a scarcity mindset — we are more likely to leave people out, isolate, and separate. And when we do, we are not creating societies and structures that are inclusive and cohesive. Such scarcity mindsets and separations do not promote nor establish social justice.

As I have been preparing to participate in the ICCS and thinking about what I might share, I have been thinking of this song a lot. I have discovered a desire to echo Newcomer's refrain:

---

[36] Awakin.org. (n.d.). Conversation with Carrie Newcomer: Awakin call. Awakin Calls RSS. Retrieved August 19, 2022, from https://www.awakin.org/v2/calls/459/carrie-newcomer/.

> *Let our hearts not be hardened to those living on the margins*
> *There is room at the table for everyone.*

At this time in history, we are conscious of upheaval. We have been talking about it throughout the whole conference. We know why our hearts could become hardened. During this conference, we discussed the current challenges: climate change, migration, poverty, racism, religious conflict, and extremism. Echo chambers online are dangerous as well. We have discussed how the COVID-19 pandemic has changed us, with over 6.48 million COVID-19 deaths worldwide. We each are impacted by the experience of personal and collective grief, fear, and isolation. Hungry and isolated and when we are not comfortable with "the other," we lose our sense of security and control. Fear is a breeding ground for extremist ideologies — for violence across divides. This is what happens when "the other" is considered a threat instead of a welcome guest.

> *Too long we have wandered, burdened and undone*
> *But there is room at the table for everyone.*

I stand before you as a white Christian Roman Catholic religious woman — a Franciscan Sister of Perpetual Adoration from the Midwest in the United States of America. As I see it, where I come from has formed my identity and influenced my perspectives.

In the Middle Ages in Italy, St. Francis and St. Clare of Assisi came to know their mission and belonging through their religious identity and community — in relationship with Jesus Christ and others.

As a Franciscan, I also understand that meaning and purpose are found in the collective, relational, and communal identity of a person. I tend to say that since I am a Franciscan, for me the meaning of life *is* relationship. The purpose of life is found in knowing and loving "the other." As intimacy is built through ordinary relationships, "the other" is less otherised; we move into kinship. We move from "the me" to "the we."

As a Catholic, I believe that every person is made in God's image and likeness, and therefore we are called to honour the dignity of everyone. The Catholic Catechism proclaims that social justice will only be obtained by respecting the dignity of all people.[37] The Holy Father Pope Francis has taught us that we will never experience true social justice if the human person is not the centre of concern.[38] And I, personally, am convinced that social justice is built upon equity, inclusion, and liberation. As we create sacred spaces of belonging and honour the dignity of everyone, we build community, and community builds justice.

> *There is room for us all, and no gift is too small*
> *There is room at the table for everyone.*

In establishing relationships with others, I have come to know how I can show up and serve. I ended up starting an intentional community that brought people together who were lonely and separated in Chicago.[39] We gather regularly for meals and for prayer and we have rhythms of shared work, but it is really our mission of offering refuge, offering a place where people can gather and share their dreams, learn from one another, renew their hearts and minds, and prevent burnout. This is really important for changemakers, creatives, artists, and activists who are changing society.

Here is what I know. Through ordinary interactions and regular commitments, community is formed. When grounded in clear values and structures, the community is strong and healthy. And when that community has a mission that is about sharing with the other, it works when the participants in the community each have their own healthy religious identity.

---

[37] #1929. Libreria Editrice Vaticana, Citta del Vaticano 1993. (2003, November 4). Catechism of the Catholic Church: Respect for the Human Person. Catechism of the Catholic Church - IntraText. Retrieved October 12, 2022, from https://www.vatican.va/archive/ENG0015/__P6O.HTM.

[38] Dicastero per la Comunicazione - Libreria Editrice Vaticana. (2020, November 30). Videomensaje del Santo padre con ocasión del encuentro internacional virtual de jueces miembros de los comités por los derechos sociales de Africa y América. Videomensaje del Santo Padre con ocasión del Encuentro internacional virtual de jueces miembros de los Comités por los derechos sociales de África y América. Francisco. Retrieved August 19, 2022, from https://www.vatican.va/content/francesco/es/messages/pont-messages/2020/documents/papa-francesco_20201130_videomessaggio-giudici-incontro.html.

[39] See www.thefireplacecommunity.org.

No matter how complex the social injustice is and no matter if we are concerned about the global or local isolation and separation, most solutions are found in the basic act of sharing: sharing space, sharing ideas, sharing materials, sharing stories, and sharing our hearts. The more we share who we are — and what really stirs us, what we are passionate about — the more we are building authentic relationships with one another and entering into communion. This is a pathway to justice.

In my formation and practice, I have come to understand that if a person develops a mature religious identity, then they are not threatened by differences. Instead, they are enlivened by what is different and interesting. Those with a healthy religious identity are concerned with and care about those outside their group, and they will reach out with compassion and joy. They will say that there is room at the table for everyone.

On the other hand, if one has an immature religious identity, they are more prone to rigidity and self-protection: "the other" is understood as an enemy — a threat — and it becomes justifiable, unfortunately, to use violence or force. Because we know and studies reveal that for the individual, being part of a group that opposes another group can clarify one's personal identity.[40]

So there is much more I could say, but to just conclude: Those with a healthy religious identity are concerned about those outside their group. They reach out to the margins and promote social justice. Faith and civic leaders can provide effective servant leadership by building healthy community and reaching out to the margins while modelling for others how to advocate for those in need while they create spaces for community building.

> *No matter who you are, no matter where you're from*
> *There is room at the table for everyone.*

[40] Müller, D. (2007). "Our Image of 'Others' and Our own Identity." In *Iconoclasm and Iconoclast: Struggle with Religious Identity*. Essay, Brill: Leide, Boston.

Chapter 3.9

VISUALS

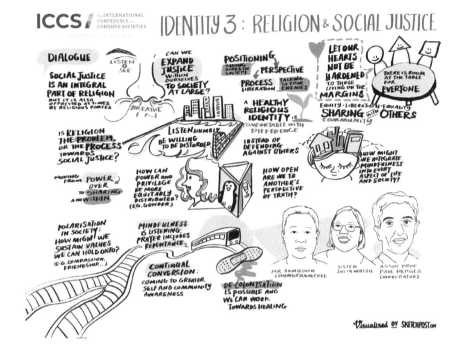

Mdm Halimah Yacob, the then President of the Republic of Singapore, delivers the Opening Address at the ICCS

"In Conversation with Deputy Prime Minister Lawrence Wong"
Deputy Prime Minister Lawrence Wong (left) and Ambassador Ong Keng Yong

Professor Lily Kong, President of Singapore Management University, delivers the "Special Presentation on Social Cohesion"

ICCS Plenary 1: How Faith Can Bridge Divides
From left to right: Professor Kumar Ramakrishna, Dr Sadhvi Bhagawati Saraswati, Lord John Alderdice, Imam Uzair Akbar, and Venerable You Guang

ICCS Plenary 2: How Diversity Can be Harnessed for the Common Good
From left to right: Assistant Professor Jack Meng-Tat Chia, Mr André Azoulay, Professor Yoshiko Ashiwa, and Dr Iyad Abumoghli

ICCS Plenary 3: How Technology Can be Leveraged to Foster Mutual Trust
From left to right: Dr Terri-Anne Teo, Mr Jasvir Singh, Associate Professor Patrice Brodeur, and Dr Shashi Jayakumar

146

Launch of the Southeast Asian Social Cohesion Radar Study Report
From left to right: Associate Professor Paul Hedges, Ms Vishalini Suresh, Mr Ravi Nadeson and Dr Jolene Jerard

Father Fiel Pareja addressing delegates from the ICCS Young Leaders Programme

Youth delegates from the ICCS Young Leaders Programme

Delegates interacting at the ICCS 2022 Conference

The VR goggles by local social enterprise Being Bridges featured at ICCS 2022 and gave users the opportunity to explore various houses of worship virtually

Delegates interacting at the ICCS 2022 Conference

Deputy Prime Minister Lawrence Wong takes a wefie with various ICCS 2022 participants

The ICCS 2022 was attended by representatives from diverse cultures, religions, ages and professional backgrounds

Briefing the ICCS 2022 delegates during visit to Wisma Geylang Serai

ICCS 2022 participants at the Silat Road Sikh Temple

Part 4

DIVERSITY

Chapter 4.1

KOPITIAM CONVIVIALITY: A STRENGTHS-BASED APPROACH TO COMMUNITY RESILIENCE IN SUPERDIVERSE SINGAPORE

Professor Selvaraj Velayutham and Professor Amanda Wise

Introduction

Ask a Singaporean what makes Singapore, Singapore. Almost without exception, their list will include Housing Development Board (HBD) flats, Singlish, food, hawker centres, and coffee shops. These are also fundamental ingredients in the 'recipe' that holds the everyday diversity of Singapore together. How might this 'recipe', which we call 'kopitiam conviviality', be harnessed to help in the next stage of Singapore's journey with diversity? In this chapter, we draw on our research on everyday multiculturalism in Singapore, current academic thinking on 'superdiversity', and 'conviviality' and link these to an action-focused everyday strengths-based approach to building community resilience.[1]

---

[1] Hammond, W. and Zimmerman, R. (2012). A strengths-based perspective. A report for resiliency initiatives, 1–18 viewed at https://shed-the-light.webs.com/documents/RSL_STRENGTH_BASED_PERSPECTIVE.pdf.

Resilient communities cope best with change, including the kinds of changes brought about by migration and diversification. Identifying and developing latent community strengths is central to current thinking on building community resilience. Though tensions and racism exist and have always existed — and should be addressed — many Singaporeans have significant strengths in coping with everyday diversity. These everyday 'old Singapore' strengths evolved over time by necessity. A resilience approach suggests the rich potential to harness and adapt these latent strengths in the next phase of Singapore's diversity journey.

We have been researching what we have termed 'everyday multiculturalism' in Australia and Singapore for over two decades and more recently drawn upon enabling concepts like superdiversity, conviviality, and community resilience to enrich our approach. We propose the metaphor 'kopitiam conviviality' to capture the everyday intercultural strengths that may be drawn upon to productively engage with Singapore's new diverse cultural landscape. Authors like Lai and Khoo have previously highlighted the socio-cultural significance of the coffee shop, also known as *Kopitiam* (in Chinese dialects) or *Kedai kopi* (in Malay) found in public housing estates in Singapore and Malaysia.[2,3] Kopitiams are places where people from all walks of life and cultural backgrounds gather to eat, drink, and chat, sometimes for hours. These are places of diversity, difference, hybridity, and multicultural conviviality.

Superdiversity, Everyday Multiculturalism, and Conviviality

The term 'superdiversity' has been circulating in academic circles for some time and has gained increasing attention among policymakers and

---

[2] Lai, A. E. (2016). The Kopitiam in Singapore: An evolving story about cultural diversity and cultural politics. In Kong, L., and Sinha, V. (eds.) *Food, Foodways and Foodscapes: Culture, Community and Consumption in Singapore*. World Scientific Publishing, Singapore.

[3] Khoo, G. C. (2009). Kopitiam: Discursive cosmopolitan spaces and national identity in Malaysian culture and media. In Wise, A., and Velayutham, S. (eds.) *Everyday Multiculturalism*. Palgrave Macmillan, London.

practitioners.[4-6] Superdiversity draws attention to the 'diversity of diversities', including the structural and inherent complexities characteristic of a culturally diverse population in a particular setting. While terms like 'multiracialism' and 'multiculturalism' invoke certain political ideologies and policy legacies, superdiversity is more an explanatory approach to understanding the many complex intersections and relations of identity, power, and inequality in immigrant-receiving societies. These not only include the standard intersections of gender, race, and class but also highlight other varieties of 'difference' such as immigrant status (visa categories, permanent residents vs Employment Pass or Work Permit for example), and the varying conditions and statuses attached to different migrant visa pathways, and the stratifications of multicultural urban citizenship these produce. In Singapore, superdiversity also accounts for the complex differences between 'old' (local) Singapore Indians and Chinese and recent 'new' Chinese and Indian immigrants. In this view, it is unsurprising that temporary migrant workers from the Philippines, India, Bangladesh, and China on highly restricted visa schemes are the most marginalised group in Singapore as compared to Employment/S-pass holders or new permanent residents and Singapore citizens.

If superdiversity signals the 'diversity of diversities' and accompanying processes of social differentiation, what does that mean for the everyday lived experience and politics of race and cultural diversity in a place like Singapore? This chapter attends to this question of multicultural coexistence and superdiversity "through" what we have previously termed everyday multiculturalism.[7,8] Like superdiversity, everyday multicultural-

---

[4] Vertovec, S. (2007). Super-diversity and its implications. *Ethnic and Racial Studies* 30(6), 1024–1054.

[5] Vertovec, S. (2019). Talking around super-diversity. *Ethnic and Racial Studies* 42(1), 125–139.

[6] Meissner, F., and Vertovec, S. (2015). Comparing super-diversity. *Ethnic and Racial Studies* 38(4), 541–555.

[7] Wise, A., and Velayutham, S. (2009) Introduction: Multiculturalism and everyday life. In Wise, A., and Velayutham, S. (eds.) *Everyday Multiculturalism*. Palgrave Macmillan, London.

[8] Wise, A., and Velayutham, S. (2014). Conviviality in everyday multiculturalism: Some brief comparisons between Singapore and Sydney. *European Journal of Cultural Studies* 17(4), 406–430.

ism is a meso-level methodological and conceptual approach to understanding the everyday relations, practices, possibilities, and outcomes of everyday living in superdiverse societies. Everyday multiculturalism as an approach has five main points of focus[9]:

1. a concern with the how (process) and why (conditions of possibility) as new communities of difference form (or not, as the case may be),
2. identifying the shape and timbre of social relations in situations of lived cultural diversity, such as how tensions and divisions brew and are challenged or worked through, as well as patterns of affinity and solidarity, disjuncture, and division in diverse contexts,
3. describing changing patterns of identity and belonging and the nature of new social ties,
4. identifying patterns of contradiction and ambivalence in coexistence, including patterns of hate and racism at the everyday level,
5. exploring the nature, malleability, inclusiveness, and resilience of new forms of community in diversity, more established urban multicultures, and the shifts and reworkings of identities and belongings over time.

The immediate methodological interest is in sites of sustained everyday encounter, such as local public spaces, neighbourhoods, apartment complexes, shopping areas, various kinds of micropublics, such as workplaces, schools, leisure activities, and spaces, formal and informal sporting/recreational activities, and craft groups, as well as welfare initiatives and civil society. It is the 'ism' in everyday multiculturalism that distinguishes the approach from alternative concepts like 'lived diversity', 'urban multiculture', or 'intercultural relations'. The -ism insists on attention to the structural and the ideological in our analyses of the everyday because they cannot be separated from lived experience. All experience is mediated, as illustrated in Figure 1.

---

[9] Wise, A. (2022). Superdiversity and the everyday. In Meissner, F., Sigona, N., and Vertovec, S. (eds.) *Oxford Handbook of Superdiversity.* Oxford University Press, Oxford.

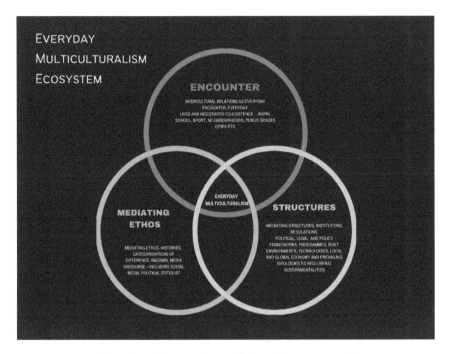

Figure 1.   The everyday multiculturalism ecosystem.[10]

Taken together, the concepts of superdiversity and everyday multiculturalism offer productive insights into the opportunity structures that influence patterns of coexistence and everyday intercultural sociality, especially in a place like Singapore. These ideas attune us to the everyday social, cultural, and structural forces that enable or limit the emergence of solidarities and affinities in diversity at the everyday level across varying axes of difference. Though both concepts overlap in their approach and orientation towards the study of living in culturally diverse societies, everyday multiculturalism's concern with everyday social relations in situations, their underpinnings, patterns, possibilities, and potential outcomes offer invaluable lessons on where and how they work or fail. With these insights, we can arm ourselves with strategies and tools to effect positive and productive social relations among strangers who must co-exist.

---

[10] *Ibid.*

Convivial Labour and Community Resilience

Diversity and difference are often celebrated for the richness and vibrancy they add to everyday life and social interaction. Yet they are also sometimes viewed as an obstacle to cohesion and the cause of social friction. Together with superdiversity and everyday multiculturalism, we enrol third concept, conviviality, as invoked by Paul Gilroy.[11] It refers to the process by which co-existence and accommodation are made possible. Writing about Britain's urban multicultures, Gilroy's take deploys the Spanish notion of *Convivencia*, which has a more nuanced meaning than the English term 'conviviality' which tends to infer 'happy', 'festive', and 'fun' forms of togetherness. Convivencia as shared life includes an emphasis on practice, effort, negotiation, and achievement. This sense of 'rubbing along' includes not just 'happy togetherness' but also negotiation, friction, and sometimes conflict. It signals belonging and new forms of community as practice, as hard labour.[12] Noble argues that we should see this hard work as 'a form of labour — not just because it is hard ... but because it is productive, transactional, and cumulative, creating things — like 'community' and 'identity' — over a period of time.'[13] Like learning any new skill — whether learning a musical instrument or learning to cook or sing, to play football, or mathematics — it takes work, practice, discomfort, and careful listening for a skill to become habit, achieving both proficiency and harmony.

Scholarship on everyday multiculturalism has identified situations, practices, places, and spaces that enable an openness to others

---

[11] Gilroy, P. (2004). *After Melancholia or Convival Culture?* Routledge, London.

[12] Wise, A., and Noble, G. (2018). Convivialities: An Orientation. In Wise, A., and Noble, G. (eds.) *Convivialities: Possibility and Ambivalence in Urban Multicultures*. Routledge, London.

[13] Noble, G. (2009). Everyday cosmopolitanism and the labour of intercultural community. In Wise, A., and Velayutham, S. (eds.) *Everyday Multiculturalism*. Palgrave Macmillan, London.

while also acknowledging that cultural intermingling can be hard work.[14–20] Approaching the 'diversity question' through the lens of 'convivial labour' captures the reality that living with and adapting to difference are not always easy. Approaching these challenges as problems that are or can be worked through acknowledges both the ambivalent and hopeful dimensions of social change and spotlights the active role demanded of all stakeholders — from individuals to the government — in fostering more hopeful communities-in-difference. Things can get tense or go awry, but working together in good faith can help turn things around.

Perhaps a story is the best place to start this accounting of everyday strengths. More than thirty years ago, my[21] family moved into a new housing estate in Taman Jurong. Singapore's ethnic integration policy meant that the proportion of Chinese, Malays, and Indian residents in the neighbourhood reflected the respective national population ratio. On our floor, there were four Chinese, three Malay, and two Indian households. Greetings and brief exchanges as neighbours encountered one another along the common corridor over time led to a comfortable familiarity-in-difference. This eventually deepened into an inclusive everyday sociality

[14] Leong, G. W. (2020). Conviviality in clementi. In Chung, S. S., and Douglass, M. (eds.) *The Hard State, Soft City of Singapore*, pp. 213–232. Amsterdam University Press.

[15] Ye, J. (2019). Re-orienting geographies of urban diversity and coexistence: Analyzing inclusion and difference in public space. *Progress in Human Geography*, 43(3), 478–495.

[16] Kathiravelu, L., and Bunnell, T. (2018). Introduction: Urban friendship networks: Affective negotiations and potentialities of care. *Urban Studies*, 55(3), 491–504.

[17] Peterson, M. (2017). Living with difference in hyper-diverse areas: How important are encounters in semi-public spaces? *Social & Cultural Geography*, 18(8), 1067–1085.

[18] Neal, S., Bennett, K., Cochrane, A., and Mohan, G. (2017). *Lived Experiences of Multiculture: The New Social and Spatial Relations of Diversity*. Routledge.

[19] Neal, S., Bennett, K., Cochrane, A., and Mohan, G. (2019). Community and conviviality? Informal social life in multicultural places. *Sociology*, 53(1), 69–86.

[20] Vertovec, S. (2015). Introduction: Migration, cities, diversities 'old' and 'new'. In Vertovec, S. (ed.) *Diversities Old and New: Migration and Socio-spatial Patterns in New York, Singapore and Johannesburg*, pp. 1–20. Palgrave Macmillan.

[21] 'My' refers in this account to the chapter co-author Selvaraj Velayutham.

based on neighbourly relations between Chinese, Indian, and Malay aunties gifting treats to neighbours' children as they pass and sharing plates of festive foods between neighbours of different faiths and races on Chinese New Year, Hari Raya, or Deepavali.

Fast forward to the 2010s, close to 70% of the original flat owners had sold their properties or were renting them out. Singapore's ethnic and cultural landscape has rapidly become much more diverse, and this new diversity is reflected in Taman Jurong. On our floor, only the Chinese family next door and us remain of the original neighbours. The other flats along our common corridor are now occupied by new residents: S-Pass and Employment Pass holders, and new permanent residents from China, India, the Philippines, and Myanmar. The easy and familiar sociality built up over time with Singapore's 'familiar others' became less so.

In October 2021, after brief illness, my father passed away suddenly. Despite the pandemic restrictions, nearly everyone in our apartment block came to pay their respects at the wake, which was held in the void deck below. The Singapore-Chinese daughter of our long-time neighbour was overcome with grief. Her family stood alongside us to carry out the final rites and, in the days and weeks following, checked on my mother regularly. My mother speaks only Tamil and a sprinkle of Malay and English words which she picked up from my father who had moved to Singapore in 1952 and worked most of his career in the Singapore Electricity Board. Similarly, our elderly Chinese neighbour speaks only Hokkien and Melayu pasar. But both have been exchanging pleasantries and checking on each other regularly.

This anecdote is nothing extraordinary — everyday encounters like these are commonplace in Singapore's HDB heartlands and so too the transformation of heartland neighbourhoods. Yet it is this kind of everyday encounters and interactions — however fleeting — sustained over time that can lead to positive and productive relationships. The picture drawn in this anecdote is backed up by our two decades of research on everyday multiculturalism in Singapore. The following are examples:

Service, gift exchange, and helping culture

Everyday reciprocities are core foundations for community connection[22]: The red packets (Ang Pows), mandarin oranges, and sweet pineapple biscuits that Chinese traditionally gift to family and friends at Chinese New Year are also gifted to Malay and Indian neighbours and sometimes employees. The practice has been adapted by Malays who often gift 'green packets' at Hari Raya (Eid el Fitri). In turn, the sweets and spicy muruku snacks favoured by Singapore Indians to share at Deepavali are gifted to Chinese and Malay friends and neighbours taking care to adapt the offering to the assumed tastes of the other two groups. Sweets for Chinese friends who traditionally don't like spicy food and spicy snacks for Malays who do. These forms of gift exchange sometimes produce interesting adaptations and appropriations. For example, the traditional Chinese pineapple biscuit has gradually become a favourite for both Hindus and Muslims to swap during their festivals. Selvaraj's mother brings plastic jars of Chinese pineapple biscuits as gifts when she visits the village back in India.

Exchanges just as frequently occur outside festive occasions. Not everything needs to be explicitly about cultural and religious differences. Just as important are everyday practices of neighbourly recognition like impromptu sharing of snacks and everyday food items (rice, bread, tin of Milo, 3-in-1 coffee sachets, and box of teabags), holding the lift, helping to carry shopping bags from downstairs, and even simple friendly gestures of greeting. Not only do these forms of exchange knit together new forms of community across differences — in ways that involve retaining one's diasporic orientations while opening out across differences and sometimes borrowing across groups — but over time they come to shape the communities involved.

---

[22] Wise, A., and Velayutham, S. (2014). Conviviality in everyday multiculturalism: Inhabiting diversity in Singapore and Sydney. *European Journal of Cultural Studies* 17 (4), 406–430.

Food

Food is also central to the everyday practices of religious accommodation.[23,24] These have become second nature in Singapore, not only in part due to a concerted state campaign to promote multiracial, multilingual, and multireligious respect and recognition but also in part due to everyday encounters between the Chinese, Malay, and Indian diasporas of Singapore. It is normal and quite unremarkable, for example, to see halal tables set up at wedding receptions, conferences, and work meetings as a gesture of recognition to Malay and Indian Muslim friends attending or not serving beef dishes in the company of Indians. These accommodations are also built into the urban fabric with halal-designated sections in hawker centres and food courts.

Language and Humour

Singapore's very own vernacular Singlish is often derided as just poor English. Yet, this local version of English cuts across class, race, and ethnicity and connects people in Singapore across all walks of life — from the Filipina migrant worker, Malay shop assistant to the Indian bus driver. More importantly, the use of words like 'uncle' or 'aunty' to address non-family members and complete strangers is unique to Singapore. Singlish is a language that has evolved for close to two centuries since migrants arrived in Singapore. From our research on everyday diversity at the workplace, we discovered Bangladeshi, Filipino, Indonesian, Burmese, Tamil, and Chinese migrant workers adopting the use of Singlish and even incorporating words from their languages in every interaction. This suggests that Singlish will continue to evolve and can serve as a language that can bridge diversity.

Along with Singlish, humour plays an important role in Singapore. In our previous research on interactional humour in Singaporean workplaces, we found there was an important strain of Singaporean humour that was light-hearted and accommodative of cultural and language

---

[23] *Ibid.*

[24] Duruz, J., and Khoo, G. C. (2014). *Eating Together: Food, Space, and Identity in Malaysia and Singapore*. Rowman & Littlefield.

differences For 'Channel Five please!' as a humorous intervention to switch to English in mixed language groups.[25]

Urban commons: Parks, HDBs, Hawker Centres, Coffee Shops, etc.

When we invoked the idea of kopitiam conviviality, we had in mind places where social interactions are more than fleeting as in the case of passing someone on the street and the possibilities for prolonged presence and exchanges can occur. The void decks, common corridors, and playgrounds in HDB estates, parks, wet markets, hawker centres, coffee shops, and community centres are some examples of public spaces in Singapore that are accessed by all walks of life.[26-31]

My late father, a retiree, would spend many hours at the void deck below our apartment block and likewise my mother, a couple of hours in the evenings at the playground/exercise area. These occasions were spent watching, greeting, and having small chats with old and frequently new neighbours. Void decks offer a cool respite from the sun and a protected area for play during the rain. Many are furnished with tables and residents hold weddings and funerals there, showcasing rituals from Muslim, Hindu, Christian, Buddhist, and Taoist traditions. In this way, the

---

[25] Wise, A., and Velayutham, S. (2020). Humour at work: Conviviality through language play in Singapore's multicultural workplaces. *Ethnic and Racial Studies* 43(5), 911–929.

[26] Ho, E. L., Liew, J. A., Zhou, G., Chiu, T. Y., Yeoh, B. S., and Huang, S. (2021). Shared spaces and "thrown togetherness" in later life: A qualitative GIS study of non-migrant and migrant older adults in Singapore. *Geoforum*, 124, 132–143.

[27] Yeo, S. J., Ho, K. C., and Heng, C. K. (2016). Rethinking spatial planning for urban conviviality and social diversity: A study of nightlife in a Singapore public housing estate neighbourhood. *TPR: Town Planning Review*, 87(4), 379–399.

[28] Ye, J. (2015). Flea markets and familiar strangers in Jurong West. In Vertovec, S. (ed.) *Diversities Old and New: Migration and Socio-Spatial Patterns in New York, Singapore and Johannesburg*, pp. 135–143. Palgrave Macmillan.

[29] Ye, J. (2016). Spatialising the politics of coexistence: Gui ju (规矩) in Singapore. *Transactions of the Institute of British Geographers*, 41(1), 91–103.

[30] Hou, J. (2017). Urban community gardens as multimodal social spaces. *Greening Cities: Forms and Functions*, 113–130.

[31] Lai, *op. cit.*

traditions and rituals of the different religions are on display in everyday familiar spaces; they are openly encountered and experienced by residents of other backgrounds. Some void decks have TVs and chairs lined up where the elderly gather to watch and socialize. Here too we encounter community events organised by Residents' Committees or Town Councils to commemorate special occasions.

The point of emphasis here is that the experience of encountering 'the stranger' is contextual — it differs from country to country, city to city, and place to place. In some places, it too often generates unease and indifference, but this holds less so for Singapore as compared to, for example, black-white relations in the US, where entrenched and hostile racial inequality and segregation have produced limited opportunities for neighbourhood intermingling and frequently a hostility towards and unease about doing so.

Coffee shops, void decks, and HDB recreation areas are parochial or 'third spaces' where people of quite different cultural and religious backgrounds encounter one another on neutral ground. These spaces easily meet the required social dimensions of Oldenburg's third places,[32] enjoyment, regularity, pure sociability/social leveller, diversity, and Klinenberg's notion of social infrastructures.[33] These distinctly Singaporean spaces are shared territory, where there is consensus and convention that the space is owned by all and none. Like anywhere, there are sometimes negotiations and struggles over aspects of such sharing, particularly around noise and smell, but by and large, such tensions are managed.

Viewing Kopitiam Conviviality through a Strengths-Based Lens

Circling back to the question of a community resilience approach, in what domains of everyday life does convivial labour occur, and what skills and

---

[32] Oldenburg, R. (1989). *The Great Good Place: Cafes, Coffee Shops, Community Centers, Beauty Parlors, General Stores, Bars, Hangouts, and How They Get You Through the Day.* Paragon House, New York.

[33] Klinberg, E. (2019). *Palaces for the People.* Penguin Random House, New York.

resources are there to build on? The research literature on community resilience suggests this must involve identifying and harnessing existing latent strengths and fostering community agency by enabling self-organization with particular attention to people-place connections. Crucially, these must be underpinned by inclusive social infrastructures, values and beliefs, knowledge and learning, social networks, and collaborative governance and leadership.[34] A related approach is what is known as Assets Based Community Development [ABCD] which sets out methods that begin with qualitative mapping the existing formal and informal assets and resources in a community that can be co-opted.[35]

Thinking about the Singapore context, what then are the situations, everyday practices, modes of governance, places, and spaces that can create an openness to others and foster new communities-in-difference? What are the existing strengths and assets in this picture we have drawn? The six core assets that are the core of the ABCD approach are as follows[36]:

1. individual resident capacities,
2. local associations,
3. neighbourhood institutions — business, not-for-profit, and government,
4. physical assets — the land and everything on it and beneath it,
5. exchange between neighbours — giving, sharing, trading, bartering, exchanging, buying, and selling,
6. stories.

In our anecdotes from everyday Singapore, we can see some common threads of practice that map easily onto these: (1) a helping culture, neighbourliness, and everyday gift exchange between the four races, especially in HDB buildings, (2) a rich diasporic food culture that also fuses different

---

[34] Berkes, F., and Ross, H. (2013). Community resilience: Toward an integrated approach. *Society & Natural Resources*, 26(1), 5–20.

[35] Kretzmann, J, P., and McKnight, J. L. (1993). *Building Communities from the Inside Out: A Path toward Finding and Mobilising a Community's Assets*. ACTA Publications, Chicago.

[36] *Ibid.*

food traditions and everyday convivial spaces where food is consumed, (3) government regulation that ensures that communal spaces like HDB's and hawker centres are inclusive by way of residential quotas and the distribution of food stalls to be representative of various races, as the provision of safe and well-designed multigenerational recreation and leisure spaces in HDB developments, (4) the lingua franca of Singlish and a distinctively Singaporean humour, (5) celebrating and making spaces for elders, and (6) a willingness and ability to make everyday religious and cultural accommodations.

Conclusions

Following a strengths-based approach highlights how existing practices can be adapted for the newly emerging cultural landscape of Singapore and how this is both in the hands of everyday people and practices and in the guiding hand of government to foster the spaces and conditions for new communities in difference to flourish. Like every nation grappling with these issues, Singapore is not perfect — the diversity project is a work in progress.[37–39] Government programmes, assistance, and accommodation are the foundation stones for Singapore's multiracial success so far, especially recognising and sponsoring hawker centre culture its intrinsic value and celebrating Singlish as a core aspect of national identity. After all, as hybrid a lingua franca, Singlish has at its heart the labour of togetherness of muddling by across differences.

---

[37] Velayutham, S. (2017). Races without racism? Everyday race relations in Singapore. *Identities*, 24(4), 455–473.

[38] Kathiravelu, L., and Dorairajoo, S. (2022). Invisible privilege in Asia: Introduction to special section. *Current Sociology*. https://doi.org/10.1177/00113921221132311.

[39] Ye, J. (2017). Managing urban diversity through differential inclusion in Singapore. *Environment and Planning D: Society and Space*, 35(6), 1033–1052.

Chapter 4.2

MOROCCO: A 3,000-YEAR HISTORY OF DIVERSITY AND EXCELLENCE

Mr André Azoulay

Good morning to all. In Morocco, many of us start the day by saying "Salam" in Arabic or "Shalom" in Hebrew.

This morning, in addressing such a prestigious audience, I took the risk to put my papers aside and try, as a Moroccan citizen, to share with you the diversity and complexity of my own identity.

Let me just start by saying that as a Moroccan, I have the privilege to introduce myself as Jewish, Amazigh, Arab, and African all at the same time. That makes me a Moroccan citizen.

I want to first say how grateful I am to the Singapore government for giving me this chance to visit this country for the first time. I have heard of Singapore since the time I was an investment banker in Paris, as it is well known for its impressive economic success story. At that time, Singapore was already a model country for bankers.

Singapore: A Model of Inclusivity

But on this visit, I discovered something more. We say that Singapore is an inclusive country for everyone, but from what I have seen in the last two days, it is not merely rhetoric or theory, or a way of being politically correct.

It is daily life, everywhere. It is so impressive considering that we are living in a time and world where we are confronted with regressive theories, exclusion, denial, archaism, and extremism.

In this country, I see what inclusiveness means, for example, when you have the Harmony Circles. You come together while retaining your differences in a convincing way. It is fascinating. I will return to my country with new ideas, more confident, and more committed to the convictions of my journey all my life.

Morocco: 3,000 Years of Diversity

You also missed something when you introduced me: I confess that I am 3,000 years old. I am saying that because I belong to my country Morocco. It is not well known that Jews in this country arrived close to 1,000 years before the Muslims. So, if I feel at home in Morocco, it is something which is deeply rooted in the history and the mindset of my people.

Morocco gave us a chance all along in those years, when you are Jewish, in a Muslim country in the Arab world.

I am sure, that you will not be really convinced by what I share this morning because you often hear on television or social media about confrontations between Jews and Muslims.

The relationship is more complex than that. My history book spans 3,000 years. It has not always been a happy book. Some pages are nice, while others are dark.

In my country, we have to tell the truth to everyone and give a chance for all narratives to be known and to be heard.

Morocco today is one of the very few countries in the world which states in its Constitution (in the version voted by the people in July 2011) that Morocco was forged first by the Berber civilisation, then the Jewish, and later by the Arab Muslim civilisations. Two-thirds of my people voted on this text. I do not know another Constitution in the world which states this.

Usually, cities in the land of Islam do not have a non-Muslim majority. In the 19th century, Morocco was very small demographically with less than seven million people. Essaouira-Mogador, my hometown, had a population of about 22,000 people of which Jews made up at its peak 16,000. For close to a century, Jews were the majority in this city.

I feel that my DNA is different because my hometown was forged by Judaism and Islam. Both are so close.

It gave me the chance not only to be at ease but also, as a full and responsible citizen, to try to speak out my voice, not only as the Adviser of His Majesty the King Mohammed VI, but also as a human being to ask others to understand how meaningful, powerful, and rich my diversity is. It is not black or white.

While it is true that Israelis and Palestinians could be confronted with challenging and difficult political issues, there is another way to deal with this. My Rabbis and my Jewish teachers have taught me that to keep alive my Judaism means first to give a chance to those who are in front of me, to enjoy the same dignity and freedom as I enjoy myself. If not, my Judaism will be at stake and risk.

This is my way to be Jewish. It is not only for political correctness that I fight for the rights of Palestinians but also for the purpose to give sense to my Judaism. The Palestinians do not enjoy the same dignity as I do. And while I am not an Israeli citizen, as a Jew, I am also responsible for giving a chance to the Israeli people and their children to enjoy peace and security.

So, I have a double commitment as a Moroccan Jew; likewise, as a Moroccan citizen, I must help the Palestinian people recover their freedom and dignity and at the same time; by doing so, I contribute to strengthen the safety and the security of the children of Israel tomorrow.

I will end by sharing with you a fascinating experience I had two years ago in Essaouira-Mogador, my hometown, at the inauguration of *Bayt Dakira*, a Memory and History Jewish House. His Majesty King Mohammed VI officiated the event, and he made a gesture that I would have never dreamed of.

He entered the synagogue in *Bayt Dakira* with me and opened the sacred place where the scrolls of the Torah were kept. He placed his hand on the scrolls for an unprecedented moment of emotion and meditation in the heart of the synagogue.

This happened in an Arab country, in the land of Islam, in Morocco. It may no longer be possible for this to happen in New York, London, or Paris, but it is still possible in Morocco, in Essaouira.

I am so proud of that.

Thank you for listening.

Chapter 4.3

FACING COMPLEXITY, OVERCOMING INDIFFERENCE FOR COMMON HUMANITY

Professor Yoshiko Ashiwa

Issues to Achieve Cohesion of Society

In recent decades, excessive globalisation has, on one hand, enhanced the high mobility of people, including exchange populations through tourism and long-term visitors to locals, which causes diversity or superdiversity, in society. On the other hand, globalisation has reinforced the realisation of the importance of striving for unity amidst such diversities and ensuring quality of life for all people in a country. Therefore, achieving the cohesion of society is an essential issue for state governance and social communities. There have been serious discussions of these matters, especially the complexified global situation due to the COVID-19 pandemic since 2020.

I believe that to achieve a cohesive society for the coexistence of diversity and unity, one of the most difficult issues is "indifference." Indifference is the mental attitude of no interest and no real commitment to the other or other worlds. Indifference to the other does not stay as it is, but it leads to indifference to oneself. The other side of the coin of indifference is indifference towards oneself. The issue of indifference exists in a closed, exclusive, and homogeneous society whose members share attributes, values, and customers and feel no need to pay attention to the others in their community. Confronting no differences in ethnicity, language, and religion, they assume that everyone is similar, thinks as they do, and is equal. So they have no need to pay attention to others. However, the existence of such a society is unimaginable in the contemporary world except for some tribal or strictly esoteric religious communities.

Then what about a society of diversity? In a heterogeneous society with countless different communities, does indifference not exist? The answer is no. Even in a multicultural, multireligious, multiethnic, and multilinguistic society or superdiverse society, indifference exists. Perhaps the degree of indifference is even higher in such a complex society because the large numbers of segments of the others, such as ethnic, religious, language, and social class communities, simply bring the multiple layers of walls of demarcations. Although people may work with others from different communities in office environments, schools, stores, and other public places, they tend to stay within their comfort communities and cultural zones. In essence, sharing public spaces as fellow citizens does not mean that people communicate as intimate friends and commit to each other by crossing these boundaries. They may work and study in the same school and office while tending to avoid intimate contact, especially in their cosy private zone. At the end of the day, they are indifferent to the different communities and ignore them.

I analyse that there are three reasons for indifference in a diverse society. First, the countless others are beyond a person's capacity to understand deeply. So, as a matter of fact, it would be easier for a person to ignore them and to be indifferent. Second, the idea of diversity and superdiversity would remain only as discourse, like the word "multiculturalism." This new all-encompassing imaginary identity that we live in a world of diversity and respect every single difference, such as gender, age, religion, ethnicity, and language, gives individuals an excuse not to have any practical commitment to other sections. As civilised people, they accept the concepts of diversity and multiculturalism only to observe political correctness without going further over the boundary to understand the other. Third, in general, people tend to avoid facing complexity, which makes them uneasy and insecure, as complexity does not fit any categories they already know. Therefore, people tend to run into simple and often dichotomised recognition using stereotypical images of others. Let us examine this matter further.

Superdiversity and Indifference

In an environment of diversity, we generally ignore the other. If so, even the newly introduced word "superdiversity" for explaining the unprecedented mixture of immigrants and moving populations in megacities, such as London, New York, and Berlin, remains just as discourse on the surface of reality. It has been pointed out that the popular concept of multiculturalism as the necessary condition of contemporary civilised city respects and counts such differences as ethnicity, religion, gender, and sexuality but does not promote serious commitment among them. This keeps people within superficial understandings. Therefore, the other side of multiculturalism is segmentation and indifference.

When we face people and situations we do not know or lack experience of, we face the following questions: "What is it?" and "Who are the others?" Then, when we keep being in such a situation of facing unknown others, we gradually start to come close to them and figure them out step by step, ultimately making us go beyond our boundary. Then, we realise that the fundamental questions have started to be raised inside ourselves: "Who am I?" "Where am I?" "Who are we?" There are questions about newly discovering oneself and others.

In fact, these processes are the core of the theory of cultural anthropology for cross-cultural understandings and the practical methodology to be trained as an anthropologist. The discovery of self can occur through the discovery of the other. In other words, understanding others enhances understanding oneself. It is very rare to have an encounter without any power unbalance with the other, an encounter expressed in Kenzaburo Oe's novel as a dialogue between his handicapped son and his grandmother, metaphorically expressed as "a movement of water on a flat tray." Contrarily, most encounters occur in the context of power asymmetries. Tzvetan Todorov states that "the postulate of difference readily involves the feeling of superiority, the postulate of equality that of indifference."[40]

It is true that reality has multiple aspects depending on the individual's interpretation. You may know some Japanese words that have entered the English lexicon, such as sushi and teriyaki, especially in the last

---

[40] Todorov, Tzvetan. (1984). *The Conquest of America: The Question of the Other*, p. 63. Harper & Row.

decade as Japanese culture became globally popular. But, interestingly, in the 1950s, another Japanese word came to be used in Europe and US. That word is "Rashomon-like." *Rashomon* is a world-famous Japanese movie directed by Akira Kurosawa, which won a gold medal at the 1951 Venice Film Festival. It is about a murder, with different testimonies given according to the three witnesses' desires. The word "Rashomon-like" in English and other languages came to signify the awareness of diverse realities. If there are diverse realities with multiple aspects stemming from different interpretations, it is no wonder that the complexity of understanding the reality of the other increases.

Standing for Complexities

Let us examine more closely the tendency to avoid complexity. Nearly a half-century ago, Edmund Leach wrote about the primordial character of human beings when they encounter the unknown cross-culturally in his brilliant book *Culture and Communication.*[41] He argued that people resort to polarisation to simplify the complexities, perplexities, and puzzlement given by the unknown world as an easy and powerful way to make oneself feel secure. Simplification leads to dichotomisations and polarisations, such as "good/bad," "white/black," "just/evil," "we/they," and even "humans/zombies." He argues that the primordial character of human beings is to polarise nature as they try to recognise the world. To simplify the complexity, perplexity, and bepuzzlement given by nature or the outer world is an easy and powerful way to make oneself understand and accept them. Simplifications, in other words, dichotomisation and polarisation, let people put themselves on the better side of the dichotomies, such as good, right, fair, and comfortable. Then, they compartmentalise the ambiguities into the box of the other and stop thinking. Here is where indifference comes in. However, unexpected issues, such as natural disasters, accidents, wars, and conflicts, always happen. In addition, people instinctively know that ambiguity is the resource for the emergence of concepts, new understanding, and new power. However, indifference will block them from stepping into the other world.

---

[41] Leach, Edmund. (1976). *Culture and Communication.* Cambridge University Press.

This tendency brings us to the very safe zone, and, of course, people place themselves on the side of "good, right, and fair," and then they put the ambiguities or complexities into the box of the other. Having done this, they no longer have to think about it. Difference comes here. And at the end of the day, indifference towards others will lead to indifference to oneself and absorb the energy for life — vita — that is always activated by communicating with others.

Religion, which produces a semiotic space for people can help those who tend to get into the simplification of dichotomy and stay in the safe cage of "us" and indifference to overcome simplification, encourage them to face the complexity, and lead them to a deeper understanding of humanity. However, I say again that the temptation to dichotomise is so strong and is often accelerated by religion. Religion dichotomises people, such as believer in our god/believer in other gods, religious believer/paganist, and believer/atheist. Even when the believers of one religion accept the believers of another, they still think their religion is better.

However, indifference towards others ultimately leads to indifference towards self. Indifference absorbs the energy for life (vita) activated by communicating with others. "Vita" is the crucial insight of Hannah Arendt, the political scientist and philosopher, regarding her political and academic struggles as a Jewish survivor of World War II. Vita exists in communication with others, in other words, in facing the complexities. People know that ambiguity is a rich resource for creating new concepts, perceptions, and ideas. And artists, in particular, know very well the ambiguities and perplexities that result from crossing boundaries of self and other. It brings a new dimension of dynamism where both sides can share something regarding common humanity. The strength of understanding others without falling into the temptation of simplification and dichotomisation derives from facing complexity.

Strength Derived from Crossing Boundaries and Facing Complexity

So how to get into the unknown other? The anthropological methodology, which is the essence of anthropology itself, will work regarding this issue.

A fieldworker should have an anthropology-like experience of fieldwork in a different culture or different sections of diversity. Interface with other communities and religious groups is the first step for facing the other, but it is not sufficient to stop there. They need to step forward. Fieldwork means that people stay in a different community for a longer period, from at least six months to a year, or sometimes even more, as a member of the community and live a life as people in the community do. The field workers' awareness and understanding of the other and self will be greatly changed through this experience. This will influence the other community too. During this period, the other community would also be in the process of coming to accept the stranger, and its people also face bewilderment and puzzlement. Their experiences of otherness in this way are the most effective in understanding not only the other but also their community, themselves, and the otherness in oneself.

It would be especially effective for societal leaders of communities, such as leaders and officers of non-government organisations (NGO) and governmental organisations, to have experiences even a short moment as a newcomer in a different community. If leaders such as teachers, policy-makers, and NGO people have these experiences in crossing the boundaries, they will face the puzzlement and uncomfortableness of complexities and, through these experiences, likely find a way to achieve common ground. Even after these leaders return to their communities, the influence on their followers will be immense. Many short-term programmes have been created by various organisations to provide such an experience, and moving forward, we can expect longer-term ones to be readied without much difficulty.

However, among the various kinds of communities, it is most difficult to create anthropology-like experiences for members of religious ones. Religious people, such as Christians and Muslims, become clerics of a particular religion because they only believe in that very religion. It would be outrageous and even unimaginable for them to live in another religious group or community that believes in another religion.

Nevertheless, it is not unheard of in history for members of one religion to take an interest in another religion and to practice and learn it intellectually, participate in its ceremonies, and live together in other religious denominations. Consider the Christian *Bible*, which has been translated into nearly every language, albeit for different purposes. To translate it, one must first study the language one is translating well and know its culture, thought, and even the religion associated with it. For example, what words are best translated for God and love? If you do not know the culture, thought, and religion of the language you are translating into, you will be unable to find optimal words for translation. Although the purpose was to propagate Christianity and convert pagans, it is undeniable that a core work of a missionary involves learning about different cultures. That said, the work of respecting other religions and seeking common ground is quite different from the work of proselytising.

By learning and practising parts of other religions, religious specialists deepen their own religiousness, seek common ground between the two religions, promote inter-religious understanding and inter-religious dialogue, and develop humanity and transcendence. Certainly, countless specialists in all religions have, throughout history, been mediators, translators, and bridges among different religions to seek common ground. Through my study of religion, I became acquainted with some of such clerics.

Let me tell you about a case I experienced recently. There is a Catholic Jesuit monastery with a history of about 100 years on the campus of Sophia University in Tokyo, Japan. In the early summer of 2022, I took some Chinese Buddhists visiting Tokyo there because I knew that they had never visited a Christian monastery in China nor had any intention to do so. I thought it would be a good chance for them to walk in the sacred space of another religion. The priest guiding us took us to the monastery's prayer room, which visitors are rarely permitted to enter. To my surprise, in the corner of the room were *zabuton* cushions used during Zen meditation practice in Buddhist temples. The priest told us that another priest interested in Zen underwent special training at a Buddhist temple for many years. He then taught Zen practice and its thoughts to interested priests at this chapel daily. The priest giving us the tour said it is not uncommon for Jesuit priests to have studied Indian philosophy or Buddhism and practised asceticism. The Buddhist believers from China were very surprised. They started asking questions, such as why a Christian priest practised Buddhism, whether there were any problems for a priest to study at a Buddhist temple, what he learned from Buddhism, and how Christianity and Buddhism could exist in the priest's mind. In this scene, the practice of Zen Buddhism started by a Jesuit priest opened a dialogue with Chinese Buddhist believers who never imagined that they could discuss such things with a Christian priest.

This discussion will let the communicators perform a crucial role at the watershed moment — either simplify, dichotomise, and be antagonistic to other religions and communities or search for common ground among them. Such communicators are also very much needed nowadays, even within their institutional religions — some of which split into numerous antagonistic sects.

For nearly forty years, I have been involved in practical peacebuilding activities in ethnic conflicts in Sri Lanka. I have encountered very few clerics who can act as communicators between Buddhism, Christianity, and Islam. However, there were always some who were excellent interreligious communicators. They played important roles in countless crucial moments in preventing small conflicts in the community from becoming large violence, even if they were not known.

These clerics were mostly Catholic, a minority religion in Sri Lanka, with no training experience, even for a short time, in a Buddhist sect, but they had the experience of daily life in Sri Lankan society, where Buddhists are the majority. They made efforts not to link ethnic conflicts with religious conflicts. It is precisely because there was a common goal of overcoming the differences among religions and ethnic groups which led them to avoid violence and enabled them to act as a bridge among religions.

From ancient times, countless religious people have acted as bridges, using their abilities to culturally interpret between religions. When modernity came during the period from the end of the 18th century to the beginning of the 20th century, religions other than Christianity were being introduced as serious religions rather than paganism, such as at the Parliament of World Religions during the 1893 world fair in Chicago. Since then, on the one hand, dialogues among religions have been enhanced, but on the other, sectarian tensions have increased within a religion, often among fundamental and liberal communities. Especially after World War II, we see not only inter-religious conflicts but also growing intra-religious sectarianism within Islam, Judaism, and Hinduism.

The issues of life and the private body, such as abortion, esthesia, and homosexuality, have become political watershed problems among religions and political parties.

The novel *Daniel Stein, Interpreter* by Ludmila Ulitskaya, narrates the life of a Catholic Carmelite priest based on the true story of Oswald Rufeisen (1922–1998).[42] It is about the life of a Polish Jew who became a Catholic priest living among multiple religions and ethnicities. He was a Catholic priest in religion and Jew in terms of ethnicity. As the novel's title suggests, his life was an "interpreter" in a symbolic sense between different peoples, cultures, religions, political systems, and memories. Daniel Stein is a Polish Jewish boy who survived the Nazi invasion of Poland with the help of nuns at a Catholic covenant and converted to Catholicism. After World War II, he became a priest. He emigrated to Israel and served at a small church for all kinds of people who cross the boundaries of existence, cannot fit premade categories, and struggle to survive, such as Palestinian Christians, married couples of different ethnicities and religions, and homosexual Jews. The book portrays his story as a life full of contradictions but with undaunted faith in humanity.

It is true, as Gandhi said, that there are as many religions as there are people. This story tells us that searching for the truth and living a life truly is done by people's own effort to reach the common humanity, which process is ultimately the religion of people.

Non-verbal Communication: Art, Music, Prayer, and Social Service

I have thus far discussed the ways by which people cross boundaries through an anthropology-like method to understand others and themselves, bear ambiguities, and derive strength by facing complexity to find common humanity and not stay in a cage of indifference.

There is no panacea. Even the common humanity as universal values you may look at will be constantly challenged, re-examined, and reconstructed by facing the other and oneself, according to the time the world

---

[42] Ulitskaya, Ludmila. (2012). *Daniel Stein, Interpreter* (translated from Russian to English by A. L. Tait). Overlook Duckworth.

changes. Under these circumstances, verbal communication is one means of communication among people, but there is a limit to what can be conveyed by words. While words convey meaning, they cannot be fully translated into the language of the receiver. Just as there are as many religions as there are people, each of us has a different context. Therefore, even among those using the same language, the entire meaning a person puts into words is not fully understood by the receiver because their context for interpretation is different. In addition, words cannot convey the real sensation.

In anthropological fieldwork, in addition to words, sharing sensations and emotions is also an important experience and means for understanding those in a different culture. This is done through non-verbal communication, such as art, music, architecture, rituals, and social activities. What happens when people encounter religious art different from theirs? They may feel a sense of incongruity, anxiety, and fear that leads them to destroy the art, as has occurred many times throughout history. But at the same time, people may be fascinated by the exotic art and realise a new sensation is being born inside them. And in some cases, they may notice commonalities with the religious art they are familiar with or a new dimension of shared artistry.[43] Some examples are the impressive geometric pattern of mosaics in Muslim mosques and stained glass in Catholic churches, the beautiful coexistence of sacredness and nature of a Shinto shrine and Hindu ashram, and the majestic altars of Catholic churches and Buddhist temples. Apart from theological doctrines and textual teaching, religions have used art such as music, architecture, murals, and statues to impart to people shared sensations of sublimity, majesty, mystery, and perfect cosmology of the universe. Ordinary people in ancient times, who did not have written text, could feel a supreme existence through artistic sensation. Religion and art have been on the same ground throughout history.

Even in people's everyday life, sensory experiences via such media as art and music work to connect different communities. Often, listening and making music together creates a totally different platform for different

---

[43] Belting, Hans. (2014). *An Anthropology of Images: Pictures, Medium, Body* (translated from Germany to English by Thomas Dunlap). Princeton University Press.

communities, dimensions of understanding by excitement and mutual joy more directly than discussing and debating in language. Here, I would like to introduce a project of non-verbal communication through music. I organised a project in post-conflict Sri Lanka over three years from 2012. The project, "Randooga: Music for Peace," was funded by the Japan Foundation and the Center for the Study of Peace and Reconciliation at Hitotsubashi University, which I directed. "Randooga" is a word created by jazz pianist and composer Masahiko Satoh, a globally renowned Japanese musician.

Randooga is a method to access a world of new communication via sound. It can be enjoyed by both individuals and groups of people, from those who have never touched a musical instrument to accomplished musicians. For a quarter century, Sri Lanka has suffered from an interethnic conflict between the Sinhalese and Tamils, the government force and LTTE-led militant group. Both groups of people spoke different languages and were unable to communicate. Furthermore, even though the war had ended, the complex and years-long experiences of both being victims and perpetrators made dialogue difficult.

Randooga has two simple rules: One, listen carefully to the sounds and rhythms of the other party and respond to them and two, no one dominates the conversation by sound. For example, if one person hits a pot with a stick to make a small rhythm or sound phrase, the other people hear it, and someone responds with an answering rhythm. Sometimes, a person makes rhythms and sounds alone, and sometimes they continue the conversation with multiple people. It is that simple. But as it continues, a very well-communicated musical conversation emerges as a whole. Even if a person makes a small sound, others hear it and respond with a similar or slightly altered sound. It is incredibly simple, but this happiness and joy springs from the bottom of people's hearts. Communication is established in a completely different dimension from the language of politics, memory, and violence. It is no wonder that after just a few hours of a Randooga workshop, all attendees felt a very close intimacy almost as if they had known each other since childhood.

The Randooga workshops, each followed by a concert, were led by Satoh and Pradeep Ratnayake, a Sri Lankan sitar player, in five Sri Lankan cities. A total of 300 people participated in the workshops, and over 2,500 attended the concerts. Although this project shared only a moment of joy in communication, it was an irreplicable experience to confirm our common humanity. It was indeed serendipity.[44] I think it is true what a participant said: "it is like a delightful prayer of sensation for all by all through music."

A practice common to all religions is prayer. All religions similarly pray for world happiness and peace, and the salvation of unhappy souls, and prayers of all religions in unity can create a great emotional force in common. Another common practice for connecting all religions is community service. Assistance and relief to the victims of natural disasters, wars, and violence, as well as to those in need due to social injustice and inequality, are the very practice of religious teachings.

The practice of these actions is not a language but a non-verbal action that shares compassion and humanity, is emotionally based, exists across religious boundaries, and connects them. Indeed, in the contemporary world, we have issues concerning all people, religions, and other diverse communities. Facing them will work to make bridges to overcome differences and not let people remain in cages of indifference.

The Issue of Social Stratification and Great Disparity

Finally, I try to share the idea of "the issue that remains." There are so many issues that remain unresolved, as mentioned above. I will focus on the issue of increasing social stratification and large disparities in all parts of the world. Global movements to identify and solve the issues have started, named "we are the 99 percent" movement. Studies of peace and

---

[44] See, Ashiwa, Yoshiko. "Emotion and Logic: The Communication Art of Randooga" https://alfpnetwork.jfac.jp/en/e-magazine003_02/. The newspaper article on Randooga is "Japanese Randooga Workshop in Colombo and Jaffna," *Daily News*, Sri Lanka, November 29, 2012, http://archives.dailynews.lk/2012/11/29/fea25.asp.

See the visual record of Jaffna concert on November 2012 on Yu-tube. https://www.youtube.com/watch?v=4psqE-Lvs7o&list=PLu5TlSItd7isy-QwhTrfdhyspK8xydHpQ&index=2 >. This is a part of five sections of a concert after a three-day workshop with ordinary people, both Sinhala and Tamil, with a group of foreign musicians.

conflict have shown that social structural issues of economic inequality underlie most communal violence. The frustrations caused by the economic gaps between poor and rich social classes have often been strategically aimed by power holders towards the issues of religious and ethnic conflicts, which often become communal violence. Even the growth of the large middle class has not resolved issues of social inequality. On the contrary, nowadays, inequality is growing within the middle class even as middle-class identity is being stripped away. The middle class is becoming divided into the poor and the rich, a growing phenomenon, especially in the last two decades.

Interestingly, around 2007, when the concept of superdiversity was suggested by anthropologist Steve Vertovec, another powerful concept was proposed by anthropologist David Graeber in his books *Debt* and *Bullshit Jobs*.[45] Graeber is one of the theorists of the Occupy Wall Street movement in 2011. The movement emphasised that in contrast to the 1% super wealthy and super rich, 99% of the people struggle with poverty in the capitalist system.

Class issues will link the diversities of multiple categories and constitute one particular class, most often, the underprivileged, suppressed, and exploited one. These people have high physical mobility as cheap labour to go to rich countries according to the demands of capitalism and the global labour market. However, their social mobility in the host countries is completely unthinkable. It is not in the development plan of the host country from the very beginning at all. The success story of guest workers in the host country simply does not exist; at most, they and their dependents may have a slightly better life than in their home countries, such as being able to send their children to school. So it is undeniable that the other side of superdiversity is a society lacking expectations of social mobility. This coexistence of social mobility among economic classes and the stability of society is a paradoxical issue and is challenging to resolve globally.

---

[45] Steven Vertovec. (2007). "Super-diversity and its implications." *Ethnic and Racial Studies* 29(6), 1024–1054. David Graeber. (2011). *Debt: The First 5000 Years*. Melville House, (2018). *Bullshit Jobs: A Theory*. Penguin.

In sum, in a society of superdiversity, intersectionality, and overlapping identities, we cannot stay in a compartmentalised, cosy space with indifference towards others, fearing ambiguity. Rather, we should communicate with others and live with them to gain the energy for life — vita — and the energy of change and seek the common ground for humanity. I would like to stress again that religions search together for common humanity.

Do experience the other rather than staying comfortably in a separate and pre-made system, societal sector, and group. By doing this, you will first find yourself and others you have never seen before. Then, we can realise that we all strive to open potentials for alternative systems and ideas of now and the future.

Searching for common humanity and acting on common ground with other communities are the key to the success of religions now and in the future. Religion, as teachings as well as organisational systems, should function to gather and allocate wealth to reduce social inequalities. Redistributing wealth will encourage shared values that enhance common humanity through the shared ground of religions, as well as social activism for such issues as the environment, peace, and disarmament.

I would like to conclude this short essay by referring to the last scene of Rashomon, the movie by Akira Kurosawa. As embodied in the word "Rashomon-like," this movie makes us realise that there are multiple realities based on the interpretations of people. However, Kurosawa chose a scene for the ending. Three people, a man who told the entire event he witnessed to the court and a thief and a monk who listened, despaired at humans whose behaviour was driven by desire. Then, they found an abandoned baby well wrapped in kimono. The thief took the kimono from the baby and ran away. The monk was shocked. Then, the man picked up the baby to raise as his child, which made the monk regain trust in humanity and religion. The movie, which makes the word "Rashomon-like" — multiple realities of ambiguity — ends by sharing the hope of common humanity with the world audience and deepened the belief of the monk. We need to make every single effort to accept the differences and multiple realities while simultaneously seeking common humanity on the same ground around the globe.

Chapter 4.4

MANY RELIGIONS, ONE SHARED RESPONSIBILITY

Dr Iyad Abumoghli

Religions have two important powers that can influence a new development paradigm that will provide for a healthy planet and the prosperity of its people. First, the power of convening and convincing where more than 84% of people believe in a religion or a spiritual belief.[46] The second is economic power, as religious institutions are the fourth largest economy in the world.[47] Religious institutions own 8% of habitable land on Earth.[48] This is 7,000 times the size of Singapore or 21 times the size of the United Kingdom.

Many religions dictate what people eat and drink and how they should walk on Earth. Therefore, religious values can impact individual and institutional behaviours towards nature and natural resources that will respectively affect production and consumption attitudes.

The summer is almost over, but it is leaving us with devastating impacts of droughts. This is threatening East Africa's food security,

---

[46] Abumoghli, Iyad. (2022). *Religion and the Environment*. Reimagining the Human-Environment Relationship. UN University and UN Environment Programme. http://collections.unu.edu/view/UNU:8838.

[47] World Economic Forum. (2017). Role of Religions, https://www.weforum.org/agenda/2017/01/religion-bigger-business-than-we-thought/.

[48] Faith for Earth. (2018). Foresight Brief No. 008, https://wedocs.unep.org/handle/20.500.11822/25452.

Europe's ecosystems with drying rivers, and Southeast Asia with disturbing floods that have left millions in despair. Climate change is a justice issue, representing the interdependence of human rights, gender equality, peacebuilding, and climate action.[49]

Role of Faith Actors

The role of faith is crucial. Faith leaders, in particular, are the key actors in humanitarian response, protection, and social cohesion and can work with actors working across the nexus of climate change, fragility, and peacebuilding to promote trust building, social justice, and equal participation in decision-making.[50]

Dignity, respect, tolerance, and peace are the principal prerequisites for cultural diversity and environmental integrity. A dialogue is needed that prevents polarisation, resolves the main concerns of globalisation, sustainable development, and the environment that we face today, and promotes respect and builds confidence among cultures.

There are real opportunities stemming from interfaith collaboration. There is a vast potential for building a more peaceful, prosperous world by bringing issues of culture to the mainstream of development thinking and practice, by complementing and strengthening one another.

Environmental degradation and climate change increasingly threaten peace and human security. UNEP's Faith for Earth Initiative addresses these universal concerns by building on the Role of Faith-based Organisations to advance environmental stewardship and facilitates interreligious dialogue to achieve shared objectives of environmental protection and sustainable development.[51]

---

[49] Patrick Huntjens, Ting Zhang, and Katharina Nachbar. (2018). *Climate Change and Implications for Security and Justice: The Need for Equitable, Inclusive, and Adaptive Governance of Climate Action*, pp. 141–176. https://doi.org/10.1093/oso/9780198805373.003.0007.

[50] Act Alliance. (Accessed 2022). The Role of Faith-Based Organizations in Humanitarian Response: A Reflection on the Unique Role of FBOs in Humanitarian Crises, https://www.christianaid.org.uk/sites/default/files/2016-03/role-of-faith-based-organizations-in-humanitarian-response-reflection.pdf.

[51] UNEP. (2018). Faith for Earth Strategy, https://www.unep.org/about-un-environment-programme/faith-earth-initiative/strategy.

Faith for Earth

The Faith for Earth programme of the United Nations Environment Programme was established in 2017 to promote interreligious and intercultural dialogue, understanding, and cooperation for peace between people and with the environment.

The Faith for Earth Initiative has three main goals:

- First, to provide faith organisations and their leaders a neutral platform to engage in policy dialogue with decision-makers.
- Second, for green Faith-Based Organisations' investments and assets to support the implementation of sustainable development goals.
- Third, to provide faith and religious communities with knowledge to understand the relationship between religions and science and to effectively communicate with decision makers and the public.

Faith for Earth facilitates multistakeholder dialogue, ensuring inclusivity of the voices of faith actors in advancing environmental stewardship. During the United Nations Environment Assembly, the highest-level intergovernmental body responsible for environmental governance, Faith for Earth, held an Interfaith Dialogue Series that gathered 700 participants, mobilising 94 religions and congregations and 180 speakers over 25 sessions. Resultantly, religions and congregations were united to adopt powerful positions towards environmental governance.[52]

Many Religions, One Shared Responsibility

Although religions come from different belief backgrounds, all agree on the human, spiritual, and moral responsibility towards Earth. The nexus of belief systems and environmental policy affirms the imperative of bringing religious actors to the forefront of environmental governance.[53]

---

[52] UNEP. (2022). Faith for Earth Dialogue during the United Nations environment Assembly, https://www.unep.org/events/unep-event/faith-earth-dialogue-unea-52.

[53] Iyad Abumoghli and Euan McCartney. (2020). The role of Environmental and Spiritual Ethics in Galvanizing Nature Based Solutions, https://wedocs.unep.org/bitstream/handle/20.500.11822/34063/1/ESE.pdf.

We know that a stable environment is essential to guarantee peace and prosperity. This should serve as a rallying call for all diverse faith actors to come together around a shared objective. All faith traditions have teachings that are directly or indirectly linked to the environment.[54] There are strong ethics of environmental care that exists across all religions. These spiritual values and ethics reflect moral values about the way humans should behave towards nature, its resources, and other living beings.

Faith actors can also provide social and spiritual support to increase resilience in communities affected by the double hardship of climate change and conflicts, supporting communities to adapt to climate change, and advocating for climate-sensitive ways of life.

Despite the great diversity of religions and faith traditions, there are a few similar attributes:

- First, they explore the relationship between humans and the natural environment.
- Second, they contain ethical mandates concerning this relationship.
- Third, they recognise that human well-being is fundamentally related to the environment.

For example, in Buddhism, climate change is presented as the ecological consequence of our own collective karma. Therefore, it is not just an ecological crisis but a spiritual one too. Hindu theology demonstrates a reverence for nature and the environment. The great forces of nature, the Earth, sky, air, water, and fire, along with all life forms, are fundamentally interconnected with each other.

In Christianity, humanity is seen to have been made in God's image and given a unique responsibility to care for the well-being of all creation. The Earth is a gift, a product of God's love. However, as God's stewards, people's dominion cannot be understood as license to exploit, abuse, or destroy God's creation.

---

[54] UNEP. (2020). Faith for Earth: A Call for Action, https://wedocs.unep.org/bitstream/handle/20.500.11822/34063/1/ESE.pdf.

Addressing climate change from an Islamic perspective is about assuming the role as trustee or steward of creation that God bestowed upon humanity. This trusteeship applies to all life forms and ecosystems in their full diversity and richness.

Daoism teaches that the *Dao*, or the great way of the universe, guides the relationship between humanity and nature, with humans expected to live in harmony with nature and nature's principles as a sacred duty.

Harnessing the Power of Religion in Environmental Care

Therefore, these common concepts make it essential for religions and faith actors to play an effective role in the following manner:

First, we need to work on religious literacy concerning the intrinsic relationship between religions and the environment and educate not only faith leaders but also the public about how environmental issues are reflected in their own religious values. This will not only enhance our moral responsibility towards nature but also increases opportunities for interreligious cooperation towards common threats and strengthen peaceful coexistence.

Second, religious voices are very important during intergovernmental negotiations. Several interfaith statements have been submitted to the climate change conventions: United Nations Environment Assembly, biodiversity convention, and Stockholm plus fifty.[55]

Third, religious institutions can be models in divesting from fossil fuel, applying moral financing principles, and greening their assets and operations.[56]

Fourth, religious institutions need to partner with scientific institutions as religions meet science on issues related to climate change, nature,

---

[55] Interfaith Statement at Stockholm +50 (2022). https://wedocs.unep.org/bitstream/handle/20.500.11822/40048/Stockholm%2B50%20Interfaith%20Statement%2025%20May%202022.pdf?sequence=1&isAllowed=y.

[56] Climate-Responsible Finance — A Moral Imperative towards Children. (2022). https://www.unep.org/events/webinar/climate-responsible-finance-moral-imperative-towards-children.

and pollution. The scientific evidence can help support the faith perspectives and religions can bring moral values to scientific findings.[57]

Fifth, youth are our best chance. Investing in young faith leaders will be key to establish peaceful understanding and collaboration on a common threat facing their future, as well as to ensure intergenerational dialogue and cooperation. Faith for Earth has launched the youth council representing 12 religions, and the young men and women are working together demonstrating the unity of purpose and future.[58]

Our selfish wants and greed to exploit nature are acts of violence against Earth, our only life support system. What we need is a peaceful non-violent revolution of ethics and values. This is similar to the concept of Ahimsa. Ahimsa is not only a concept of Jainism, Hinduism, and Buddhism but also a concept of all other religions believing in living in peace with one another and with our surroundings.

This unification of concepts provides an excellent opportunity for all believers to unify and correct the course of humanity that is taking us to a bleak future. Engagement of faith-based organisations and faith leaders can be a tool for addressing peace and security challenges. This can be achieved through mediation, dialogue, and working towards one global goal to protect our one and only planet.

Environment and peace are cross-cutting issues that are intrinsic to sustainable development. While natural resources are vital to achieving sustainable development, they are also increasingly acting as drivers of fragility, conflict, and violence. Interfaith efforts can help resolve or avoid disputes, as well as improve the conditions of millions in civil strife.

---

[57] Iyad Abumoghli. (2022). Reimagining the Human-Environment Relationship: Religion and the Environment, http://collections.unu.edu/eserv/UNU:8838/UNUUNEP_Abumoghli_RHER.pdf.

[58] Faith for Earth youth Council, https://www.unep.org/faith-earth-youth-council.

Chapter 4.5

WORKING TOGETHER: RELIGION, RESILIENCE, AND COHESION FROM BUDDHIST, MULTICULTURAL, AND MULTIFAITH PERSPECTIVE

Venerable Chi Kwang Sunim

This is a very wonderful opportunity for us to all reflect on what it is we do in our communities and how we serve in some way to better our inter-religious and inter-Buddhist engagement and interfaith relationships. Since 2000, shortly after returning to Australia after living many years abroad, I connected with both faith communities and Buddhist organisations in the state of Victoria, Australia, along with many other ordained Sangha from various traditions. I discovered at that time, interfaith relationships were serving and supporting the broader community needs, including Buddhists for the common good, multicultural harmony, and greater communal peace.

I had lived as a Buddhist monastic for over 20 years in the mountain monasteries of South Korea, studying and practising as a Korean Seon (Zen) Buddhist nun. In 1998, I found myself back in Australia and settling near Melbourne. Due to being alone much of the time while creating a centre in a country town, I realised it was important to work with both the local interfaith community and to reach out to other Buddhist organisations in Australia. We often came together at events, such as the Chinese

New Year, Buddha's Birthday, and Kathina, and at other times to discuss the needs of their diverse cultural communities. Often with limited English, they were trying to work with local councils and on government policies with complex legal guideline. There were many issues regarding the location of religious centres and building cultural temples in less sympathetic neighbourhoods, the supporting associations needed help. Even for Western monastics, there were so many regulations and everchanging rules surrounding monastic and employment visas. So, in 1996, the Buddhist Council of Victoria (BCV) formed to serve these Buddhist community needs, based on the model, then Chair of New South Wales Buddhist Society, Graham Lyall had established. Later, other states, Queensland, South Australia, and West Australia, followed suit.

I joined the Buddhist Council of Victoria (BCV) in 1999 shortly after it was formed. It has developed over the years to be a more representative body that not only acts on behalf of Buddhists in Victoria with education resources or in the training of chaplains for various services, but it has become an avenue for governments and local councils to disseminate regulatory information and relevant proposals to the broader Buddhist community. BCV is also engaged in broader community representations on interfaith boards, including the current Victorian Multicultural Advisory Group in supporting the government office of Multicultural Victoria.

Multicultural Victoria Act

Since the mid-1800s, Chinese Buddhists and Taoists, European Christians, and Jews and even Northern Indian Muslims, Hindus, and Sikhs arrived in Australia to mine, trade, and transport goods across Australia. They were living and practising their faith in various cultural communities throughout the country. However, it was not until 1993 that the Victorian Multicultural Act was created and since 2004, the legislation has been amended yearly. The legislation states the following:

> "The Australian Government has supported and promoted the principles of multiculturalism by recognising all individuals in Victoria are entitled to mutual respect and understanding, regardless of their cultural, religious, racial and linguistic backgrounds. The Act is there to promote and

preserve diversity, cultural heritage and also to promote regard for the shared laws, values, aspirations and responsibilities."[59]

Multiculturalism was first presented as the basis for migrant settlement, welfare, and social-cultural policy in Australia in a 1973 paper entitled *A Multi-Cultural Society for the Future.* Its popularity lessened due to the fears of terrorism in the 2000s and during the Iraq war. From 2003, *United in Diversity* became the slogan and no new policies were added to the Multicultural Act until 2007.

In 2007, while I chaired the Buddhist Council of Victoria, I became a BCV representative on the Victorian Multicultural Advisory Council for one year. 'The Council', as it was called then, was tasked with providing advice to the government, not only for the practical needs of a fast-growing multicultural society but also on how to promote social cohesion. The aim was to overcome growing racism and intolerance by highlighting the value of diversity in multicultural and multifaith communities. We participated in many shared festivals, celebrating all the holy days and culturally significant events.

Over the years, greater respect and understanding have grown within our multicultural society, through a broader understanding of faith and cultural issues since the *United in Diversity* policy of 2003. Now the renamed 'Multicultural Advisory Group' (MAG) continues to create solutions and offers recommendations to government, policymakers, and community organisations to make public services and government recommendations more inclusive and accessible.

The current BCV representative on the MAG is Dr Di Cousens, the Vice Chair of the Buddhist Council of Victoria. There are roughly 30 other faith leaders in the group which is led by Victorian Multicultural Commission's Chair, Viv Nguyen, AM. Together, they work on contemporary matters affecting all faith communities. They provide advice to government departments on a range of issues, such as family violence policy, COVID response, the rights of faith communities, forced marriage, and human trafficking.[60]

---

[59] www.legislation.vic.gov.au/as-made/acts/multicultural-victoria-act-2004.
[60] www.multiculturalcommission.vic.gov.au/multifaith-advisory-group.

Australian Sangha Association (ASA)

In 2000, I became a founding committee member of the Federation of Buddhist Councils (FABC) and in 2005, along with Ajahn Brahm and other monks and nuns of different Buddhist traditions, we formed the Australian Sangha Association (ASA). It became representative body for monks and nuns of all Buddhist traditions in Australia.

The intention of ASA is to maintain good relations, communication, connection, harmony, and understanding within the Buddhist Sangha nationwide.

The early committee of ASA observed that, as the number of Buddhist monastics grew in Australia, so too did their needs, especially with regard to acquiring their long-term visa status. Whereas for monastics who are already Australian citizens, it was more about practical and social support to meet their needs. The ASA's incorporated intention is as follows:

> "Represent, liaise and protect the monastic traditions; To resolve communal and inter-Sangha issues; and to respect other monastics and their orders by creating harmony and non-discrimination among the three main lineages, Theravada, Mahayana and Vajrayana."[61]

Federation of Buddhist Councils (FABC)

The FABC is a peak body, comprising Buddhist Councils from the states of New South Wales, Victoria, Western Australia, Queensland, and South Australia. It represents more than 200 Buddhist temples and organisations at a government level and is closely associated with ASA.

Over many years, the FABC committee has engaged in government consultations regarding draft legislation before parliament, which is likely to impact Buddhist and other faith communities. The main concern for Buddhists and some other religious communities is to ensure that any government legislation is to protect the freedom of all religions to practice their faith as long as it is not harming others and that it also provides protection

---

[61] www.australiansangha.org.

to people of faith who identify as gender and/or sexually diverse. One recent issue that raised many concerns throughout faith communities, as drafts became public, was the proposed Religious Freedoms Bill.

Religious Freedom Bill

In August 2019, the FABC and ASA submitted their first response to the Australian government's Religious Freedom Bill on the Consequential Amendments to the Bill and the Human Rights Legislation Amendment (Freedom of Religion) Bill 2019. As the first draft of this bill received substantial critical response, a second draft was released for comment in 2020. The ASA and FABC lodged a joint response again to the revised draft in February 2020 and continue to express concern over the possible consequences of the proposed legislation.[62]

Together, the Australian Sangha Association (ASA) and the Federation of Australian Buddhist Councils (FABC) commented that the re-definition of the objects clause now expressly makes clear that all human rights have equal status under International Law. We are also grateful that the term "vilify" has now been defined in the legislation. We also affirm the rights of individuals and organisations to be protected from discrimination on the basis of religion and spirituality.

However, we do not support or affirm the right of religious individuals or organisations to preference and or discriminate on the basis of religion and spirituality. If this bill was passed, under the new draft, we have the following:

- *A professor can be denied a job because he is a Jewish.*
- *A doctor can be refused employment at a hospital because he is a Muslim.*
- *A school student can be expelled or not accepted in a school because he is an atheist.*
- *A homeless person could miss out on a bed in a shelter because he is a Hindu.*

---

[62] www.buddhistcouncil.org.au/.

- *A charity worker can be rejected for promotion because he is a Buddhist.*
- *An aged care employee can lose shifts because he is an agnostic.*

ASA and FABC committees also agree the following:

"Any religious public benevolent institution which seeks to preference their charity or service to only those of similar faith, should be legally made to publicly declare their intention to do so, in order that the public can conscientiously preference who they donate funds to, or wish to support through volunteer work and the like. So too, when receiving financial support from state or federal government; via taxation benefits or funding or grants, should have such financial support limited".

The ASA affirmed the following:

"it is the role and duty of men and woman, lay or ordained people of faith, religion and spirituality in Australia, to help build a future where Buddhist and diverse faiths, cultures and lifestyles, can live together harmoniously, be in complete acceptance, wisdom, love and compassion for each other".[63]

Interfaith

The FABC, ASA, and the Buddhist Council of Victoria (BCV) are represented on various committees of interfaith organisations in Australia. This includes *Religions for Peace, the Victorian Interfaith Network, the Faith Communities Council of Victoria (FCCV), the Australian Partnership of Religious Organisations APRO,* and *Religious Advisory Committee to the Services (RACS).*

The Partnership of Religious Organisations (APRO) is comprised of representatives appointed by the peak bodies of seven major religions in Australia, as well as multicultural, and interfaith community organisations, at the national level and it includes academics with expertise in

---

[63] www.australiansangha.org/statements.

interfaith and intercultural relations. APRO holds an annual National Religious Leaders Roundtable; the last one was on '*Love over Hate: Faith in times of crisis.*'

The aims of APRO are threefold. The first is to promote and advocate for interfaith harmony, understanding and respect between the adherents of the various religions in Australia. The second, is to identify a means to combat religious prejudice and discrimination, through shared values and interests of the various religions, is to identify a means to combat religious prejudice and discrimination. Third is to explore and address matters of mutual concern.

One proposal that has been broadly supported was setting up an Interfaith Consultation Council at the federal government level. To this end, Prof Abd-Elmasih Malak, APRO's Convenor said *Australia enjoys and celebrates religious diversity and is rightly recognised as a leading example of fairness, tolerance and inter-communal harmony and cooperation.*

Religious Advisory Committee to the Services (RACS)

Several years ago, the previous Chair of the Australian Sangha Association, Ven. Bom Hyon Sunim, was invited to represent ASA on RACS. In her long-standing role in education for spiritual care and chaplaincy. Sunim engages with suitable Buddhist practitioners, who are requesting to serve as Defence Force chaplains, reflecting the growing religious and cultural diversity of the Defence Force.

The Chief of Defence, General Angus Campbell stated the following:

> "Physical, mental, and spiritual health are essential for the building of Defence Force's capability through its people. In an increasingly multicultural Defence Force, it is important we are able, to meet the Service-related spiritual and religious needs of all our members."

RACS provides advice to the Defence Forces on religious matters and is also responsible for selecting, supporting, and accrediting chaplaincy candidates. Until recently, only Christians and Jewish members (post World War II) were included on the RACS committee. Ven Bom Hyon Sunim, advocated for the inclusion of Hindus, Muslims, and Buddhists to also be trained as chaplains to serve the needs of their faith. Three Buddhists have recently been accepted into the Navy, another has joined the Army Chaplaincy team, and a current Airforce officer will complete his chaplaincy training at the end of 2023. Several other Buddhists are also undertaking Buddhist chaplaincy training.

ASA Representative Signs the Joint Resolution of Religious Organisations in Support of the 'Uluru Statement from the Heart'

On May 27th 2022, faith leaders from across Australia gathered at Barangaroo in Sydney to endorse the 'Uluru Statement from the Heart'. It has been five years since the first statement was first released to the First Nations National Constitutional Convention, which formally endorsed the Uluru Statement of the Heart. Aboriginal elders have now called for a 'Voice': a representative body to help shape policy directed at First Nations people. They ask for it to be enshrined in Australia's constitution. Australian Prime Minister Anthony Albanese and his government have promised to action the statement.

A Buddhist monk, Bhante Sujato, representing the ASA added, *Now is a time to build a better democracy' Sometimes people from the outside think that all these religions are so different, but the people within it don't really see those differences as so important. For us, what matters is compassion, empathy, and humanity. We've got to create a broad consensus among the political class, as we have already among the religious leaders.*

Melbourne Archbishop Peter Comensoli commented: *I am personally moved by the deep yearning expressed in the Statement from the Heart, and I am so encouraged that faith leaders have offered a response from the heart of their own spiritual traditions.*[64]

---

[64] www.abc.net.au/news/2022-05-27/religious-leaders-back-referendum-on-indigenous-voice/101104568.

Role of the Buddhist Council of Victoria (BCV)

The BCV is comprised of its executive committee and members who are engaged in various Buddhist programmes, such as education, chaplaincy, healthcare, and community. The BCV works with Buddhist leaders and their member temples to engage in interfaith and cultural events and in partnership with pilot projects to serve their communities and the state. The BCV serves the Buddhist and broader interfaith communities in many ways.

Education

The Daylesford Dharma School has been affiliated with and supported by the BCV since it began in 2009. It is the first Australian primary school to develop a school based on Buddhist principles, ensuring that mindfulness and meditation are at the core of each day. It is also an independent, not-for-profit school with extremely low school fees and a 10 to 1 teacher-to-student ratio. The school believes that education is a right, not a privilege. The school's community is at the heart of how the children grow and flourish. The motto of the school is as follows: *'honesty, authenticity, and inner awareness' in building a new way of learning.*[65]

Religious Instruction (RI)

RI was sadly removed from the Victorian State curriculum in 2015 in favour of a programme on respectful relationships. Other states in Australia still value Religious Instruction classes with training offered through their Buddhist Councils. Rules in these states are perhaps more strongly regulated for the safety of the children and to prevent proselytising. Some BCV-trained teachers still teach after school and on weekends and the well-developed course material has been shared worldwide. The RI in a school states the following:

---

[65] https://dharmaschool.com.au.

"Awakening mind skills and values are ones we all cherish, for now and for the future of our world and our children. By making Buddhist understandings available in Victorian schools, is not only for greater knowledge and to encouraged acceptance, but Buddhist children can feel that their religious and cultural backgrounds are being recognized and respected in mainstream education".[66]

Buddhist Library

I am currently working with other BCV members on the BCV Buddhist Library. The BCV office facility has a library room and other useful spaces including; a shrine room for meditation, Buddhist teachings and to host multicultural events. A large collection of Dharma books has been donated by the prominent Buddhist scholar, the late Lawrence Mills (formerly Phra Khantipalo), along with books from other community members, and these are being catalogued.

A monk of many years and well-known Buddhist author Phra Khantipalo was an influential teacher for me in the late 1970s during my early years on the path. He was instrumental in my going to South Korea to train and ordain. I assisted him, his co-teacher, Ilsa Lederman — who became the nun Ayya Khemma — and the growing community of Wat Buddha Dharma during its first two years. The Wat is situated in the Dharug National Park at Wisemans Ferry in New South Wales, Australia.

Chaplaincy

For many years, the Buddhist Council of Victoria has provided the capacity to enable qualified members to train as volunteer chaplains to work in hospitals, aged care, and primary schools. Buddhist prison chaplains are funded by the state government.

Healthcare

Healthcare Chaplaincy, or Spiritual Health as it is now becoming known, is offered in hospitals and aged care facilities to support the physical,

---

[66] https://bcv.org.au/308-2/.

mental, and emotional well-being needs of patients, especially during their last stages of life.

During 2012–2013, while working with the BCV and the Healthcare Chaplaincy Council of Victoria, Ven. Bom Hyon Sunim developed a curriculum and offered training to many Buddhists, a number of whom went on to work in healthcare and prisons. Several have since completed advanced training and currently, there are three Buddhists who are qualified as Clinical Pastoral Educators (CPE). Ven. Thong Phap, an Australian-born monk ordained in the Vietnamese Mahayana tradition, was the pioneer on this path and has conducted many CPE training sessions for Buddhists and has provided CPE training to university institutions in New South Wales.

The BCV has also produced education pamphlets for healthcare professionals. One example is a booklet produced by the BCV, *Buddhist views on Healthcare and Buddhist Healthcare Principles for Spiritual Carers,* which seeks to inform healthcare staff about Buddhist principles underlying Buddhist healthcare and approaches to patient care.[67]

Australia has a very diverse multicultural Buddhist population, so the spiritual care requirements of Buddhist patients in primary health and aged care facilities can vary considerably; it can, however, be challenging at times to find a suitable monastic for end-of-life support. The widely published booklet *Buddhist Care for the Dying* by Di Cousens provides culturally sensitive end-of-life support.[68]

Prisons

The Department of Criminal Justice and Community Safety, Corrections Victoria, allocates financial support for prison chaplains. This has enabled the Buddhist Council of Victoria to coordinate Buddhist prison chaplaincy in Victorian prisons since 2002 when it was first approached by Corrections Victoria to bring Buddhist chaplains into the prisons. There are 11 government-run prisons in Victoria and two private prisons. The small number of Buddhist chaplains, mostly lay people from different Buddhist backgrounds, are committed to bringing the Buddha Dharma

---

[67] These guidelines are available on the BCV and ASA websites: https://bcv.org.au/news.
[68] www.academia.edu/23015392/Buddhist_Care_for_the_Dying.

and pastoral care to those who seek it and work under the Chaplaincy Advisory Committee and Corrections Victoria.

Prisoners from the Buddhist faith constitute only a small percentage of the total prison population, less than 5% or in numerical terms a little over 200 prisoners. Ven. Hōjun Futen is a Senior Chaplain and Chaplain Coordinator for the Buddhist Council of Victoria (BCV). He coordinates chaplains from several different Buddhist communities and traditions who visit prisoners on a regular and 'as-needs' basis.[69]

When I first returned from Korea, I worked for two years as a chaplain in the Loddon Prison, not far from where I lived. I discovered there were prisoners interested in learning about mindfulness and meditation as well as Buddhist methods to deal with mental and emotional pain. For many, it was just about engaging in a space where there was no judgement or expectations so as to explore new ways to interact with themselves and others in a kinder, more honest, gentler, and less reactive way.

Buddhist View of Organ Donation

Organ donation can be a difficult decision, especially for family who are greiving, or those unclear about how organ donation interacts with their religious beliefs, such as rebirth. We believe that the act of organ donation, when motivated by a sincere wish to contribute to the well-being of others, reflects the highest ideals of Buddhism. First, the act of donation informs that there is a vow by the donor to overcome the attachment to their body. Second, the generosity of giving up our bodies after death for the well-being of others acknowledges the continuity of life and that we give back what we take from this world. Finally, after making a vow to donate our bodies after death, we begin to face death with calm and dignity. Making a vow allows us to become settled in our intention and mind, to follow through with our promise. This vow and its fulfilment orientate the donor on the way of good practice. The BCV developed a protocol on organ donation for the benefit of the Buddhist community and medical practitioners, particularly hospitals.[70]

---

[69] https://bcv.org.au/prison-chaplaincy/.
[70] https://bcv.org.au/news/.

Promoting the auspicious symbol of Swastika and banning the Hakenkreuz

In 2022, Victoria became the first Australian state to ban Nazi symbols, in particular the Hakenkreuz, so as to arrest far-right sentiments and anti-semitism. The Hakenkreuz refers to the swastika used in a Nazi context. The swastika, however, has been considered an auspicious symbol among Hindus, Jains, and Buddhists for thousands of years but was tragically misused by the Nazis and became identified with their atrocities during the Second World War.

Due to concerns raised regarding an initial proposal for the outright banning of the swastika, as causing harm to Hindu, Buddhist, and Jain communities, the BCV representatives worked with Hindu and Jewish leaders and government officials to come to an agreeable arrangement. The swastika is a symbol of peace, love, and auspiciousness for the Hindu, Buddhist, and Jain communities and is an important symbol for these faiths. However, after growing interest in the use of the Nazi Hakenkreuz as a symbol of division, and with rising anti-semitism, concerns grew for the safety of the Jewish community in Victoria.

The Victoria Government noted the following:

> "The Bill recognises the cultural and historical significance of the swastika for the Buddhist, Hindu, Jain and other faith communities as an ancient and sacred symbol of peace and good fortune. The Bill does not prohibit the display of the swastika in such religious and cultural contexts. The ban will be supported by a community education campaign to raise awareness of the origins of the religious and cultural swastika, its importance to the Buddhist, Hindu and Jain communities and its distinction to the Nazi symbol."[71]

Recently, the state government has decided to run a public education campaign about the new legislation banning the abuse of the swastika. The Buddhist Council, Hindu Council, Jain Council, and Jewish Community Council have each been given funding to assist in the delivery of the education programmes. Among other tasks, the councils

---

[71] www.premier.vic.gov.au/nation-leading-reform-banning-hate-symbols-victoria.

will work with the Australian Multicultural Foundation, communication specialists, and other peak organisations to deliver on programme objectives.

They will inform and support the delivery of the state-wide campaign, co-designing products and undertaking consultation with community members, and providing relevant content as needed. Specifically, they will lead activities within their respective communities and initiate and take part in interfaith activities and joint initiatives. The councils will assist in the distribution of key messages and resources through existing networks, share learnings, and reflect on the effectiveness of activities to continually improve attendance and participation on the Steering Committee.

Faith communities supporting healthy family relationships

The Buddhist Council is in its fourth year of engaging with government departments and community leaders to address the growing issue of Family Violence in Australia. The project was initially established by the Multifaith Advisory Group (MAG) based on recommendations 163 and 165 of the Victorian Royal Commission into Family Violence.

Data from the United Nations suggest that an average of 137 women across the world are killed by a partner or family member every day.[72] It is known that spiritual advisors in Buddhism, as in other religions rarely report known cases of verbal abuse, family violence, or coercion to the appropriate authorities nor raise awareness of the issue in their communities.

In a pilot project conducted between 2019 and 2021, the BCV worked with the Department of Premier and Cabinet Multicultural Affairs and Social Cohesion Division (MASC) to deliver a pilot project to build the capacity of the Buddhist faith community. The University of Melbourne and the Multicultural Centre for Women's Health partnered with the Victorian Government to support the programme design and evaluation. Dr Di Cousens from the BCV and Associate Professor Anna Halaffof

---

[72] www.bbc.com/news/world-46292919.

from Deakin University will present an academic paper at the upcoming Sakyadhita International Conference in Seoul in 2023 about the project.

The pilot project has been extended by two years. The current project aims to support community leaders to recognise, respond, and refer disclosures of family violence and learn about gender inequality as the driver of violence against women. It will support men to be active leaders in promoting gender equality and build the capacity of community and faith leaders to lead the programmes in their respective communities. Additionally, the project also aims to create culturally appropriate resources, provide information on preventing and responding to family violence, promote healthy and respectful relationships among children, support reciprocal learning between the faith and specialist family violence sector, and increase information sharing by Buddhist chaplains. This will help improve the safety of victim-survivors and increase accountability of perpetrators of family violence.

With other Buddhist leaders, we participated in creating a video, speaking on the broader issues and long-lasting implications of family violence. Another online material was created along with face-to-face and online workshops and the making of help cards, posters, and fact sheets. The videos had subtitles in various languages, and they help inform Buddhist communities on how they can better respond to and prevent family violence.[73]

BCV Inter-Buddhist and Interfaith Events

Since its inception in the late 90s, the Buddhist Council of Victoria (BCV) has co-operated with many Buddhist communities for cultural celebrations, such as Chinese Lunar, Tibetan and Thai New Years, *Vesak* (Buddhas Birthday), *Magha Puja day* (Sangha Day), *Ullambana* (deliverance from suffering day), and *Kathina* (end of the Rains Retreat). They are colourful, fun-filled cultural celebrations that invite the wider public to participate and learn about Buddhism.

In 2007, when I was chairing the BCV committee, we opened the first Theravada Bhikkhuni Hermitage, which paved the way for the Newbury

---

[73] faithsafe.org.au/images/buddhist-toolkit-bcv.pdf.

Buddhist Retreat Centre. Newbury now houses communities of monks and nuns, and at present, a lay retreat centre is being built. The exhibition *Buddha 2550* was created in partnership with the City of Melbourne Local Government Council. Thanks to the generosity of the Lord Mayor, John So, and Buddhist communities, in February of 2007, the longest and possibly largest inter-Buddhist event was held in the Melbourne Town Hall to celebrate 2,550 years of the Buddha's life and his teaching.

Thousands came through the doors to participate in an extraordinary week of Buddhist cultural exhibitions and events. There were beautiful displays of cultural iconography, Dharma talks, workshops, and a mini conference, all complimented with traditional entertainment, food, and ending in a long lantern parade. It certainly strengthened the relationships between the many Buddhist communities and local Victorian monastics.

BCV Creating Interfaith Relationships

The BCV has always had an engaging presence in interfaith dialogues and inter-religious cultural events since its inception. Positive interaction and friendships have grown over the years, between people of different faiths, when cooperation and opportunities for constructive dialogue and collaboration were created.

The BCV, ASA, and FABC committee members are often invited to speak or participate at inter-religious and interfaith ceremonies and at political or national events, such as the promotion of the 'Uluru Statement of the Heart'.

The Interfaith Centre of Melbourne (ICM)

The centre, founded by Helen Summers in 2000, has long been a friend of the BCV. ICM offers spiritual events, ceremonies, celebrations, collaborations, and world peace prayers. Along with interfaith seminars, forums, and meditation, Helen and her ICM team have created art exhibitions and displays of the sacred arts.[74]

---

[74] https://interfaithcentre.org.au/.

Other members of BCV and I have collaborated with and participated in many of the ICM programmes over many years and we have also invited Helen to our Buddhist celebrations, ceremonies, and conferences. Recently, I was invited to speak on mindfulness to her and other chaplains at RMIT University in Melbourne. I realised the practices of mindfulness, from a traditional Buddhist perspective are less known.

Currently, the BCV interfaith representative is Dr Di Cousens. She along with other members are often invited to contribute or participate on behalf of the BCV at interfaith and multicultural events.

Much has been achieved in the past two decades through healthy collaborations between Buddhist and other Faith Peak bodies in liaison with the government. However, there are great concerns for organisations throughout Australia with the growing lack of committed volunteers. Exacerbated by the ongoing impact of COVID-19 and its economic strain on community and public services, the future of many small yet important community organisations with their broader social impact remains to be seen.

Chapter 4.6

LANGUAGE AND BELONGING: THE INSULATION AND ISOLATION INTERNATIONAL STUDENTS FROM NON-ENGLISH SPEAKING BACKGROUNDS EXPERIENCE IN AUSTRALIA

Professor Catherine Gomes

Introduction

International students from culturally and linguistically diverse countries across all education sectors (e.g., higher education, vocational and technical training, and schools) are arguably attracted to Australia as a place to study because English is not only the medium of instruction but also the national language in this monolingual country. English is a significant skill to possess because students see this language as a passport for greater professional and educational mobility not only in Australia but also elsewhere. Possessing good English-language skills is thus a necessary social and professional lubricant for long-term residency in Australia as well as for working and living in the cosmopolitan capitals of the English-speaking world.[75] Additionally, students consider themselves 'global

---

[75] Gomes, C. (2017). *Transient Mobility and Middle Class Identity: Media and Migration in Australia and Singapore*. Palgrave Macmillan, Singapore.

citizens' because they are mobile actors who venture beyond their countries of birth for education.[76] Hence, students in Australia become heavily invested in bettering their English-language skills. By interviewing 47 international students in Australia, this chapter argues that although international students desire to better their professional prospects outside their home countries by improving their English communication skills, the methods they utilise to do so leave them insulated within their own international student networks and ultimately isolated from immersing themselves among native English-speaking Australians. The result thus is a lack of belonging within the host country through a desire, ironically to communicate with the citizenry.

Not Permanent Settlers: International Students as Transient Migrants

While migrants of any kind — settlers and non-settlers — face similar challenges such as adapting to the culture/s of the receiver nation and sometimes more sinister issues such as racism, both these broad groups of migrants, who are defined by their temporal status, are inherently different. Traditional migration theoretical and analytical frameworks which almost wholeheartedly examine permanent migrant(ions) specifically in the areas of economics, race and ethnicity, social structure, and political or public policy should not be used to interpret and understand the agendas and aspirations of international students.

International students are transient migrants and hence have different agendas and aspirations from permanent settlers (new citizens and permanent residents) and more so from first (or multi) generation citizens. Their agendas and aspirations are different to settler migrants who want to make Australia a permanent home for themselves, their children, and sometimes wider family (e.g., parents). While permanent settlers may be concerned about issues of citizenship, such as a sense of belonging in the adopted country and societal acceptance by the citizenry, international

---

[76] Gomes, C, (2015). Negotiating everyday life in Australia: Unpacking the parallel society inhabited by Asian 2015, international students through their social networks and entertainment media use. *Journal of Youth Studies* 18, 515–536.

students are not bound by such anchoring.[77–79] Instead, as transient migrants, international students' residency status is determined by the temporary (student) visa they are on. However, transient migrants are open to their own (im)mobilities and residencies:

> Some transnational transient migrants may not, for instance, want to prolong their overseas experience in the receiver country while others may want to settle more long term as permanent residents or even as citizens. The term transient migration thus allows for manoeuvring of visa and residency statuses within these two categories, for example, individuals on international student visas may shift to working professional visas. Transient migrants thus are transient within the temporary migrant space as they move and upgrade their visa statuses and conditions. In other words, while "temporary" implies a direct and opposing situation to permanence, "transient" is not so limited and instead allows for mobility within the term itself.[80]

International students' agendas thus are fuelled by their aspirations of (im)mobility. In other words, international students may want to be immobile by staying in the destination country whether in the short term or for longer periods of time, be mobile then immobile by returning to the home country and possibly being mobile again, or continue their mobilities by going elsewhere with the prospect of anchoring outside the home and current country they are transient in. Because international students and permanent settlers have different agendas and aspirations, approaches to language should not be framed from a non-settler/citizenship structure. Most academic writing in Australia concerning language, particularly English as a language of communication for non-native speakers within

[77] Wise, A. (2014). Everyday multiculturalism. In *COMPAS Anthology of Migration*. Oxford University, Oxford.

[78] Fozdar, F. (2012). Social relations and skilled Muslim refugees in Australia: Employment, social capital, and discrimination. *Journal of Sociology* 48(2), 167–18.

[79] Hebbani, A., Colic-Peisker, V., and Mackinnon, M. (2017). Know thy neighbour: Residential integration and social bridging among refugee settlers in greater Brisbane. *Journal of Refugee Studies*, 1–22

[80] Gomes, C. (2018). *Siloed Diversity: Transnational Migration, Digital Media and Social Networks*, pp. 3–4. Palgrave Macmillan, Singapore.

the multiculturalism and diversity framework, argues that the Australian cosmopolitan society needs to be accepting that different migrant communal societies speak languages other than English, sometimes almost exclusively.[81]

In this chapter, I thus point out that the English language provides a pivot in the way in which we understand the agendas and aspirations of international students, thus adding another level of understanding of the different experiences and planes of transnational migration and mobility.

English Language Learning in Australia

Proficiency in the English language is considered by non-English speakers as an incredibly important skill to possess. This is because English is deemed to be the currently accepted language for communication and for professional and business mobility.[82] Moreover, English language proficiency is thought to be a social currency in some cultures. In Japan, for instance, knowing English is looked upon in a positive light even though it is not a language that might be used as a language of communication in Japan.[83] In Asia, Latin America, Africa, and Europe there are growing numbers of both foreign and locally owned private and public (government-funded) service providers specialising in teaching English as a foreign language. The British Council, for example, is perhaps the most respected English language teaching organisation with over a hundred centres around the world. The British Council — 'the United Kingdom's international organisation for cultural relations and educational

[81] Matthews, J. (2008). Schooling and settlement: Refugee education in Australia. *International Studies in Sociology of Education*, 18:1, 31–45. DOI: 10.1080/09620210802195947. https://www.universitiesaustralia.edu.au/Media-and-Events/media-releases/One-in-half-a-million--Australia-reaches-International-student-milestone#.Wz1sKtIzbIV.

[82] Universum College. (2017). What significance does the English language today? *Research*, n.d., viewed 12 July 2018, http://www.universum-ks.org/blog/en/hulumtime/cfare-rendesie-ka-gjuha-angleze-sot-2/.

[83] Tsuboya-Newell, I. (2017). Why do Japanese have trouble learning English? *The Japan Times*, 29 October, viewed 12 July 2018, https://www.japantimes.co.jp/opinion/2017/10/29/commentary/japan-commentary/japanese-trouble-learning-english/#.W0ROtdIzbIU.

opportunities' (The British Council, 2018) — not only teaches English but also administers the International English Language Testing System (IELTS). IELTS is a well-regarded and universally recognised English language test for non-native English speakers for the purpose of further education in English and international mobility in English-speaking countries, such as the United Kingdom and Australia.[84] Often, the British Council and other language learning service providers employ native speakers from the United Kingdom and Australia as English teachers.

International students from culturally and linguistically diverse countries across all education sectors (e.g., higher education, vocational and technical training, and schools) are arguably attracted to Australia as a place to study because English is not only the medium of instruction but also the national language in this monolingual country.[85] Learning and improving language skills through non-language specific courses is not a new phenomenon with international students travelling to places where they would like to improve their spoken and written abilities with countries where English is a native language being the most popular destination for such purposes.[86]

Likewise, in her work on English-language skills transnational education, Phan Le-Ha notes that even students who enrol in Western 'English'

---

[84] The British Council. (2018). *The British Council*. Viewed 12 July 2018, https://www.britishcouncil.org.

[85] While there is literature on permanent residents and international students in Australia pointing to education as a pathway for residency (e.g., Baas, 2010; Soong, 2015), a recently released report by the Australian Government (2018) on migration trends tells another story. Here, the report noted that in the period 2000–2014, only 16% of international students converted their status to permanent resident. Previous studies made links between international education and permanent residence primarily because ethnographic work was confined to former international students who were already permanent residents (Soong, 2015) and the focus on specifically students who expressed aspirations for permanent residency (Baas, 2010).

[86] While non-English speaking countries such as France and China attract international students who study non-language-related courses in these places as part of their own desires and aspirations for language learning — in this case French and Mandarin — countries where English is not the native or national language also offer English-language courses in order to attract international students. China increasingly offers English language courses despite Mandarin being its national language.

institutions in their home countries do so because both parents and students feel that they will be getting an 'English' degree and that they will be improving their language skills. This is because courses are taught in English and both parents and students have an expectation that enrolled students will also be conversing in English.[87] So when Western institutions from English-speaking Australia and the United Kingdom open campuses in non-Western countries (Dubai, Vietnam, and Singapore), they become attractive to local (international) students. Students, in other words, enrol not for the courses but to improve their English-language skills, since English is viewed as a language of social-employability and mobility. Clearly, English language skills are significant not only for the present but also for the professional futures of international students.

However, international students who are not very well versed in the language also struggle in their courses — particularly at university — with their spoken and written English.[88] This has resulted in unfortunate grievances by both teaching staff and domestic student peers who find this lack of English language proficiency difficult for teaching and learning. The result are calls for language proficiency courses to be incorporated into university courses for international students.[89] The negativity surrounding international students and their English language skills, is not limited to the education space but is a widely held view by the Australian general public.

To improve their English language skills, international students enrol specifically in English language courses in Australia. Before the COVID-19 pandemic, 20% of Australia's 792,422 enrolled international students — some of whom are enrolled in two or more courses — are in institutions offering ELICOS (*English Language Intensive Courses for Overseas Students*) courses in order to improve their language

---

[87] Phan, H. L. L. (2017). *Transnational Education Crossing 'the West' and 'Asia': Adjusted Desire, Transformative Mediocrity, and Neo-colonial Disguise*. Routledge, London and New York.

[88] Arkoudis, S., and Doughney, L. (2014). *Good Practice Report: English Language Proficiency*. Canberra: Office for Learning and Teaching. http://www.olt.gov.au/resource-good-practice-report-english-language-proficiency-2014.

[89] Arkoudis, S. (2015). More international students should mean more support for communication and interaction. *The Conversation*, 20 April, viewed 12 July 2018, https://theconversation.com/more-international-students-should-mean-more-support-for-communication-and-interaction-39914.

skills.[90],[91] ELICOS courses prepare and test students on a number of popular English language tests which include IELTS, TOEFL IBT (Test of English as a Foreign Language Internet-Based test), PTE (Pearson Test of English), and CAE (Academic Cambridge English): Advanced test (also known as Certificate in Advanced English), OET (Occupational English Test), and TOEFL PBT (TOEFL Paper-Based Test are accepted in a number of institutions.[92] Most students enrol in ELICOS courses before embarking on the next stage of their education journey, often in higher education institutions in Australia while others just want to improve their language skills and they see Australia as the best place to do so.

In this chapter, I look at the significance of English language proficiency among a group of international students living in Melbourne in the state of Victoria and the strategies they take to improve their language skills. In the state of Victoria, international education is the biggest export earner and, in 2017, it was worth $9.1 billion to the state economy while supporting 58,000 jobs.[93] International education has also changed the ethnographic and urban landscapes of Melbourne City and the surrounding suburbs which support universities and private colleges, both of which have ELICOS courses. In 2016, there were 200,000 international students studying in the state with a quarter of the students living in the Melbourne Central Business District while a third living in neighbouring suburb of Carlton.[94] These areas in Melbourne are host to building developments

---

[90] This number is inflated because while there were over 624,000 international students in Australia in 2017, some of these students were also enrolled in other courses, thus they were 'enrolled international students'.

[91] Australian Government. (2018). Research Snapshot: Export income to Australia from international education activity in 2017, *Department of Education and Training*, June, viewed 12 July 2018, https://internationaleducation.gov.au/research/Research-Snapshots/Documents/Export%20Income%20CY%202017.pdf.

[92] Elicos. (2018). Study English in Australia. *Elicos*, viewed 12 July 2018, http://www.elicos.com/.

[93] Victoria State Government. (2018). *International Education*, 18 April, viewed 12 July 2018, https://economicdevelopment.vic.gov.au/priority-industries-sectors/international-education.

[94] Australian Bureau of Statistics. (2014). Where do Migrants Live? *Australian Social Trends 2014*, viewed 12 July 2018, http://www.abs.gov.au/ausstats/abs@.nsf/Lookup/4102.0main+features102014.

and businesses catering to the growing numbers of international students, such as accommodation and retail.

Methodology

Between 2013 and 2014, I embarked on a transnational qualitative and quantitative study looking at the everyday lives of transient migrants (international students, exchange students, working holiday visa holders, skilled temporary knowledge workers and bridging visa holders) in Australia and Singapore. Altogether I interviewed 201 respondents and surveyed 385 transient migrants across both countries. While I found that my participants were resilient in navigating their everyday lives in their respective host countries, I also found that the Asian international students I met in interviews in Australia considered English language proficiency as a significant skill to have and resorted to various ways of improving their language abilities.

For the purpose of this chapter, I specifically look at data pertaining to international students in Australia. Here I report on forty-seven Asian international students studying at Melbourne higher education institutions: universities and colleges. Ethics approval for this study was granted by the RMIT College Human Research Advisory Network committee (CHEAN A-2000827-01-13). Respondents were recruited through advertisements in the Australian online classified website Gumtree, through colleagues from various Victorian universities (e.g., RMIT University, La Trobe University, and Melbourne University), through international student society groups, through the City of Melbourne (a municipal government whose precinct includes the Melbourne central business district which is home to large numbers of international students), and through the snowball effect where respondents brought along their friends for scheduled interviews with the researchers. The advertisements requested for respondents over the age of 18 and who had lived in Australia for a minimum of 3 months. Participants were remunerated with a $30 shopping gift voucher each for their time.

The respondents were interviewed in focus groups, small groups, and as individuals in addition to a short survey which captured their background information, such as age, gender, country of birth/citizenship, ethnicity(s), number of years in Australia to date, course of study/work, media use, and hobbies. Two focus groups with 3 and 7 international students, respectively, took part in the pilot study of this project. There were 13 individual interviews while the rest were interviewed in small groups of no more than 2 respondents each. The data in this chapter reflects the open-ended questions I asked pertaining to respondents' social networks (friendship networks/groups), their impressions of Australian society, and their entertainment media consumption. The duration of the interviews ranged from 30 minutes to 60 minutes, depending on the willingness of the respondents to go into more depth with their answers. I amended my research strategy from focus groups to individual and small groups because I found that the focus group sessions ran for between 90 minutes and 150 minutes longer than the expected 1 hour.

Table 1 provides a demographic breakdown of the students interviewed. It shows that international students pursue a variety of diploma/degree programmes across a wide cross-section of disciplines and come

Table 1. Demographic breakdown of Asian international students.

Gender	M (18)
	F (29)
Age Range	19–24 yrs (28)
	25–29 yrs (15)
	30 yrs and more (4)
Education Pursuit	ELICOS (8)
	Bachelor's degree (19)
	Master's degree and higher (20)
Home Country	Bangladesh (2)
	China (8)
	India (6)
	Indonesia (3)
	Japan (1)
	South Korea (4)
	Malaysia (5)
	Pakistan (3)
	Singapore (8)
	Vietnam (6)
	New Zealand, originally China (1)

(*Continued*)

Table 1.   (*Continued*)

Length of stay in Australia at time of interview	3 months (3)
	3.1–6 months (5)
	6.1 months–1 year (7)
	1 year 1 month–2 years (15)
	2 years 1month–3 years (7)
	3 years 1 month–4 years (8)
	4 years 1 month and more (3)

from a range of countries from Asia. Table 1 also indicates that most participants have been studying in Australia for more than a year while half work in part-time jobs.

An issue I encountered with the interviews which is relevant to this chapter, is that some students had problems understanding some of my questions, particularly those connected to identity. For instance, some participants could not understand what was meant by 'identity' in terms of the concept itself. Hence, I ended up re-framing the question to: 'Who do you think you are?' While those who had difficulty with their English language skills may have struggled a little during interviews, they persevered and were keen to answer the questions as best as they could. Moreover, these participants insisted on conversing in English despite being in focus or small groups with others. I also learned about the bond wanting to improve their English skills creates among international students as they desire to better their language skills. I also learned about how the participants I spoke to practised their language skills with other international students who themselves desired to improve their language skills.

I interviewed two university-going international students who were friends with each other, meeting in an ELCOS class a year earlier. One was a female postgraduate from South Korea and the other a male postgraduate from China. The South Korean participant found understanding some of my questions challenging because they were in English. However, whenever she had difficulty, she turned to her Chinese friend for help with understanding what I was asking. Her friend attempted to help her by reiterating my questions into simpler English so that she might understand. Both participants also told me that their close friends at the time of our interview were fellow students they met during ELICOS classes and who were now studying at various universities in Melbourne.

Insulated and Isolated from Australian Society

Living in a parallel society — International student networks

I have argued before that international students form a parallel society in Australia.[95–98] By parallel society, I mean that while they may live in Australia and among Australians, they set themselves apart by creating groups and communities made up of other international students whether these are groups made up of students from the same country, region, and/ or elsewhere. Hence, while the international students I spoke to may do similar activities as Australians (e.g., having coffee in cafes), they do so with each other and not with domestic students who are coursemates, in tutorials, or lectures.

Moreover, the international students I spoke to see 'Australian' as 'white'. By 'white' they also include anyone who is not broadly of Asian or African appearance. So often, Australians of Middle Eastern and Mediterranean heritage would be considered 'white'. Likewise, while the participants acknowledged that there are Australians who are Asian-born or who grew up in Australia, these groups of Australians were not their friends despite speaking English well. In a separate study of 6,699 international

---

[95] Gomes, C. (2015). Negotiating everyday life in Australia: Unpacking the parallel society inhabited by Asian 2015, international students through their social networks and entertainment media use. *Journal of Youth Studies* 18, 515–536.

[96] Gomes, *op. cit.*

[97] Gomes, *op. cit.*

[98] Gomes, C. (2022). *Parallel Societies of International Students in Australia: Connections, Disconnections, and a Global Pandemic* (1st ed.). Routledge. https://doi.org/10.4324/9781003129981.

students in Australia with 67.45% identifying themselves as from Asia, my colleagues and I asked international students whether they had friends who were Australian who were of the same ethnicity as them. Less than 1% admitted to having friends who were of the same ethnic group as them.[99] The assumption here is that Asian international students do not see Asian Australians — those born or who grew up in Australia — as friends.

International students form strong bonds with other international students, often co-nationals but increasingly with international students from other countries, particularly from their own region (e.g., Asian international students with other international students from the region) and then from elsewhere. These bonds are formed based on a common identity as an international student with similar experiences as foreigners studying in Australia. However, because international students are only maintaining friendship groups with other international students, they insulate themselves away from domestic students and Australians as a whole.[100] While international students may have do similar activities as Australians such as going to pubs and cafes, they do these with other international students; and not with domestic students. In other words, international students become insulated within their own international student networks.

Excluding themselves from Australian society has long-term effects on Australia the more diverse it becomes particularly if international students choose to stay longer after graduation as temporary skilled workers, permanent residents, or citizens. Those international students I spoke to who expressed a desire for permanent residency after they completed their studies explained that their reason for wanting this was because they felt that the pace of life in Australia was more to their liking. A Singaporean student in his second year of undergraduate study, for instance, explained that he felt that if he returned to Singapore, he would have to work long hours, just like other Singaporeans. Australia, he explained, was much more 'laid back'. He felt that Australia, in other words, was less stressful

---

[99] Gomes, C., Chang, S., Jacka, L., Coulter, D., Alzougool, B., and Constantinidis, D. (2015). Myth busting stereotypes: The connections, disconnections and benefits of international student social networks. In *26th ISANA International Education Association Conference*, Melbourne, 1–4 December 2015.

[100] Gomes, *op. cit.*

a country to live and work in than Singapore. None of the international students in my study discussed about how they were attracted to Australia because of its people. If they were already living in a parallel society as international students, would they continue doing so with other international students-turned-permanent migrants? However, a more troubling issue which international students face is isolation.

Isolation

Research on international students' well-being in Australia and elsewhere often expresses concern on the mental health and wellbeing of international students. The research often points out that being in a foreign country while separated from family and friends can lead to emotional and social dissonance, such as loneliness and homesickness.[101,102] While research has shown that over time international students learn to cope with living away from home and loved ones, for some international students however, experience mental health and wellbeing issues. Isolation particularly is an issue of concern which international education stakeholders must address. Again, in the previously mentioned study of 6,699 international students, my colleagues and I found that 4% of respondents admitted that they did not have any friends in Australia. While this percentage may seem small, this group is still a matter of concern due to a lack of friendship groups in the host country.

Various studies in the past decade have increasingly shown that international students suffer from mental health and wellbeing issues due to being in a culturally and linguistically foreign country away from the familiar faces of family, friends and community.[103,104] Moreover, some may face direct, indirect, or perceived forms of racism resulting in them

---

[101] Sawir, E., Marginson, S., Deumert, A., Nyland, C., and Ramia, G. (2008). Loneliness and international students: An Australian study. *Journal of Studies in International Education* 12, 148–180.

[102] Hendrickson, B., Rosen, D., and Aune, R. K. (2011). An analysis of friendship networks, social connectedness, homesickness, and satisfaction levels of international students. *International Journal of Intercultural Relations* 35(3), 281–295.

[103] Sawir, Marginson, Deumert, Nyland, and Ramia, *op. cit.*

[104] Hendrickson, Rosen, and Aune, *op. cit.*

withdrawing into their own worlds even more. A male respondent from Singapore in his second year of undergraduate study, for instance, told me that the Australians he meets are in his tutorials. However, after classes, his tutorial mates go their separate ways. He explained that they do not invite him for coffee a gesture he interprets as a form of racism. As international education in Australia recovers with more face-to-face classes incorporating online learning styles built in known as blended learning, would international students become once more disconnected from the wider student community since they are able to engage in their courses without leaving their residences in Australia.

Conclusion: Practical Implications

In this chapter, I discuss the significance of English language skills for international students in Australia. I highlight how international students in Australia value English language as a skill to have not only for every-day living in Australia but also for their futures. Additionally, I describe how international students resort to both conventional and creative yet informal ways of improving their language skills which they incorporate into everyday living in Australia. The conventional ways of improving their English language skills primarily relate to enrolling in ELICOS courses an acronym for English Language Intensive Courses for Overseas Students while the creative yet informal ways include social relations between international students and turning to English language entertainment and news media from the United States, the United Kingdom, and, at a lesser level, Australia to improving English proficiency. So, what practical implications can we develop from knowing that English has meaningful significance for international students that go beyond study?

In yearly international student satisfaction surveys such as the International Student Barometer which are conducted in key English-speaking Western international education destinations such as the United Kingdom, Australia, the United States, and Canada, international students often say that while they are largely satisfied with their study experience in Australia yet unhappy that after their entire degree or diploma, they did not make any Australian friends.[105] Moreover, such surveys also reveal that international students who are not satisfied with their study experience are a source of negative publicity for countries and institutions since respondents admit that they would actively dissuade potential students from enrolling. The classroom (and lecture theatre) environment, ironically where international and domestic students meet, is the environment where students from both sides barely talk to each other.

Research into international student well-being often notes that having meaningful relationships with domestic students leads to happier and more adjusted international students who otherwise might suffer from emotional and mental issues connected with being away from family, friends, and the familiarity of home country, culture, and society. To plug this friendship gap, institutions could devise programmes — possibly introducing them at orientation — to help international students with language. Such programmes openly facilitate mixing between international and domestic students, hence allowing international students the opportunity to make inroads into possible meaningful relationships with domestic students in a more conducive environment arrangement outside of the classroom.[106]

---

[105] i-Graduate International Insight. (2014). *The International Student Barometer.* i-Graduate International Insight, viewed 12 July 2018, https://www.i-graduate.org/services/international-student-barometer/.

[106] A version of this chapter appeared in Gomes, C. (2020). Outside the Classroom: The Language of English and its Impact on International Student Mental Wellbeing in Australia. Journal of International Students, 10(4), 934–953. https://doi.org/10.32674/jis.v10i4.1277

Chapter 4.7

LANGUAGE AND HEALTH: INDIGENOUS TONGUE REVIVAL, CULTURAL IDENTITY, SENSE OF BELONGING, AND WELL-BEING

Professor Ghil'ad Zuckermann

This chapter postulates heritage language as core to people's identity, sense of belonging, well-being, spirituality, happiness, and social cohesion. Language is crucial for health. Hallett, Chandler, and Lalonde reported a clear correlation between lack of conversational knowledge in the native tongue and youth suicide.[107] However, so far, there has been no systematic study of a correlation in the other direction, i.e., the impact of reconnecting with one's heritage language towards *empowered* well-being, *improved* mental health, and *reduction* in suicide. This is partly because language reclamation is still rare.[108,109] This chapter demonstrates that just as language loss *increases* suicide, language gain *reduces* suicide,

---

[107] Hallett, D., Chandler, M. J., and Lalonde, C. E. (2007). Aboriginal language knowledge and youth suicide. *Cognitive Development* 22(3), 392–399.

[108] Waldram, James B. (1990). The persistence of traditional medicine in urban areas: The case of Canada's Indians. *American Indian and Alaska Native Mental Health Research* 4(1), 9–29.

[109] Chandler, Michael J., and Chris E. Lalonde. (2008). Cultural continuity as a protective factor against suicide in first nations youth. *Horizons — A Special Issue on Aboriginal Youth, Hope or Heartbreak: Aboriginal Youth and Canada's Future* 10(1), 68–72.

improves well-being, and increases sense of belonging and cultural identity.

This chapter introduces the Barngarla Aboriginal language of Eyre Peninsula, in South Australia, Australia. Barngarla became a 'Dreaming, Sleeping Beauty' tongue in the 1960s. It belongs to the Thura-Yura language group, which is part of the Pama-Nyungan language family that includes 306 out of 400 Aboriginal languages in Australia, and whose name is a merism deriving from the two endpoints of the range: the Pama languages of northeast Australia (where the word for 'man' is *pama*) and the Nyungan languages of southwest Australia (where the word for 'man' is *nyunga*). I have been facilitating the Barngarla reclamation since 14 September 2011.

Introduction: Revivalistics

Revivalistics is a new global trans-disciplinary field of enquiry that comparatively and systematically studies both *universal* constraints and global mechanisms and *particularistic* peculiarities and cultural relativist idiosyncrasies that are apparent in linguistic reclamation, revitalisation, and reinvigoration.[110–113]

---

[110] Zuckermann, Ghil'ad. (2003). *Language Contact and Lexical Enrichment in Israeli Hebrew*. Palgrave Macmillan, Houndmills.

[111] Zuckermann, Ghil'ad. (2009). Hybridity versus revivability: Multiple causation, forms and patterns. *Journal of Language Contact, Varia* 2, 40–67.

[112] Zuckermann, Ghil'ad. (2020). Revivalistics: From the Genesis of Israeli to Language Reclamation in Australia and Beyond. Oxford University Press, New York.

[113] Zuckermann, Ghil'ad, and Michael Walsh. (2011). Stop, revive, survive: Lessons from the Hebrew revival applicable to the reclamation, maintenance and empowerment of aboriginal languages and cultures. *Australian Journal of Linguistics* 31(1), 111–127. Also published as Chapter 28 in Susan D. Blum (ed.). (2012). *Making Sense of Language: Readings in Culture and Communication*, 2nd edn. Oxford University Press, Oxford.

[114] Zuckermann, Ghil'ad and Michael Walsh. (2014). "Our Ancestors Are Happy!": Revivalistics in the Service of Indigenous Wellbeing. Foundation for Endangered Languages XVIII: Indigenous Languages: Value to the Community, 113-9. Naha, Ryukyuan Island, Okinawa, Japan: Foundation for Endangered Languages.

What is the difference between reclamation, revitalisation, and reinvigoration? All of them are on the revival spectrum. Following are my specific definitions:

- *Reclamation* is the revival of a Dreaming, 'Sleeping Beauty' tongue, i.e., a no-longer natively spoken language, as in the case of Hebrew, Barngarla (the Aboriginal language of Eyre Peninsula, South Australia), Bayoongoo (the Aboriginal language of Coral Bay, Western Australia), Wampanoag, Siraya, and Myaamia.
- *Revitalisation* is the revival of a severely endangered language, for example, Adnyamathanha of the Flinders Ranges in Australia, as well as Karuk and Walmajarri.
- *Reinvigoration* is the revival of an endangered language that still has a high percentage of children speaking it, for example, the Celtic languages Welsh and Irish, and the Romance languages Catalan and Quebecoise French.

Language endangerment has little to do with absolute numbers. Rather, it has to do with the percentage of children within the language group speaking the language natively. A language spoken natively by 10 million people can be endangered (as, say, only 40% of the children speak it). A language spoken natively by 3,000 people can be safe and healthy (as 100% of them are native speakers).

Table 1 describes the difference between reclamation, revitalisation, and reinvigoration.

Needless to say, reclamation, revitalisation, and reinvigoration are on a *continuum*, a cline. They do not constitute a *discrete* trichotomy. That said, the distinction is useful. For example, the Master-Apprentice (or Mentor/Apprentice) method can only be used in the case of revitalisation and reinvigoration, not in reclamation. This method was pioneered by linguist Leanne Hinton at the University of California, Berkeley, who had been working with a wide range of Native American languages spoken or, in some cases, remembered or documented, across California.[115] In many

---

[115] Hinton, Leanne. (1994). *Flutes of Fire: Essays on California Indian Languages*. Heyday Books.

Table 1   Comparison of Reclamation, revitalization, and reinvigoration.

Reclamation	Revitalisation	Reinvigoration
There are NO native speakers when the revival begins.	Severely endangered. The percentage of children within the group speaking the language natively is very low, e.g., 10%, but there are still adults speaking the language natively.	Endangered. The percentage of children within the group speaking the language natively is lower than 100%.
For example, Hebrew, Barngarla, Bayoongoo, Wampanoag, Siraya, Myaamia, and Tunica (Central and Lower Mississippi Valley, USA)	For example, Adnyamathanha, Karuk, and Walmajarri	For example, Welsh, Irish, Catalan, and Quebecoise French

cases, she was working with the remaining handful of ageing fluent speakers of languages, such as Karuk. It is a difficult proposition to ask an elderly speaker to come into a school classroom and teach children when they themselves are not trained teachers and, in some cases, may never have had an opportunity to attend school themselves. Even if they were able to teach their languages in a school setting, will this really ensure that their language continues into future generations? Probably not.

What is more effective is to ensure that highly motivated young adults who are themselves owners-custodians of the language gain a sound knowledge of, and fluency in, their language. This is achieved through the Master-Apprentice (or Mentor/Apprentice) approach: A young person is paired with an older fluent speaker — perhaps a granddaughter with her grandmother — and their job is to speak the language with each other without resorting to English. It does not matter what they do — they can weave baskets, go fishing, build houses, or fix cars together — so long as they speak the language with each other.[116]

Revivalistics is *trans-disciplinary* because it studies language revival from *any* angle. For example, law, mental health, linguistics, anthropology, sociology, geography, politics, history, biology, evolution, genetics, genomics, colonisation studies, missionary studies, media, animation

---

[116] Zuckermann, Ghil'ad, *op. cit.*

film, technology, talknology (talk+technology), art, theatre, dance, agriculture, archaeology, music education, games (indirect learning), pedagogy, and even architecture.[117,118]

Consider architecture. An architect involved in revivalistics might ask the following 'location, location, location' question, which is, of course, beyond language:

- Should we reclaim an indigenous language in a natural indigenous setting to replicate the original ambience of heritage, culture, laws, and lores?
- Should we reclaim an indigenous language in a modern building that has Indigenous characteristics, such as aboriginal colours and shapes?
- Should we reclaim an aboriginal language in a Western governmental building to give an empowering signal that the tribe has full support of contemporary mainstream society?

Why Should We Reclaim Dormant Languages?

Approximately 7,000 languages are currently spoken worldwide. The majority of these are spoken by small populations. Approximately 96% of the world's population speaks around 4% of the world's languages, leaving the vast majority of tongues vulnerable to extinction and disempowering their speakers (when the percentage of children speaking the language is lower than 100%, see above). Linguistic diversity reflects many things beyond accidental historical splits. Languages are essential building blocks of community identity, cultural autonomy, intellectual sovereignty, and sense of belonging.

With globalisation of dominant cultures, homogenisation, and Coca-colonisation, cultures at the periphery are becoming marginalised, and more and more groups all over the world are added to the forlorn club of the lost-heritage peoples. One of the most important symptoms of this cultural disaster is language loss.

---

[117] Grant, Catherine. (2014). *Music Endangerment: How Language Maintenance Can Help*. Oxford University Press.

[118] Hinton, Leanne. (2011). Language revitalization and language pedagogy: New teaching and learning strategies. *Language and Education* 25(4), 307–318.

A fundamental question for revivalistics, which both the tax-paying general public and the scholarly community ought to ask, is why does it matter to speak a different language? As Evans puts it eloquently in the introduction to his book *Dying Words*[119]:

"you only hear what you listen for, and you only listen for what you are wondering about. The goal of this book is to take stock of what we should be wondering about as we listen to the dying words of the thousands of languages falling silent around us, across the totality of what Mike Krauss has christened the 'logosphere': just as the 'biosphere' is the totality of all species of life and all ecological links on earth, the logosphere is the whole vast realm of the world's words, the languages that they build, and the links between them."

Evans ranges over the manifold ways that languages can differ, the information they can hold about the deep past of their speakers, the interdependence of language and thought, and the intertwining of language and oral literature.[120] Relevant to revivalistics, it concludes by asking how linguistics can best go about recording existing knowledge so as to ensure that the richest, most culturally distinctive record of a language is captured for use by those wanting to revive it in the future. Brenzinger emphasises the threats to knowledge on the environment and conceptual diversity as a crucial loss in language shifts.[121–125]

---

[119] Evans, Nicholas. (2010). *Dying Words. Endangered Languages and What They Have to Tell Us*. Wiley-Blackwell, Malden and Oxford.

[120] *Ibid.*

[121] Brenzinger, Matthias; Bernd Heine and Ingo Heine. (1994). *The Mukogodo Maasai. An Ethnobotanical Survey*. Rüdiger Köppe, Cologne.

[122] Brenzinger, Matthias. (2006). Conceptual Loss in Space and Time: Vanishing Concepts in Khwe, a Hunter-Gatherers. *Language, Ajia Afurika Gengo Bunka Kenkyujo Tsushin* 116, 71–73.

[123] Brenzinger, Matthias. (2007). 'Vanishing conceptual diversity: The loss of hunter-gatherers' concepts, Jornades 15 anys GELA (Grup d'Estudide Llengües Amenaçades), Recerca en llengües amenaçades (Published on CD by GELA).

[124] Brenzinger, Matthias. (2018). Sharing thoughts, concepts and experiences: Fieldwork on African languages. Hannah Sarvasy and Diana Forker (eds.) *Word Hunters: Field linguists on fieldwork*, pp. 45–60 (Studies in Language Companion Series 194). John Benjamins, Amsterdam — Philadelphia.

[125] Heine, Bernd and Matthias Brenzinger. (1988). *Plants of the Borana (Ethiopia and Kenya)*. (Plant Concepts and Plant Use, Part IV). Breitenbach, Saarbrücken.

The following is my own *why* trichotomy of the main *revivalistic* reasons for language revival. The first reason for language revival is *ethics*: It is right. The second reason for language revival is *aesthetic*: It is beautiful. The third benefit for language revival is *utilitarian*: It is socially beneficial.

Ethical Reasons

A plethora of the world's languages have not just been dying of their own accord; many were subject to linguicide: language killing. They were destroyed by settlers of the land where the languages belong. Many Aboriginal Australians believe in a trinity: not *il padre, il figlio e lo spirit santo* (the Father, the Son, and the Holy Spirit) but rather *Land, Language, and People*. The language and the people belong to the land. When you speak to a kangaroo in Galinyala (Port Lincoln), Eyre Peninsula, South Australia, you are supposed to speak in the Barngarla Aboriginal language as both the language and the kangaroo belong to the same land.

Deontologically, we owe it to the Aboriginal and Torres Strait Islander people to support the maintenance and revival of their cultural heritage simply because these languages were subject to linguicide. According to the international law of human rights, people belonging to ethnic, religious, or linguistic minorities have the right to use their own language (Article (art.) 27 of the International Covenant on Civil and Political Rights (ICCPR)). Thus, every person has the right to express themselves in the language of their ancestors, not just in the language of convenience that English has become.

Through supporting language revival, we right the wrong of the past, allowing people to reconnect with their linguicided tongues. By supporting language revival, we appreciate the significance of Indigenous languages and recognise their importance to Indigenous people and to Australia.

Aesthetic Reasons

The linguist Ken Hale, who worked with many endangered languages and saw the effect of loss of language, compared losing language to bombing the Louvre: 'When you lose a language, you lose a culture, intellectual wealth, a work of art. It's like dropping a bomb on a museum, the Louvre' (*The Economist*, 3 November 2001). A museum is a repository of human artistic culture. Languages are at least equally important since they store the cultural practices and beliefs of an entire people. Different languages have different ways of expressing ideas and this can indicate which concepts are important to a certain culture.

For example, information relating to food sources, surviving in nature, and dreaming/history is being lost along with the loss of Aboriginal languages. Consider the practice known as singing to the sharks was an important ritual in Barngarla Aboriginal culture in Eyre Peninsula, South Australia. The performance consisted of men lining the cliffs of bays in the Eyre Peninsula and singing out, while their chants were accompanied by women dancing on the beach. The aim was to enlist sharks and dolphins in driving shoals of fish towards the shore, where Barngarla fishermen in the shallows could make their catch. This technique expired when the last speaker of Barngarla passed away in the 1960s.

A study by Boroditsky and Gaby found that speakers of Kuuk Thaayorre, a language spoken in Pormpuraaw on the west coast of Cape York, do not use 'left' or 'right' but always use cardinal directions (i.e., north, south, east, and west).[126] They claim that Kuuk Thaayorre speakers are constantly aware of where they are situated and that this use of directions also affects their awareness of time.[127] Language supports different ways of 'being in the world'.

Such cases are abundant around the world. An example of a grammatical way to express a familiar concept is *mamihlapinatapai*: a lexical item in the Yaghan language of Tierra del Fuego in Chile and Argentina. It refers to 'a look shared by two people, each wishing that the other would offer something that they both desire but have been unwilling to suggest or offer themselves'. This lexical item, which refers to a concept that many have despite lacking a specific word for it in their language, can

---

[126] Boroditsky, Lera and Alice Gaby. (2010). Remembrances of times east absolute spatial representations of time in an Australian aboriginal community. *Psychological Science* 21(11), 1635–1639.
[127] *Ibid.*

be broken down into morphemes: *ma-* is a reflexive/passive prefix (realized as the allomorph *mam-* before a vowel), *ihlapi* 'to be at a loss as what to do next', *-n*, stative suffix, *-ata*, achievement suffix, and *-apai*, a dual suffix, which has a reciprocal sense with *ma-* (circumfix).

Three examples of beautiful concepts that most people might never imagine are as follows: (1) *nakhur*, in Ancient Persian, refers to 'camel that will not give milk until her nostrils have been tickled'. Clearly, camels are very important in this society and survival may have historically depended on camel milk; (2) *tingo*, in Rapa Nui (Pasquan) of Easter Island (Eastern Polynesian language), is 'to take all the objects one desires from the house of a friend, one at a time, by asking to borrow them, until there is nothing left'; (3) *bunjurrbi*, in Wambaya (Non-Pama-Nyungan West Barkly Australian language, Barkly Tableland of the Northern Territory, Australia), is a verb meaning 'to face your bottom towards someone when getting up from the ground'.[128,129]

Such fascinating and multifaceted words, *maximus in minimīs*, should not be lost. They are important to the cultures they are from and make the outsiders reflexive of their own cultures. Through language maintenance and reclamation, we can keep important cultural practices and concepts alive. Lest we forget that human imagination is often limited. Consider aliens in many Hollywood films, despite approximately 3.5 billion years of DNA evolution (and the world being finite), many people still resort to the ludicrous belief that aliens ought to look like ugly human beings with two eyes, one nose, and one mouth.

Utilitarian Benefits

Language revival benefits the speakers involved through improvement of well-being, mental health, general health, and cognitive abilities.[130]

---

[128] De Boinod, Adam Jacot. (2005). *The Meaning of Tingo: And Other Extraordinary Words from around the World*. Penguin, London.

[129] De Boinod, Adam Jacot and Ghil'ad Zuckermann. (2011). *Tingo: Language as a Reflection of Culture*. (The Israeli translation of Adam Jacot de Boinod's The Meaning of Tingo). Tel Aviv: Keren. (Three chapters by Zuckermann, pp. 193–222).

[130] Zuckermann, Ghil'ad, *op. cit.*

Language revival also reduces delinquency and increases cultural tourism. Language revival has a positive effect on the mental and physical well-being of people involved in such projects. Participants develop a better appreciation of and sense of connection with their cultural heritage. Learning the language of their ancestors can be an emotional experience and can provide people with a strong sense of pride and identity.

There are also cognitive advantages to bilingualism and multilingualism. Several studies have found that bilingual children have better non-linguistic cognitive abilities compared with monolingual children, as well as improved attention and auditory processing: the bilingual's 'enhanced experience with sound results in an auditory system that is highly efficient, flexible, and focused in its automatic sound processing, especially in challenging or novel listening conditions'.[131,132]

Furthermore, the effects of multilingualism extend to those who have learned another language in later life and can be found across the whole lifespan. This is relevant to the first generation of revivalists, who might themselves be monolingual (as they will not become native speakers of the revival language). The effects of non-native multilingualism include better cognitive performance in old age, a significantly later onset of dementia, and a better cognitive outcome after stroke.[133–136] Moreover, a measurable improvement in attention has been documented in participants

---

[131] Kovács, Ágnes Melinda and Jacques Mehler. (2009). Flexible learning of multiple speech structures in bilingual infants. *Science* 325(5940), 611–612.

[132] Krizman, Jennifer, Viorica Marian, Anthony Shook, Erika Skoe and Nina Kraus. (2012). Subcortical encoding of sound is enhanced in bilinguals and relates to executive function advantages. *Proceedings of the National Academy of Sciences* 109(20), 7877–7881.

[133] Bak, T. H., Nissan, J., Allerhand, M., and Deary, I. J. (2014). Does bilingualism influence cognitive ageing? *Annals of Neurology* 75(6), 959–963.

[134] Alladi, S., Bak, T. H., Duggirala, V., Surampudi, B., Shailaja, M., Shukla, A. K., Chaudhuri, J. D., and Kaul, S. (2013). Bilingualism delays age at onset of dementia, independent of education and immigration status. *Neurology* 81(22), 1938–1944.

[135] Alladi, S., Bak, T. H., Mekala, S., Rajan, A., Chaudhuri, J. R., Mioshi, E., Krovvidi, R., Surampudi, B., Duggirala, V., and Kaul, S. (2016). Impact of bilingualism on cognitive outcome after stroke. *Stroke* 47, 258–261.

[136] Paplikar, A., Mekala, S., Bak, T. H., Dharamkar, S., Alladi, S., and Kaul, S. (2018). Bilingualism and the severity of post-stroke aphasia. *Aphasiology*. Published on-line 15/1/2018.

aged from 18 to 78 years after just one week of an intensive language course.[137] Language learning and active multilingualism are increasingly seen as contributing not only to psychological well-being but also to brain health with a potential of reducing money spent on medical care.[138]

Further benefits to non-native multilingualism are demonstrated by Keysar *et al.*[139] They found that decision-making biases are reduced when using a non-native language, as follows:

> "Four experiments show that the 'framing effect' disappears when choices are presented in a foreign tongue. Whereas people were risk averse for gains and risk seeking for losses when choices were presented in their native tongue, they were not influenced by this framing manipulation in a foreign language. Two additional experiments show that using a foreign language reduces loss aversion, increasing the acceptance of both hypothetical and real bets with positive expected value. We propose that these effects arise because a foreign language provides greater cognitive and emotional distance than a native tongue does."

Thus, language revival is not only empowering culturally but also cognitively, and not only the possibly envisioned native speakers of the future but also the learning revivalists of the present.

Language Loss and Youth Suicide in British Columbia, Canada

Language is core to people's well-being. But it is one thing to have a qualitative statement about the importance of language for mental health,

---

[137] Bak, T. H., Long, M. R., Vega-Mendoza, M., and Sorace, A. (2016). Novelty, challenge, and practice: The impact of intensive language learning on attentional functions. *PLoS One*. Published online 27 April 2016.

[138] Bak, T. H., and Mehmedbegovic, D. (2017). Healthy linguistic diet: The value of linguistic diversity and language learning. *Journal of Languages, Society and Policy*. Published online 21 May 2017.

[139] Keysar, Boaz, Sayuri L. Hayakawa and Sun Gyu An. (2012). The foreign-language effect thinking in a foreign tongue reduces decision biases. *Psychological Science* 23(6), 661–668.

it is another to have the statistical, quantitative evidence that governments so often require to implement policies that will affect cultural and social well-being.

One fundamental study, conducted in 2007 in British Columbia, Canada, began that evidence gathering: Hallett, Chandler, and Lalonde reported a clear correlation between youth suicide and lack of conversational knowledge in the native tongue.[140] They matched seven cultural continuity factors and measured them against reported suicide from 150 indigenous Inuit communities and almost 14,000 individuals. These cultural continuing factors were self-governance, land claims, education, healthcare, cultural facilities, police/fire service, and language. Of all the communities that research sampled, the results indicated that those communities with higher levels of language knowledge (over 50% of the community) had lower suicide levels when compared to other communities with less knowledge. The 16 communities with high levels of language had a suicide rate of 13 deaths per 100,000 people compared to low levels of language which had 97 deaths per 100,000. The suicide rate in high-language communities was six times lower than the other communities. When coupled with other cultural protective factors, there was an even higher protective effect against suicide. Hallett, Chandler, and Lalonde demonstrated that youth suicide rates dropped to zero in those few communities in which at least half the members reported a conversational knowledge of their own native tongue.

That landmark research was the first to study the correlation between language knowledge and mental health. However, so far, there has been no study of a correlation in the other direction, i.e., the impact of language *revival* on *improved* mental health and *reduction* in suicide. This is partly because language reclamation is still rare.[141,142]

This chapter suggests that just as language loss *increases* the suicide rate, language gain *reduces* the suicide rate, improves well-being, and increases sense of belonging, spirituality, and happiness.

---

[140] Hallett, Chandler, and Lalonde, *op. cit.*

[141] Waldram, *op. cit.*

[142] Chandler, Michael J. and Chris E. Lalonde, *op. cit.*

Language Revival and Empowered Spirituality and Sense of Belonging in Australia

Due to invasion, colonisation, globalisation, and homogenisation, there are more and more groups losing their heritage. Linguicide results in the loss of cultural autonomy, intellectual sovereignty, spirituality, well-being, sense of belonging, and the 'soul'.[143] The dependence of the linguicided group on the coloniser's tongue further increases the phenomena of disempowerment, self-loathing, and suicide.[144,145]

According to the 2008 National Aboriginal and Torres Strait Islander (ATSI) Social Survey, 31% of indigenous Australians aged 15+ experienced high or very high levels of psychological distress in the four weeks prior to interview. This is 2.5 times the rate for non-indigenous Australians.

I arrived in Australia in 2004. My main goal has been to apply lessons from the Hebrew revival, of which I have been an expert, to the reclamation and empowerment of indigenous languages and cultures. Throughout my revivalistic activities in the field in Australia and globally (e.g., Eastern Tibet and Inner Mongolia in China, Thailand, New Zealand, Namibia, South Africa, Canada, Israel, Fiji, Norfolk Island, Cook Islands, Mauritius, Muscogee Native Americans in Georgia, and Cherokee Native Americans in Alabama), I have noticed, *qualitatively*, that language reclamation has an empowering effect on the community well-being and mental health of the people directly involved, as well as on their extended families. Participants in my revivalistic workshops have developed a better appreciation of, and sense of connection with, their identity and cultural heritage.

---

[143] Zuckermann, Ghil'ad, *op. cit.*

[144] Biddle, Nicholas and Hannah Swee. (2012). The relationship between wellbeing and Indigenous land, language and culture in Australia. *Australian Geographer* 43(3), 215–232.

[145] King, M., Smith, A., and Gracey, M. (2009). Indigenous health part 2: The underlying causes of the health gap. *The Lancet* 374(9683), 76–85.

The Barngarla Aboriginal Language of Eyre Peninsula, South Australia

Barngarla is a 'Dreaming, Sleeping Beauty' tongue belonging to the Thura-Yura language group, which also includes Adnyamathanha, Kuyani, Nukunu, Ngadjuri, Wirangu, Nawoo, Narangga, and Kaurna. The name Thura-Yura derives from the fact that the word for 'man, person' in these languages is either *thura* or *yura* — consider Barngarla *yoora*. The Thura-Yura language group is part of the Pama-Nyungan language family, which includes 306 out of 400 Aboriginal languages in Australia and whose name is a merism derived from the two endpoints of the range: the Pama languages of northeast Australia (where the word for 'man' is *pama*) and the Nyungan languages of southwest Australia (where the word for 'man' is *nyunga*). According to Bouckaert *et al.*, the Pama-Nyungan language family arose just under 6,000 years ago around Burketown, Queensland.[146]

Typically, for a Pama-Nyungan language, Barngarla has a phonemic inventory featuring three vowels ([a], [i], [u]) and retroflex consonants, an ergative grammar with many cases, and a complex pronominal system. Unusual features include a number system with singular, dual, plural, and superplural (*warraidya* 'emu', *warraidyalbili* 'two emus', *warraidyarri* 'emus', and *warraidyailyarranha* 'a lot of emus') and matrilineal and patrilineal distinction in the dual. For example, the matrilineal ergative first person dual pronoun *ngadlaga* ('we two') would be used by a mother and her child, or by a man and his sister's child, while the patrilineal form *ngarrrinyi* would be used by a father and his child, or by a woman with her brother's child.

During the 20th century, Barngarla was intentionally eradicated under Australian 'Stolen Generation' policies, with the last original native speaker dying in 1960. Language reclamation efforts were launched on 14 September 2011 in a meeting between myself and representatives of the Barngarla people (Zuckermann, 2020). During the meeting, I asked the Barngarla representatives whether or not they were interested in

---

[146] Bouckaert Remco, Bowern Claire, and Atkinson Quentin. (2018). The origin and expansion of Pama–Nyungan languages across Australia. *Nature Ecology & Evolution*. 2. 10.1038/s41559-018-0489-3.

reclaiming their Dreaming, Sleeping Beauty tongue and improving their well-being, mental health, cultural autonomy, intellectual sovereignty, spirituality, sense of belonging, and educational success. They told me: 'We've been waiting for you for fifty years!'

Since then, I have conducted dozens of language reclamation workshops to more than 120 Barngarla people. The primary resource used has been a dictionary, including a brief grammar, written by the German Lutheran missionary Clamor Wilhelm Schürmann (Schürmann 1844), which I improved.

Published resources for Barngarla, non-existent 10 years ago, are now emerging. Two examples are *Barngarlidhi Manoo* ('Speaking Barngarla Together'), a Barngarla alphabet book/primer compiled by Ghil'ad Zuckermann in collaboration with the nascent Barngarla revivalistic community, as well as *Mangiri Yarda* ('Healthy Country': Barngarla Well-being and Nature).[147,148]

In May 2013, my Barngarla learners expressed clear feelings of empowerment during an interview on SBS 'Living Black' Series 18, Episode 9 (Linguicide) about the Barngarla revival.[149]

Language reclamation increases emotions of sense of belonging, well-being, and pride among disempowered people, who fall between the cracks, feeling that they are neither *whitefellas* nor in command of their own Aboriginal heritage. As Fishman puts it[150]:

> "The real question of modern life and for RLS [reversing language shift] is [...] how one [...] can build a home that one can still call one's own and, by cultivating it, find community, comfort, companionship and meaning in a world whose mainstreams are increasingly unable to provide these basic ingredients for their own members."

---

[147] Zuckermann, Ghil'ad. (2019). *Barngarlidhi Manoo: Speaking Barngarla Together*. Barngarla Language Advisory Committee (BLAC) (2nd edn. 2021).

[148] Zuckermann, Ghil'ad and Emmalene Richards. (2021). *Mangiri Yarda: "Healthy Country": Barngarla Wellbeing and Nature*. Revivalistics Press, Adelaide.

[149] See https://www.youtube.com/watch?v=DZPjdNaLCho. Accessed 19 October 2022.

[150] Fishman, Joshua A. (2006). Language loyalty, language planning, and language revitalization: Recent writings and reflections from Joshua A. Fishman. In Nancy H. Hornberger and Martin Pütz (eds.) vol. 59. Multilingual Matters, Clevedon.

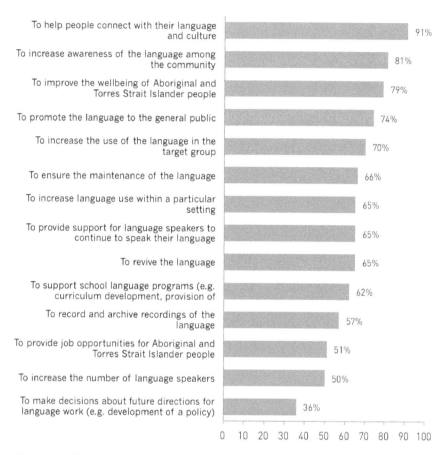

Figure 1. Goals of language activities; data drawn from the second, most recent, National Indigenous Languages Survey (NILS2) report and analysed by Marmion, Obata & Troy.[150]

The language revival process is as important as the revival goals. The reward is in the journey. Figure 1 shows that more Aboriginal Australians see 'improving well-being' as more important than 'increasing language use' (79% vs 70%/65%, respectively).

During 2017–2021, Alex Brown and I, together with the Barngarla Aboriginal people, conducted research with funding through a grant from

---

[151] Marmion, Doug, Kazuko Obata and Jakelin Troy. (201). *Community, Identity, Wellbeing: The Report of the Second National Indigenous Languages Survey.* Australian Institute of Aboriginal and Torres Strait Islander Studies (AIATSIS), Canberra, Australia.

the National Health and Medical Research Council (NHMRC) to assess *quantitatively* (not only *qualitatively*) the correlation between language revival and mental health. As Brown said (personal communication):

> "What scientists hold stock in is only what they can measure. But you can't measure the mind or spirit. You can't weigh it, you can't deconstruct it. But only if we do will they see that Aboriginal people are spectators to the death of their culture, their lives [...]. We watch as our culture dies. How are you going to measure that?"

The quantitative instruments we employ have already been validated: *Health and Well-being Survey Instrument* consists of already-validated questionnaires selected from the ABS National Aboriginal and Torres Strait Islander Health and Social Survey and the Longitudinal Study of Indigenous Children (LSIC). Most importantly, however, the well-being measurement must be created together with the Aboriginal people themselves. And what we have done so far is exactly that: We have so far determined — together with the Aboriginal people themselves — how to assess their well-being. Indigenous assessment offers both an enhanced understanding of psychological constructs in their cultural context and the potential to enrich universalistic psychological models.

As Cheung and Fetvadjiev argue, the need for indigenous assessment tools that are sensitive to the cultural context becomes increasingly apparent with globalisation and international mobility trends.[152] The inadequacies of translating Western tests that 'coax the observed pattern behaviour to fit the imposed model and ignore the local conceptualisation of the observed pattern of behaviour' have been recognised by cross-cultural psychologists.[153] After all, establishing test equivalence and local norms for standardised translated tests demands considerable efforts in building a research programme. Instead of 'cutting one's toes to fit the [imported]

---

[152] Cheung, F. M., and Fetvadjiev, V. H. (2016). Indigenous approaches to testing and assessment. In Leong, F. T. L., Bartram, D., Cheung, F. M., Geisinger, K. F., and Iliescu, D. (eds.) *The ITC International Handbook of Testing and Assessment*, pp. 333–346. Oxford University Press, New York, NY.

[153] Cheung, F. M., Cheung, S. F., Wada, S., and Zhang, J. X. (2003). Indigenous measures of personality assessment in Asian countries: A review. *Psychological Assessment* 15, 280–289. doi:10.1037/1040-3590.15.3.280.

shoes', there would be a greater incentive to develop indigenous psychological tests that fit the local needs. It is not only professional ethics that stipulate the use of culturally relevant and psychometrically reliable and valid tests; in some countries, such as South Africa, it is a legal requirement to adhere to such criteria.

The main purpose of our NHMRC project has been to assess the effectiveness of language reclamation in improving mental health.[154] Key outcomes also include the following:

- Establish the first formal test of a causal relationship between language revival and mental health.
- Provide a model for language revival to be used by communities all over the world. My MOOC (Massive Open Online Course) *Lang101x: Language Revival: Securing the Future of Endangered Languages* has so far attracted 20,000 learners from 190 countries. On average, I receive an email message once a week from a minority or an indigenous group, e.g., from Africa and South America, hoping to reclaim its language.
- Promote language rights globally, e.g., by defining Aboriginal languages as the official languages of their region and by proposing 'Native Tongue Title' the enactment of an *ex gratia* compensation scheme for the linguicided tribes.[155] Although some Australian states have enacted *ex gratia* compensation schemes for the victims of the 'Stolen Generations' policies, the victims of linguicide are largely overlooked by the Australian Government. Existing competitive grant schemes to support Aboriginal languages should be complemented

---

[154] Sivak, Leda, Seth Westhead, Emmalene Richards, Stephen Atkinson, Jenna Richards, Harold Dare, Ghil'ad Zuckermann, Graham Gee, Michael Wright, Alan Rosen, Michael Walsh, Ngiare Brown and Alex Brown. (2019). '"Language breathes life" — Barngarla community perspectives on the wellbeing impacts of reclaiming a dormant Australian aboriginal language. *International Journal of Environmental Research and Public Health* 2019, 16, 3918; doi:10.3390/ijerph16203918. https://res.mdpi.com/d_attachment/ijerph/ijerph-16-03918/article_deploy/ijerph-16-03918.pdf.

[155] Zuckermann, Ghil'ad, Shakuto-Neoh, Shiori and Quer, Giovanni M. (2014). Native tongue title: Compensation for the loss of aboriginal languages. *Australian Aboriginal Studies (AAS)* 2014/1, 55–71.

with compensation schemes, which are based on a claim of right. I believe that language is more important than land (cf. 'Native Title'), despite its intangibility.

While continuing to support the reclamation of Barngarla (I am currently training Barngarla people to teach Barngarla, replacing me), our NHMRC project has sought to find out systematically whether there is an interdependence between language revival and important benefits, such as personal and community empowerment, improved sense of identity and purpose, and enhanced mental health, thus closing the health gap between indigenous peoples and others. The systematic measuring of these significant aspects of life has the potential to create a change not only in Australia but also all over the globe.

Concluding Remarks

More and more indigenous and minority communities seek to reinstate their cultural authority in the world. However, many of them lack not only their heritage language but also the revivalistic knowledge required for language reclamation, reconnection, and empowerment.

One should listen to the voice of Jenna Richards, a Barngarla Aboriginal woman who took part in my Barngarla reclamation workshop in Port Lincoln, South Australia, from 18–20 April 2012. She wrote to me the following sentence in an unsolicited email message on 3 May 2012:

> "Personally, I found the experience of learning our language liberating and went home feeling very overwhelmed because we were finally going to learn our "own" language, it gave me a sense of identity and I think if the whole family learnt our language then we would all feel totally different about ourselves and each other cause it's almost like it gives you a purpose in life."

As Barngarla woman Evelyn Walker (née Dohnt) wrote to me following the same reclamation workshop: *Our ancestors are happy!*

Chapter 4.8

VISUALS

Part 5

TECHNOLOGY

Chapter 5.1

THE UNBEARABLE LIGHTNESS OF "OTHERING"

Dr Leong Chan-Hoong

The world before us has never been so interwoven and yet emotionally divided. For as long as human civilisation has existed, our connection with a fellow human remains highly influenced by a well-defined catalogue of social identities, often demarcated by nation-states, political ideologies, wealth, religion, or ethnic heritage.

While the industrial revolution that began two centuries ago in Anglo-Saxon countries has led to remarkable technological advancement and quality of life, the idea of a unified global community remains an elusive and distant goal. On the contrary, the body of empirical evidence in the last decade has consistently pointed to a fragmented consortium of social identities that have limited intersection with the "Others".

The COVID-19 pandemic has further brought the 'Othering' dynamic to the fore. People with opposing socio-political values, communities with distinct ethnocultural profiles, transnational migrants, and generally anyone beyond the demography are commonly essentialised, compounded by a layer of prejudice and hostility and amplified through social media. It did not help that our political institutions, societies, and the mainstream consortia have evolved to become increasingly volatile and polarised. Members from the majority culture who have learned to empathise with the stigmatised "Others" are also sidelined by some, euphemistically termed as "cancelled".

With the protracted war in Europe, rising tensions between the United States (US) and China, and a fragile global economy on the brink of major recession, the global sentiment has never been so bleak and uneasy. In the midst of these struggles, our social contour today is besieged by a myriad of cultural contestations not seen in recent decades. Religious divides, racial discords, economic class segregation, and the rise of right-wing nationalism and xenophobic hostility are all but signposts of "Othering": a binary "we" versus "them" prism that essentialises a person or group on the basis of some disposition.

To be sure, the contemporary economic and political quagmire we now observed is not entirely unexpected, and it was all but part of a developmental trajectory momentarily punctuated by the end of the last cold war between the Communist block and US-led Western democracies some 30 years ago. Francis Fukuyama, Harvard political scientist, then posited a world where personal freedom and civil rights would flourish to eclipse feudalism, fascism, and communism.[1] Samuel Huntington on the other hand argued that the post-Cold War climate will not necessarily be a collegial one but that the emerging conflicts will be primarily driven by cultural and religious identities.[2] The future wars will be fought between cultures, not countries.

Both conjectures have predicted the course of history albeit in different forms. In line with Fukuyama's thesis, the world and its inhabitants today remain dazzled by the promise of democracy, even among the most despotic regimes. But as Huntington postulated, we have also witnessed the explosion of culture war and the growingly corrosive quality of public discourse, particularly in the online space.

In the widening list of schisms and controversies (which includes but is not limited to political ideologies, racial and religious identities, nationalist movements, and since the COVID-19 pandemic, the freedom to choose over mandatory vaccination), the middle ground has largely vanished as the populace gravitated in either direction. Both ends of the

---

[1] Francis Fukuyama. (1992). *The End of History and the Last Man.* Free Press. ISBN 978-0-02-910975-5.

[2] Huntington, S. P. (1996). *The Clash of Civilizations and the Remaking of World Order.* Simon & Schuster, New York. ISBN 0-684-84441-9.

spectrum accuse their opponents (i.e., the outgroup) of undermining communal social fabric, while concomitantly shut themselves from socialising with the opposing outgroup, choosing instead to indulge in the safety of their respective Internet echo chambers.

From Europe to Americas, populist right-leaning parties and politics have surged to prominence among traditional Western liberal democracies. National leaders from the global North, such as Donald Trump (United States), Marine Le Pen (France), Viktor Orban (Hungary), and Giorgia Meloni (Italy), have all but shaped the global "Othering" discourse in one way or another. Their corrosive rhetoric on religious stereotypes, racial prejudice, and immigrant's marginalisation has further fuelled the sense of insecurity among the middle-class and consequent discrimination of people who are considered the outgroup.

Why is the "Othering" an endemic toxin?

To understand the genesis and orbit of "Othering", we first need to recalibrate the analytical lens towards a more individual-centric prism.

False Dichotomy: Beggar thy Neighbour?

Psychology tells us that we are cognitive misers. As humans, we rely extensively on heuristics, or mental shortcuts, to help us make sense of the complex world around us, and one effective strategy is to view our environment through a binary lens, e.g., black versus white, good versus evil, and friend versus foe. To label someone as an "Other" not only implies that the target is a member of the outgroup but that the person also has all the attributes — mostly negative ones — that are commonly associated with the collective. Suffice to say, this optical lens does not do justice to the plurality of our universe today.

The preference for dichotomous thinking is a divine primitive imprint among the homo sapiens. It is hard-wired in our cognition to relieve us from the burden of processing massive amount of information, particularly so when confronted with a problem or an existential threat like making a split-second decision to "fight or flight" from an intruder.

To be sure, there is nothing inherently wrong with binary thinking. It is after all a mental shortcut like others. This tool however becomes a controversial instrument if it is utilised to cause harm, embarrassment, discord, or injustice to a collective target. For instance, it is not uncommon for airlines to design their inflight food catering according to their clients' racial profile and home domiciles; it will be however a contentious practice if airlines perform their security screening based on these attributes.

This binary paradigm is not merely a cog in human heuristics, but it is also the lynchpin in intergroup dynamics. In this regard, holocaust survivor Henri Tajfel's pioneering research in social identity theory offers influential insights into the psychological science of prejudice.[3] According to Tajfel, humans are habitual creatures, we have an innate proclivity to define ourselves according to dispositions that matter to us: ethnicity, nationality, and gender are examples of some. Moreover, we aim to derive positive personal and group esteem when we compare positively with members of the outgroups.

When the status of our social ingroup is threatened (regardless of real or imaginary competition from an outgroup), a feeling of antagonism and outgroup bias tends to follow. The outgroup members are commonly stereotyped as homogenous, membership loyalty is assumed among people from the ingroup, reinforcing a false separation in dispositions, behaviours, and motivations. Crucially, the mere distinction as members of different arbitrary groups is sufficient to trigger ingroup favouritism, inflicting harm and prejudice to the "Other", even at the expense of the ingroup.[4]

To illustrate what this means, consider the story of Vladimir's choice, a well-known Eastern European mythology:

> *Vladimir was a dreadfully impoverished peasant. One day, God came to Vladimir and said: "Vladimir, I will grant you one wish; anything you wish shall be yours!" Naturally, Vladimir was very pleased at hearing*

[3] Tajfel, H., and Turner, J. C. (1986). The social identity theory of intergroup behaviour. In Austin, William G., and Worchel, Stephen (eds.) *Psychology of Intergroup Relations* (2nd ed.), pp. 7–24. Nelson-Hall, Chicago. ISBN 978-0-830-41075-0.

[4] Sidanius, J., and Pratto, F. (1999). *Social Dominance: An Intergroup Theory of Social Hierarchy and Oppression.* Cambridge University Press. https://doi.org/10.1017/CBO9781139175043.

this news. However, God added one caveat: "Vladimir, anything I grant you will be given to your neighbour twice over." After hearing this, Vladimir stood in silence for a long time, and then said, "OK, God, take out one of my eyes".[5]

Vilifying the Other as a Hegemonic Control

The history of "Othering" has consistently demonstrated the profound ways in which we rationalise the vilification of selected minorities. The script to prejudice does not change even if the profiles of the protagonist are altered.

In the 1950s, driven by the deep anxiety of enemy filtration from the then Soviet Union, the US embarked on a protracted witch hunt to purge itself from all domestic communism sympathisers. The Americans pursued what was coined as the McCarthyism strategy — named after Senator Joseph McCarthy — by making false and unfounded accusations of subversion and treason among public employees, political figures, and citizens. Many of the accused were innocent victims but as a result of the relentless attack and scrutiny, have lost their jobs and lives.

In the immediate years, post September 11, the Muslim communities in liberal democracies came under much unwarranted scrutiny. They were perceived by many as enemies of the state, sympathisers if not sponsors of global religious extremism. Since 2016, the civil unrest in Syria and the middle east has drove millions of refugees across western Europe in search for refuge. The arrival of the refugees was welcomed by some in the receiving societies but also despised by many for the purported criminal activities they bring. Even in Singapore, a soft-authoritarian state known for its meritocratic, multiracial, and inclusive policies, bigotry frictions have surfaced from time to time, and more so over periods where there are seismic shifts in economic and geopolitical conditions. At the peak of the COVID-19 pandemic outbreak in 2021, there were few notable incidents of minority harassment in public spaces, and the general

---

[5] Sidanius, J., Haley, H., Molina, L., and Pratto, F. (2007). Vladimir's choice and the distribution of social resources: A group dominance perspective. *Group Processes & Intergroup Relations*, 10(2), 257–265. https://doi.org/10.1177/1368430207074732.

discourse on racial diversity and inclusion was perceptibly more worrisome.

All of the above underline two common denominators in "Otherings". First, there is a perceived disruption in either normative values or some standard of familiarity over time. Second, there is an asymmetrical power differentiation, where there is some latent tension between a numerical majority and a sizeable, sometimes visible minority. Moreover, there is an attempt among some members of the mainstream majority to insinuate a causal link between the presence of the stigmatised collectives and the purported threats to public security and/or the social rituals.

Consciously or subconsciously, the stereotypes and vitriol charged against stigmatised minorities offer a convenient framework to explain our socio-economic woes. Importantly, the cognitive dichotomy gives us a false sense that we could in some way control the source of our misery.[6,7] Vilifying the "Others" helps alleviate this discomfort by reassuring us that we are on the right side of history, thus preserving the moral status of the ingroup.

Why Faith, Ethnicity, and Nationality Still Matter?

It is often said that global trade liberalisation, market-driven economies, labour and capital movement, and technological transfers across borders will eventually lead nation-states to converge along the economic and socio-political contours. The intersections between countries will be expanded as the proportion of middle-class families rises and the culture of consumerism sinks its roots. While this conjecture has largely proven correct on the economic front, the impact on national heritage and other aspects of our social identities remains elusive.[8]

---

[6] Matute, H., Blanco, F., Yarritu, I., Díaz-Lago, M., Vadillo, M. A., and Barberia, I. (2015). Illusions of causality: How they bias our everyday thinking and how they could be reduced. *Frontiers in Psychology*, 6, 888. doi: 10.3389/fpsyg.2015.00888.

[7] Eyal, N. (February 25, 2022). Why the illusion of control is hurting your goals. *Psychology Today*. Retrieved January 1, 2023, from https://www.psychologytoday.com/sg/blog/automatic-you/202202/why-the-illusion-control-is-hurting-your-goals.

[8] Friedman, T. L. (2000). *The Lexus and the Olive Tree*. Anchor Books, New York.

In fact, contrary to expectations, religion, ethnicity, and nationality remain highly influential in shaping societal systems on perceived equality, justice, and state-citizenry social compact within and across nation-states. More right-wing populist parties were elected to office in recent years[9]; regardless of cohorts, people are becoming more religious as they age,[10] and faith and religiosity had invariably deepened since the pandemic outbreak in 2020.[11] In other words, it is within such identities that 'Othering' most often appear and take root.

In the US today, many White Americans regard themselves as the real victims of racism. They view progress gained on racial equality in the past decades as all but a zero-sum game. The conservatives, in particular, believe they are on the losing end of a crusade.[12-14] Minority's (i.e., Black) achievement in jobs, education, etc. is perceived to be at the expense of the White majority, disguised in the form of affirmative actions, fuelled by the public rhetoric on parity imperatives. It did not help

---

[9] Pew Research Center. (October 6, 2022). Populists in Europe – especially those on the right — have increased their vote shares in recent elections. Retrieved 1 January 2023, from https://www.pewresearch.org/fact-tank/2022/10/06/populists-in-europe-especially-those-on-the-right-have-increased-their-vote-shares-in-recent-elections/.

[10] Psychology Today. (February 16, 2016). Why Are Old People So Religious? Retrieved 1 January 2023, from https://www.psychologytoday.com/us/blog/culture-conscious/201602/why-are-old-people-so-religious.

[11] Pew Research Center. (April 30, 2020). Americans far more likely to say coronavirus crisis has strengthened their faith, rather than weakened it. Retrieved 1 January 2023, from https://www.pewresearch.org/fact-tank/2020/04/30/few-americans-say-their-house-of-worship-is-open-but-a-quarter-say-their-religious-faith-has-grown-amid-pandemic/ft_2020-04-30_covidworship_01/.

[12] Norton, M. I., and Sommers, S. R. (2011). Whites see racism as a zero-sum game that they are now losing. *Perspectives on Psychological Science*, 6(3), 215–218. https://doi.org/10.1177/1745691611406922.

[13] Wilkins, C. L., and Kaiser, C. R. (2014). Racial progress as threat to the status hierarchy: Implications for perceptions of anti-White bias. *Psychological Science,* 25(2), 439–446. https://doi.org/10.1177/0956797613508412.

[14] Rasmussen, R., Levari, D. E., Akhtar, M., Crittle, C. S., Gately, M., Pagan, J., *et al.* (2022). White (but Not Black) Americans continue to see racism as a zero-sum game; White Conservatives (but Not Moderates or Liberals) see themselves as losing. *Perspectives on Psychological Science*, 17(6), 1800–1810. https://doi.org/10.1177/17456916221082111.

that many Americans are disenfranchised by their domestic partisan politics, and globalisation had further marginalised their employability and status back home. The quintessential American dream is increasingly out of reach for this majority collective even though nearly all socio-metric indicators still point unanimously to the multiple advantages enjoyed by the White majority relative to their Black counterparts. The zero-sum belief solidifies the false dichotomy, reinforcing the "Othering" lens on how we view ethnocultural plurality.

The US is not alone in this culture war. Beyond racial divide, we see the traces of a zero-sum imprint on religious dialogues and immigrant acculturation and naturalisation, where the "Others" are blamed for the social ills in the broader society.

Promulgating a Narrative of Heritage Maintenance and Common Space

Contact with a dissimilar outgroup is inherently an intimidating task. It induces anxiety, which makes us prone to rely on negative stereotypes for sensemaking, and we are worried if the presence of an outgroup will lead to greater competition for economic resources and/or erode our social status hierarchy. The reliance on the false dichotomy is a function of our cognitive limitation as much as the motivation to understand the environment around us.

So where do we go from here? There is no magic bullet, but studies in the social psychology of intercultural relations and migration offer a few snapshots of the possible interventions.

According to Canadian eminent acculturation scholar John W. Berry, the lynchpin to building a strong, cohesive society rests on the assurance that ethnocultural identities will not be displaced even as plurality grows. That said, in order for inclusion to flourish, the different ethnocultural groups would need to compromise from time to time in order to co-create secular spaces for the "Others".[15] Importantly, ethnic and

---

[15] Berry, J. W. (2020). How shall we all live together? In Safdar, S., Kwantes, C., and Friedlmeier, W. (eds.) *Wiser World with Multiculturalism: Proceedings from the 24th Congress of the International Association for Cross-Cultural Psychology.* https://scholarworks.gvsu.edu/iaccp_papers/284.

religious maintenance and the imperatives to building a common ingroup discourse are not mutually exclusive. When both the majority and minority groups believe that their heritage and cultural identities are preserved and that their community is treated in a respectful and procedurally equitable way, there is an organic incentive to reach out to outgroups for mutual gains.

This social compact is best encapsulated in Singapore's developmental history. In this city-state, racial and religious rituals are managed using a "light touch", i.e., minimal interference from the authority; engagement with the outgroup, on the other hand, is actively promoted through secular policies that shape the lived experiences. When an ethnocultural ritual jeopardises the stability of the social fabric, the state will intervene using draconic and often intrusive programmes to safeguard a non-exclusionary space for all.

In the context of public housing, for instance, a racial quota is set aside for each apartment block based on national ethnic statistics to mitigate against the instinct for segregated housing along racial lines.[16] On education — notwithstanding the distinct Chinese majority (74%) population — English is taught as the first language in schools in addition to learning a mother tongue language that matches the racial profile of the student (e.g., Mandarin for Chinese).[17] Regardless of background, all Singaporean men at the age of 18 will be conscripted to serve two years in a military or law enforcement unit. The harsh military training and regimental routines provide a universal leveller and is perceived by many as a rite of passage to adulthood.[18]

Overall, Singapore's strategies for governing social plurality ensure there are opportunities for meaningful intercultural exchange but, at the

[16] Leong, C. H., Teng, E., and Ko, W. (2020). The state of ethnic congregation in Singapore today. In Leong C. H., and Malone-Lee L. C. (ed.) *Building Resilient Neighbourhoods: The Convergence of Policies, Research, and Practice*, pp. 29–49. Springer, Singapore. https://doi.org/10.1007/978-981-13-7048-9_3.

[17] Leong, C. H., Rueppel, P., and Hong, D. (2014). Managing immigration and integration in Singapore. In *Migration and Integration: Common Challenges and Response from Europe and Asia*, pp. 51–72. Konrad Adenauer Stiftung.

[18] Leong, C. H. (2019). Re-imagining national service in the era of hyperculturalism. In Ho, S. H., and Ong-Webb, G. (ed.) *National Service in Singapore*, pp. 155–172. World Scientific, Singapore. https://doi.org/10.1142/9789813149229_0007.

same time, emphasise the hereditary ethnocultural influence of race and religion within the overarching national identity. More crucially, the approach underscores the commitment and sacrifice for a secular, non-partisan state, where the individuals, the groups they belong, and the state each play a role in support of harmonious co-existence.

This social compact for a common space provides the foundation for building a robust and cohesive community. It is also a testament to the remarkable social trust that people have in the city-state in tackling the barrage of existential threats on the domestic and regional fronts. The Indonesian Konfrontasi in 1966, oil crisis in the 1970s, economic recession in 1985, financial crises in 1998 and 2008, and the Jemaah Islamiyah terrorist plot in 2001, Singaporeans have but confronted them all in their stride with minimal disruptions to the long-term survival and economic prognosis.

The evidence is clear, and the COVID-19 pandemic has just gifted the world another invaluable lesson in nature. How diverse communities come together to avert a public health crisis speaks volume in terms of resilience. Countries that promulgate an inclusive common space emerge stronger and more cohesive from the predicament. Natural calamities do not make a distinction between the "Us" and the "Others" like the way humans do.

Chapter 5.2

TECH FOR COMMUNITY: THE CASE OF THE SOUTH ASIAN HERITAGE MONTH

Mr Jasvir Singh

Good morning, everyone and "Sat Sri Akal" as the Sikh community would say. I am going to talk about a practical example of how it is possible to use social media and other forms of technology to foment a sense of community building.

The example I am going to use is something that I have used as a co-founder of South Asian Heritage Month, a British-based movement which was set up in 2020. It has only been around for three years, but during that time, it has grown exponentially, and social media has been the force that allowed it to thrive in the way that it has. The month has an underlying element of faith. South Asian Heritage Month is not focused on faith, it is focused on identity, but faith is one of the threads which runs all the way through it.

So, what is South Asian Heritage Month? It is an awareness month that runs each year, and it is organised by the South Asian Heritage Trust, which is a British-based registered charity. It is also a wholly volunteer-run grassroots organisation.

There are three things that it aims to do:

- first is to celebrate stories and commemorate the shared history between the South Asian communities and Britain,

- second is to be a resource for British communities to find out more information and support about South Asians,
- third is to highlight opportunities to create a more inclusive British society.

You may not know where South Asia is. The region is made up of eight countries, namely Afghanistan, Bangladesh, Bhutan, India, the Maldives, Nepal, Pakistan, and Sri Lanka. And each of those countries has a distinct relationship with Britain. They were either part of the British Empire or they had their foreign policy dictated by the British government for a period of time.

The dates of 18th July–17th August are particularly important for the Indian and Pakistani communities in the United Kingdom (UK). The date 18th July 1947 is when the Indian Independence Act gained Royal Assent, that is, when it was signed into law, and 17th August 1947 was when the line was drawn which said where the border would be between India and Pakistan. Bangladesh at that time was part of Pakistan — it was known as East Pakistan. Those dates conveniently form one calendar month and that is the reason why we have chosen 18th July–17th August each year as the dates of South Asian Heritage Month.

One fact that you may not be aware of is that 40% of people who are not White in the UK are of South Asian backgrounds. That is at least 40% of the non-White community in Britain. Nineteen percent are from an Indian background, 15% from a Pakistani background, and 6% from a Bangladeshi background. The available data sadly does not include the other five countries or people of heritage from those other five countries. One thing that is clear is that the history of South Asian identity and heritage is intrinsically part of British society and British identity.

Here is an example. There was a famous film that came out in early 2020 called '1917', and it is set during the First World War. A British commentator — a former actor — called Laurence Fox, said that there was institutional racism as a result of including one Sikh soldier — just a single Sikh soldier — in this entire film. 'Institutional racism', that is what he said. He said there is something institutionally racist about forcing diversity on people in that way. The reality is that in 1917, one soldier in every six fighting for the British in the First World War came from India.

One soldier within every six within the British Army was Indian. And on the front lines, the number was even higher. And that photograph you see there is of a French woman pinning some flowers onto a Sikh soldier in 1918 to show her thanks for the work that was being done.

So, South Asian Heritage Month talks about various stories. We talk about Noor Inayat Khan, who was a British spy and an Indian princess. She was based in France during the Second World War, and when she was executed by gunfire, her final words were *"liberté"* — freedom.

We then have the Ayahs' House. Ayahs were nannies who were looking after the families and children of the British based in India during the Raj. They would often have to travel to the UK in order to assist the British families and allow the children to settle back into British life. The Ayahs' House was based in London and it was where the nannies would stay before they caught the ship back to India.

We then have Nadiya Hussain. Is there anyone who watches the Great British Bake Off or the Great British Baking Show? If you do, you will know that she was one of the winners from a few years ago, and that was a pivotal moment within British society because it was the first time that someone in a hijab had won the competition. A woman in a hijab became a national icon overnight.

We talk about other stories as well. Freddie Mercury belongs to the Zoroastrian community and very few people know that he was fluent in Gujarati — he could speak it flawlessly. Polo as a game originates from royal games that were played in India. We then have the paisley fabric and the design, which is now named after a Scottish town, which finds its origins in Kashmiri designs.

This year, there were two major anniversaries — and this was the focus for South Asian Heritage Month this year — the events of 1947 but also 50 years since the Ugandan Asians were expelled by Idi Amin from Uganda.

South Asian Heritage Month, as I have said, only exists in the way that it does in the UK because of the large South Asian population, and I am now going to talk now about social media and how much of an impact that has had.

Our first year was 2020, Britain was in lockdown, and no events were being held in person. We had absolutely nothing when it came to social media until about six weeks before we launched, and we really hit the zeitgeist. We really captured people's attention.

We had a reach of 31 million and we had 87 million impressions in year one. In year two, we went up to 77 million reach and 269 million impressions. So within the space of a year, we had grown exponentially. This year, a few weeks ago, was the end of South Asian Heritage Month 2022, and the figures you see are even more impressive. It is increasing year on year — a 405 million reach across social media platforms. That includes Facebook, YouTube, Twitter, Instagram, and TikTok. It is impressive but it is even more impressive when you realise that the team behind it are fully volunteers, and it is a project driven by passion. People are involved in it because we are so passionate about what it achieves.

Our YouTube channel was our main means of showing and showcasing the work that we do. Forty percent of the people who have been making use of it are 25–34 year olds. Thirty-seven percent were the older generation — 55–64 year olds — so we found a means by which to engage with people across generations in a way that may not have been previously possible.

Our Twitter presence this year has been incredible. We have had the England and Wales cricket team talk about South Asian Heritage Month. Cambridge University, Ernst and Young (EY), the Law Society, if any of you are football fans, Tottenham Hotspur and other football teams as well, and Sky Sports, which is a major broadcaster in the UK.

But the faith-based tweets are where it becomes interesting, and this is how people engage with it from a faith perspective. So you have Historic England talking about the earliest purpose-built mosque in the UK. You have Hong Kong and Shanghai Bank Corporation (HSBC) using an image which contains people of all faiths that can be considered to be connected to South Asia. You have images of Parvati, the Hindi goddess, used by Sutton Heritage. You had the National Archives of the UK talking about photography and using an image of a mosque. You have references from the British Army — the British Legion, who runs something called the Poppy fund — they have spoken about the South Asians who fought in the First and Second World Wars.

And then you have news stories such as this which we share, "A Sikh Soldier Pulled Me Out of the Rubble", talking about how Sikhs and

Hindus and Muslims all suffered during the Partition of India but how they all helped each other as well.

We have had an impressive output on Facebook as well, with people connecting with us, such as Disney Plus, Spotify, and Instagram. We have had posts from Channel 4 which is another national broadcaster in the UK. We have had posts from Audible which runs audiobooks, and we have had posts by the Ministry of Sound, a major music industry player in the UK. And then we have the Instagram Faith posts.

And again, it is the ways in which people are engaging with South Asian Heritage Month which come across as being the most game-changing, for a lack of a better word. It is a secular movement, but faith communities feel part of it, and they are made to feel included. This is why the Manchester Museum promoted the children's picture book 'In My Mosque'; which is why the Bodleian Libraries, based within the University of Oxford, have used images of Buddhist scriptures in order to showcase what they are doing; which is why the Wellcome Collection, which is a medical-based organisation based in London, talks about its own records and uses this image of the Hindu goddess Durga to showcase their engagement with faith communities. And finally, the Royal College of GPs has showcased a turban-wearing Sikh woman, very few of whom ever get the chance to be in the spotlight or to be highlighted in such a way.

Now that was a whistle-stop tour. Please have a look at the website for South Asian Heritage Month at www.southasianheritage.org.uk.[19] Have a look at our Instagram and Twitter accounts as well.

I am going to end with these thoughts — when you are thinking about what to create, and when you are thinking about how to do something practical, there are lots of opportunities out there. But finding something which captures the zeitgeist, which has a non-religious-based outcome, does not necessarily mean that you cannot have religion as part of it. Think of secular society, think of something that works and something which engages the mainstream and engages people more generally. But also think of the ways in which you can use that project to connect the faiths, highlight people of faith wherever possible, and ensure that

---

[19] https://www.southasianheritage.org.uk/.

interfaith work and intrafaith work can be carried out through those sorts of mainstream projects.

Thank you very much.

Chapter 5.3

FOSTERING MUTUAL TRUST THROUGH DEEPER AND MORE EFFECTIVE ONLINE DIALOGUE

Professor Patrice Brodeur

New technologies are transforming lives across the world. They open possibilities for different and broader forms of dialogue that can address the most fundamental challenges — notably building trust. This chapter highlights four examples that offer promise for how to combine in-person and new online technologies to engage more people in dialogue, often across vast geographical distances, reducing the cost and carbon footprint of long aeroplane travels. As a preface, two cautions are important to point out so that these new forms of technology can be leveraged to foster mutual trust through deeper and more effective online dialogue that take into consideration different speed of access to the Internet as well as different modes of learning.

Gap between Those with and Those without Access to Good Internet Services

First, when we are talking about online, new platforms, new media, social media, etc., we need to understand who today has access to these platforms. We need to contextualise how widespread and at what depth their access is. There is a major gap between those people with access to the

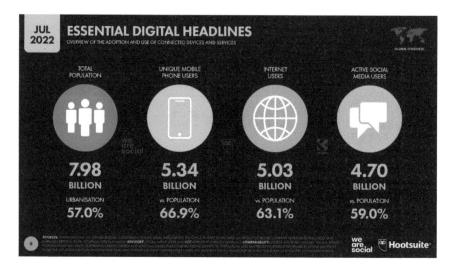

Figure 1.

https://wearesocial.com/uk/blog/2022/07/the-global-state-of-digital-in-july-2022/.

Internet and those without it. Recent statistics (Figure 1) show that between 2 and 3 billion people in the world still do not have access to the Internet, or in very limited ways, let alone any of the countless new forms of technologies it enables. Therefore, it is ethically important to be cognisant of this ongoing big gap in how we proceed with our investments in developing better online tools to promote social cohesion. The contexts thus vary greatly from one region of the world to another, as well as within many regions, especially where such access requires money beyond the reach of masses. Singapore falls at one end of the spectrum, where good Internet services are easily accessible and often free. As we heard yesterday, the local statistics say that more than 50% of young people are using social media to network. Young Singaporeans in particular, are therefore contributing directly to this growing new social reality worldwide, despite big gaps here and there across the world.

Role of Neuroscience

Second, when we are discussing how to develop better tools online to bring more people together and to create better mutual trust, we need to be aware of new knowledge in the Neurosciences, including the basic fact that while there is much neuro-diversity and indicates that not all human beings are wired the same way in our brains, the fact remains that neuro-plasticity allows for each person's multiple identity factors and unique set of diversity intelligences to learn best through the use of diverse dialogue practices, whether in-person, online, or a hybrid combination of both. When we are an infant, we slowly begin to build an "I" for ourselves. This individuation process is essential to develop sound and mature human beings. As we grow older and develop our multiple identities as human beings, this individuation process continues to unfold within the context of collective dynamics — from the family initially, then to the schools, the neighbourhoods, to the workplace, to the world, via the media mostly and, for some, travels, etc.

By the time we reach full adulthood, the balance between the "I" and the "we" becomes particularly important. In order to reach a sound "we," one particularly important competence to acquire is that of dialogue. Through dialogue can emerge the trust necessary to function collectively as a constructive "we". Dialogue is thus a competence to be fostered through all forms of education, whether in person or in various forms of hybrid or purely synchronous online learning encounters. Following are four different examples.

Soliya: Virtual Exchange Program

A first practical example to address directly our topic today is the organization called Soliya, an American non-profit organisation working trans-nationally. In the aftermath of 9/11, it emerged to develop a *Virtual Exchange Program* in order to reduce the tensions and the stereotypes between the Arab world and the United States. Soliya was at the forefront of developing one of the best methodologies for creating a virtual dialogue exchange that allows its participants to become more open to the other in a mutual dynamic that is truly transformative. This has been possible through its creative new online platform that allows the participants to explore their respective stereotypes of each other, a problem made more acute in the aftermath of 9/11.

Through its new *Virtual Connect Program* — which they eventually offered in both a long-term and a short-term version, they trained facilitators to create virtual spaces of real dialogue. The role of these facilitators has been crucial to the transformative success of this programme. Indeed, when dialogue is practised in small groups of people, it becomes clear that facilitators are needed to ensure the quality of communication between all participants. Their role is even more critical when communicating in a virtual space. Over the years, Soliya collaborated not only with the United Nations in various ways but also, surprisingly, with the Massachusetts Institute of Technology's Social Cognitive Neuroscience Lab. Out of this latter collaboration emerged a creative research project that eventually proved the viability of using the online setting as a virtual space for human transformation, when properly facilitated for meaningful dialogue to occur.

In their latest *Virtual Exchange Impact and Learning Report*,[20] one can find a study done throughout 2020 and 2021 that compared a group of students that were part of their *Virtual Exchange Program* with a similar cohort of students that were not involved in such a programme. The results of this comparison were enlightening because they proved how their particular programme was transformative in the following five foundational ways: knowledge of the Other; perspective taking, cross-cultural collaboration, self-other overlap, and warm feelings (Table 1 of above Report).

This report also presents a number of valuable practices and common challenges that are linked to virtual exchange. If you intend to improve or start new virtual exchange programmes to promote dialogue for social cohesion, this report is invaluable and avoids reinventing the wheel. For example, a common challenge that virtual exchange experiences face is that of inattentive facilitation, rendered more acute in a virtual space than in regular in-person dialogue because of the challenge to remain focused on the on-screen participants while other activities may occur in a participant or facilitator's immediate environment.

KAICIID International Dialogue Centre

A second example comes from the KAICIID International Dialogue Centre, which has been at the forefront of developing a variety of different

---

[20] https://www.stevensinitiative.org/wp-content/uploads/2022/02/2022-Impact-and-Learning-Report-English.pdf.

dialogue programmes for social cohesion over the last 10 years. I am interested in showing you, in particular, its online Dialogue Knowledge Hub. First, in their work in the Arab region, which was developed because of the urgency of addressing the rise of radicalisation in the wake of DAECH, a dialogue-training programme emerged with special focus on how to bring dialogue to social media. They developed a unique approach to turning the social media space into a space for dialogue. Over the last five years, they have trained 446 trainees from 11 Arab countries to become more effective social influencers, intervening in virtual spaces through a dialogue strategy to reduce stereotypes and false information that extremists of one group or another so often use. The trainees, mostly Arabs living in the Arab region, are taught how to intervene effectively online through dialogue techniques in order to redress misinformation about both Islam and Christianity, as well as other minority religions in the Arab region. They also address false representations of 'the West' and other regions of the world. This programme thus promotes hands-on intervention using keyboards and computer screens, to combat violent extremism in various social media.

The KAICIID International Dialogue Centre has also developed a key online tool, with manifold resources: the *Dialogue Knowledge Hub*. It is a virtual platform that offers not only a variety of webinars and free

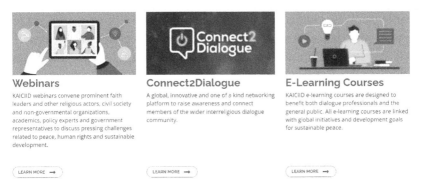

E-Learning and Online Resources

KAICIID's E-Learning and Online Resources include digital knowledge tools, e-learning courses and thematic webinars, which teach dialogue as a tool to solve global issues. All e-learning courses are linked with global initiatives and development goals for sustainable peace. Additionally, the Connect2Dialogue online networking platform fosters best practices and knowledge exchange by connecting interreligious dialogue practitioners and experts from across the globe.

Webinars
KAICIID webinars convene prominent faith leaders and other religious actors, civil society and non-governmental organizations, academics, policy experts and government representatives to discuss pressing challenges related to peace, human rights and sustainable development.

LEARN MORE →

Connect2Dialogue
A global, innovative and one of a kind networking platform to raise awareness and connect members of the wider interreligious dialogue community.

LEARN MORE →

E-Learning Courses
KAICIID e-learning courses are designed to benefit both dialogue professionals and the general public. All e-learning courses are linked with global initiatives and development goals for sustainable peace.

LEARN MORE →

Figure 2.
https://www.kaiciid.org/dialogue-knowledge-hub.

e-learning courses but also a new space for online community networking called *Connect2dialogue* (see Figure 2).

In addition, one can find different databases that contribute to virtual education opportunities. Here are two examples: the *Peace Map*, with over 650 organisations working internationally to promote dialogue in one form or another and the *Promising Practices,* replete with great summaries of successful dialogue projects and programmes from all regions of the world, with a special focus on youth and youth-led ones. This *Dialogue Knowledge Hub* is a key virtual tool not only to learn more about inter-religious dialogue globally but also to seek out opportunities to network and collaborate with like-minded organisations and people, hopefully, located or working close to your own areas. Whether we are local activists, organisational leaders or policymakers at municipal, national, or international levels, we can all save a lot of time and energy by discovering who is who in dialogue and what organisations we can learn from and potentially collaborate with. Indeed, there is no reason to reinvent the wheel, especially given the great challenge to invest more in scaling up existing promising practices.

FAS Research Lab

A third example comes from a relatively recent and unique collaboration between the FAS Research lab in Austria and Porticus, an International Foundation. Their *Network Study on Interreligious Study* interactively maps hundreds of interreligious/interfaith organisations, providing a meaningful visual understanding of their interconnections as well as their relative importance in scale. This map complements in many ways the KAICIID Peace Map, with some overlaps. One of the major advantages of the FASRL-Porticus map is that users can easily discover how, by a series of simple clicks, organisations are networked to one another. This unique feature is very important because interreligious/interfaith work cannot happen in isolation. We need to locate our own initiatives, however local they may be, into a broader interconnected network of people and organisations sharing our dialogue values and objectives. In Figure 3, the size of the dots represents the relative importance of the networks cultivated by different interreligious or interfaith organisations world-

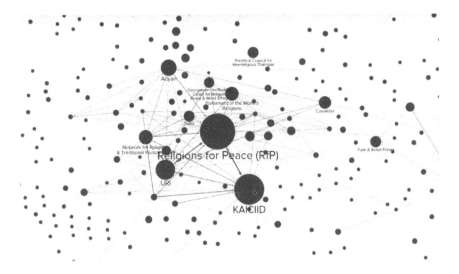

Figure 3.
https://www.fas.at/fasresearch-network-study-on-interreligious-dialogue.

wide, according to the results of in-depth interviews with 134 experts in the field of dialogue. This map thus presents a first glance at the interreligious/interfaith movement worldwide.

European Union

A fourth and last example comes from the Europe Union, where they work on strengthening democracy through inclusive, deliberative, and effective citizenship participation — where the word "deliberative", i.e., deliberation, means 'collective dialogue'.[21] From the EU's multiple forms of practising deliberative democracy emerges the fact that the development of the common good in any society can, indeed, be greatly enhanced through a more widespread use of new technologies, if strong political will and popular support go hand in hand through close political and civil society collaborations, including with religious communities when appropriate. Because technology can also be used for exclusive benefits, the

---

[21] Reber, Bernard. (2016). *Precautionary Principle, Pluralism and Deliberation: Science and Ethics*. Wiley.

natural search for belonging does not necessarily result in identities that promote participation in promoting inclusive and cohesive societies. For example, a person may rather choose instead to join a local gang, a vigilante group or even an extremist organisation. We heard yesterday from Dr Kong about the four key elements necessary to promote social cohesion — a sense of community, a sense of solidarity, an enduring sense of trust, and developing shared loyalties. Paradoxically, these four elements are found not only in the dynamics of well-integrated communities within larger pluralist societies but also in more extremist groups.

So what is the difference? The difference lies principally in the goals and discourses of any given identity group, their perceptions of geographical boundaries and history, and especially in their attitude towards a variety of others. Does a group display characteristic of openness, tolerance and respect towards others, or does it show exclusivist claims and intolerant behaviours towards others, condoning and even promoting violence as a means towards achieving their aims? While the four elements promoting social cohesion are the same in all cases, the above differences are what need to be addressed directly, thus the need for collective dialogue or deliberation.

This particular European Union example demonstrates that developing and sustaining a loyalty towards a sense of multilayered common citizenship, from the municipal and national to the EU level (in this case) and beyond (the UNESCO concept of 'global citizenship'), is a challenge that requires using dialogue/deliberation between the various segments within often complex multilateral, transversal, and multi-identity group dynamics. Indeed, collaboration between policymakers and leaders of all identity groups seeking inclusion in any given society requires the use of dialogue. Trying to make such dialogical processes ever more inclusive to ensure the participation of groups or individuals who may not initially trust the process is a major challenge. In such cases, the in-person dialogue is essential, as a prelude to a future participation in online dialogues. But given the large nature of these groups, both in human numbers and in geographical distance from one other (whether in real terms or symbolically even if there is physical coexistence), dialogue can no longer only happen through in-person encounters: it must also be practised through hybrid formats of online platforms. These new online dialogue pedagogies and communication techniques must reach an ever increasing number of both formal and non-formal educational settings, as well as an infinitely large number of work/cultural/religious/etcetera organisational contexts.

Conclusion

As we combine empirical and anecdotal evidence — feeding both the left and the right parts of the brain — it is not so important whether we prefer the concept of 'dialogue' over that of 'deliberation', or vice versa; or whether we prefer 'active listening' instead of 'compassionate listening', or vice versa: all these terms are equally valuable depending on various contexts. Moreover, whether we prefer intercultural, interreligious, inter-civilisational, interspiritual, interconvictional, or interworldview forms of dialogue — all different words that have their own specific use — the data emerging from solid monitoring and evaluation as well as evidence-based research of various dialogue programmes and the efforts to map them reveal five key points:

- First, the global map of interreligious dialogue organisations reflects increasingly broad and diverse patterns of interconnection, and this ICCS directly fosters such a worldwide transformation.
- Second, a deep transformative individual online experience is possible, therefore the need to up-scale existing promising practices and inventing new larger scale online ones.
- Third, such online endeavours are not enough: the combination of sustaining online dialogue programmes together with, when possible, in-person dialogue experiences (i.e., a hybrid approach) — even if it is more at the local level — is likely therefore to contribute to greater degrees of positive transformation.
- Fourth, in all three cases (in-person, hybrid, or only online), the identification of key objectives as well as monitoring and evaluation practices towards evidence-based research are invaluable to turn transformative dialogue initiatives and programmes into impactful

dynamics often beyond their initial set of participants and geographical contexts, with rippling 'glocal' effects towards positive peace.

- Fifth, these positive effects might lead to increased long-term social networking and active national/global citizenship engagements, all of which is necessary for sustainable and inclusive social cohesion to happen.

In closing, I recall the beautiful quote that we heard yesterday from the President of Singapore (2017–2023), Her Excellency Halimah Yacob: "We are all human beings at the end: equally fragile, equally resilient." If that is so, then my central question is simply a challenge to us all: how, when we have the privilege of accessing good-speed Internet, do we use it to build mutual resiliency among all human beings? To answer this question requires not only more open critical thinking but also more inclusive compassionate engagement.[22]

Thank you. 谢谢. Terimah Kasih.

---

[22] For an explanation by this author on the concept of 'compassionate engagement', see the following segment on the YouTube Q&A period of the ICCS-2 Plenary 3 session: https://www.youtube.com/watch?v=hNpkaEJppKY (from: 1:09:20).

https://doi.org/10.1142/9789811285387_0026

Chapter 5.4

SOCIAL MEDIA AND A POLARISED GENERATION

Dr Shashi Jayakumar

Why is it that we increasingly feel that we live in an age where we cannot talk to each other rationally where the broad middle seems to have been eviscerated?

I would like to offer you some thoughts over the next 10 minutes on these issues that I have studied while I was in government studying radicalisation and terrorism. In think tanks, we have expanded the study and my personal interests have also moved to cohesion, intolerance, and social media. In some of what follows, I should highlight that I am not going to offer a silver bullet or a Panacea.

New Dimensions of a Polarised Era

We have moved from a cooperative political age to an era where difference is essentialised along identity lines. This kind of polarisation destroys norms of tolerance and moderation, and it turns politics into a zero-sum game. It affects many societies, but it is particularly dangerous in diverse societies where a strong middle is needed to build bridges across races and creeds.

It also cuts into issues such as class and politics. In Europe, there is certainly a precarity which is happening — swingeing cuts to budgets, financial crises, growing discontent, and increasing disillusionment with the political systems which were traditionally practised. In the United

States, studies have shown effective polarisation is where citizens feel more negatively towards other political parties than towards their own. This has clearly, according to studies, been exacerbated since the late 1970s. And in Singapore, according to various studies — including a YouGov survey for Channel NewsAsia last year which you can find online — among all the respondents, 64% felt that they have experienced increased polarisation of views online in the last five years.

The hollowing out of the middle ground space for dialogue, for civil discourse, is fertile ground for polarisation and extremism. You may have individuals, some at the fringe, some even at the top of governments elsewhere, ideologues, or demagogues who feed this insecurity and paranoia — the idea that your way of life is fundamentally at stake. What we find within this hollowing out of basic norms for civil discourse is not just intolerance, but a sense of victimisation. This can take the form of blame on the "corrupt" political establishment or the "rigged" mainstream media and all that is going wrong. Meaning, radical action and change are needed to fix things. These actors can also feed a sense of conspiracy or the idea of "the Big Lie" or even encourage thinking generally that things are going downhill and action is needed. The pandemic had acted as an accelerant — encouraging further conspiracist theories and vaccine-related disinformation.

All these forces, if left unchecked, can pose serious threats, in particular, to multicultural societies which thrive only because there are bridges across divides. Social media should not be seen as a neutral force. It is a key to get messages and propaganda across, enable mobilisation for certain causes, and feed into polarisation. And I think it is true to say that the shortcomings of social media platforms in dealing with this kind of disinformation have been especially salient during these times, i.e., times of stress. Fact-checkers and debunkers are generally playing catch-up, unfortunately.

Pluralisation of Sources

The Internet's growth has led to a pluralisation of sources. Studies in Singapore have suggested that the various content of Facebook discussion groups have shown that the online quality of discourse is generally poor, with discourse skewed more positively for alternative media rather than for mainstream media. And this is something that needs to be watched. Various thinkers including Francis Fukuyama have argued that there is a kind of anti-elite or peer-driven information creation and dissemination which plays a critical role in contributing to this decline of trust in integrating institutions.

Some of what I am trying to say is captured accurately by Dr Vivian Balakrishnan, Singapore Minister for Foreign Affairs. Speaking in 2016 at a major conference, APPSNO (the Asia-Pacific Conference for Senior National Security Officers), he observed the following:

> "We now live in a world of fragmented echo chambers – we hear what we want to hear, we ignore what we don't want to hear or inconvenient truths are not heard. And in fact from an academic point of view, this leads to a 'shallowing' of discourse, a world in which there's a dearth of deep thought and cogent discussion across diverse perspectives. You get a more monochromatic world and a narrowing of minds."

Some countermeasures and online counter-narrative tools seem to hold some promise, but they are not a silver bullet. Some of you are very familiar with the Redirect method pioneered by Jigsaw and others. It targets individuals who originally look for ISIS content online and it redirects them towards alternative messaging and YouTube videos which either give alternative and more balanced views or which debunk extremist ideologies.

There are many other efforts which seem to hold promise. One is Gov-zero (g0v), a decentralised civic tech community in Taiwan. It has engineered a pol.is[23] platform designed by civic thinkers from g0v which hosts mixed-reality skilled listening exercises as a new way, and quite promising, to encourage politically critical discussions. You, as a citizen, are invited into an online space for debate — civil debate — and it shows different kinds of agreement and dissent as they emerge.

---

[23] https://pol.is/home.

Redesigning Social Media

So there is some possibility of a fundamental redesign of social media — the ability to mend the social media's fabric for a polarised generation. But there are also powerful forces working against this. Consider cancel culture, which started out, one could say laudably, as a tool to boycott or de-platform powerful people who have gone wrong. But unfortunately, this has gone in a certain direction which has not been positive. Surveys, including a recent Black Box survey in Singapore, show that online shaming, cancelling, is justified in the view of many some of the time; in addition, one in five claimed to have shamed someone online.

National resilience is going to become increasingly important, both in response to grey zone and hybrid threats and to incidents and events that might cause fissures in the body politic. One example is the viral social media campaign ("Kami Tidak Takut", or "We are not afraid") in 2016 in Indonesia following a terrorist attack there. Above all, when such campaigns take place, it is preferable that they are led by organic, ground-up movements. There are such movements in Singapore. Roses of Peace (ROP), led by my friend Mohamed Irshad, who is here, is one of them. ROP ambassadors are equipped with tools to compassionately engage with people from different views and the interventions as far as I understand it is both online and offline. And this is very useful.

The point is that such organisations will have a critical role in building a resilient society which can stem the tide in the context of polarisation across more diverse identity lines. Preserving this middle civil ground for dialogue is going to be absolutely critical.

But neither these groups nor government can do it alone. I want to end with a quote by a friend of RSIS, Professor Sir David Omand, who is the former head of Government Communications Headquarters (GCHQ), the United Kingdom signals intelligence agency. You might be asking, why are you introducing the ideas of a security expert when this conference is about cohesion?

Here is what he says:

"The goal of national security strategy is increasingly seen as the maintenance of conditions of normality, providing confidence to the public that the many major risks — threats and hazards — can be managed so normal every life can continue, against a backdrop of market stability, trade, innovation and the flourishing of industries ..."

This is spot on. But to add some thoughts from my perspective: there is this danger of taking for granted the normalcy that government and the security agencies provide us. Many people think everything is "super normal" and that nothing of note security-wise, no violent incidents, and terrorist attacks ever happened in Singapore. My conviction (and I think this is what Sir David Omand is trying to say) is that the government's role in time to come, given all the stresses and polarisation that we see, is going to be maintaining the conditions of normalcy. Some of the initiatives that you have just seen in the previous slides, where grassroots actors come together in a non-artificial, natural, and non-forcing fashion, sometimes facilitated by government, but in a non-artificial fashion, about what the threats are and what we can do about these issues — these are going to be very important. Because it is in my view, unfortunately, going to be a very dark and insalubrious neighbourhood and wider world. And the people will have that much of a greater role to play. They cannot always be relying on the government all the time.

Thank you very much.

Chapter 5.5

HATE AND CONSPIRACY ONLINE

Father Philip Larrey

In my introductory remarks, I would like to lay the groundwork for what we are going to be speaking about. Conspiracy theory is an explanation of certain facts that are not based on empirical evidence but rather on an idea. It is an idea that oftentimes cannot be either proven or disproven. That is the beauty of a conspiracy theory — if you can disprove it, it is no longer a valid theory; if you can prove it, it is no longer a conspiracy.

Conspiracy Theories

Some of the greatest conspiracy theories in recent times have to do with the Vatican. Dan Brown sold 60 million copies of his book based on a conspiracy theory and there are several theories within the book itself.[24] The primary conspiracy theory is that Jesus Christ (the founder of Christianity) had a son with Mary Magdalene and thus began a lineage that went throughout history, coming down to our present day. The book kicked off a movement, in which millions of people have visited the sites mentioned in the novel (such as the supposed tomb of Mary Magdalene in France). Dan Brown made much money from the sales of the book, and Tom Hanks starred in the movie which was a box office success. However, the evidence supporting the theory is scanty at best. The genius of Dan Brown was to weave a (somewhat credible) story that people had interest

---

[24] See D. Brown. (2003). *The Da Vinci Code*. Random House, New York.

in learning about. This is why the whole idea is called a theory. The famous group called the "Illuminati" come out of this theory.[25] I have actually met some people who are convinced they belong to a secret group that has ties to the Vatican. I have tried to convince them that it is just a story, but they are convinced it is part of history and not just a novel.[26]

Another interesting conspiracy theory has to do with the death of Pope John Paul I. This is now being replayed in the press because on Sunday (September 4th, 2022), Pope Francis beatified Pope John Paul I, who was Pontiff for only 33 days and died in mysterious conditions in 1978. In 1978, this was a huge conspiracy theory. Who killed the Pope? Did somebody assassinate Pope John Paul I? And to complicate the situation even more, the Vatican did not allow an autopsy to be done on the body. Thus, up until now, we do not know exactly how he died.[27] We do know that he died around 5:30 in the morning in the Apostolic Palace, St. Peters, with a dossier in his hand referring to the Vatican Bank.[28] At the time, the Vatican Bank — and this is not a secret, this is well known — was being accused of money laundering. The Mafia supposedly had accounts in the Vatican Bank and the Pope was about to reform that, and therefore the Mafia allegedly killed Pope John Paul I. This is the most accredited conspiracy theory referring to the death of Pope John Paul I. We can thus see how even the Vatican is not immune to the idea of a conspiracy theory or even hate speech.

---

[25] See D. Brown. (2003). *Angels and Demons*. Atria Books.

[26] Dan Brown has testified in a court of law in the UK that he does not believe "The Da Vinci Code" to be based on true facts, reversing his original stance. The reason he testified that way was to avoid a law suit brought by the authors of another book, *The Holy Blood and the Holy Grail*. "Two British authors, Michael Baigent and Richard Leigh, are suing *The Da Vinci Code* publisher, Random House, for copyright infringement. They claim Brown, an American, stole the central theme for his religious thriller from their 1982 book, *The Holy Blood and the Holy Grail*." See https://www.theguardian.com/uk/2007/mar/28/danbrown.books. Brown would have lost the law suit if he had testified that his book was historical fact, and not a novel. As the *Guardian* article shows, Brown won the suit.

[27] See https://www.npr.org/2022/09/04/1121039937/john-paul-i-beatified-pope-francis-sainthood.

[28] The "Vatican Bank" is actually not a bank. Its official title is "Istituto per le Opere di Religione" (IOR), and it is located at Cortile Sistus V, just inside the Vatican.

However, let us look at the case of the death of Pope John Paul I — the "cause" of death cannot be either proven or disproven. There is no way of proving that the Mafia killed the Pope and there is no way of disproving it because we are not completely certain regarding the cause of death.[29] There are good theories — he had a heart condition and he forgot to take his medicine that night, so that is probably the best theory out there as to how he actually died. But when you have a Pope for only 33 days, it does create curiosity.

Analysis

We can now turn to an analysis of online conspiracy theories. The most notorious website in terms of conspiracy theories is Infowars.[30] This (now, infamous) website was created by Alex Jones. Most of us have heard of Alex Jones because just two weeks ago, he lost an important lawsuit in Austin, Texas.[31,32] He has since filed for bankruptcy. InfoWars.com has a terrible reputation — Twitter has banned it, Spotify has banned it, Facebook has banned it — because it is filled with malicious stories and hate speech and, of course, conspiracy theories. What is the one that brought him down? Several years ago, there was a massacre at Sandy Hook Elementary School in Connecticut. Twenty children lost their lives and six teachers were also killed. It was one of the worst massacres in the United States. As you know, every month or so there are shootings some-where in the States and people die, but the death of twenty schoolchildren was a terrible tragedy.

Alex Jones came up with the idea that, in fact, there was no massacre, and that in reality, it was a hoax because the United States government was trying to control gun laws. This was his idea and again, he made it all

---

[29] The official statement from the Vatican regarding the cause of death was that the Pope suffered a heart attack.

[30] See www.infoWars.com, operated by Alex Jones.

[31] The initial lawsuit that he lost took place in August, 2022 and Jones was ordered to pay $ 45 million in damages to the parents of one of the victims of the Sandy Hook Elementary School massacre. See https://www.npr.org/2022/08/05/1116099506/alex-jones-infowars-sandy-hook-lies-45-million-in-punitive-damages.

[32] See https://www.npr.org/2022/12/02/1140349600/alex-jones-bankruptcy.

up. The parents of one of the students sued him for emotional harassment and hardship, and they won. It took about two years for the trial to end. In all of this, one of the interesting things is that the website has seen a significant increase in traffic. This is precisely how Alex Jones generates money — he sells publicity on his website.[33] Thus, although he lost several lawsuits (and has been publicly discredited), the number of people viewing the content of his website has increased exponentially. The reason behind the increase is that Alex Jones is very smart and creative: people are attracted to the content he puts out because they want to believe that the conspiracy theories are actually true. The content he spews out is false, but he manages to convince people that it is real.

Let us examine another example. Christopher Blair hosts a website and also a Facebook page called "America's Last Line of Defence."[34] The first phrase that you read on the website is, "Nothing on this web page is real." What Christopher Blair and his associates are doing is not a conspiracy theory. It is just satire. It is like *The Onion*, which started in the early part of 2000 in Wisconsin, and now has a great website and there is nothing real on that site either. But the stories are brilliantly written, and that is why they seem real.[35] Christopher Blair has decided to create content on digital media which is absolutely absurd and yet, people believe that what he writes is true. In order to avoid fines and legal implications, he says "nothing on this website is true", and then he proposes all kinds of interesting stories.

Blair has been interviewed by the *Washington Post* and he stated: "What are the two stories you're most proud of, having made them up but which people believed to be true?"[36] He responded by saying: number one — "Barack Obama dodged the Vietnam draft at the age of nine". As we know, the "draft" is the simple name given to mandatory military service, which the United States Government did away with after the

---

[33] Jones sells specialty items through the website as well (such as nutritional elements).

[34] See https://www.facebook.com/ALLODSatire/.

[35] For an excellent analysis and historical context of this phenomenon, see https://www.bbc.co.uk/news/resources/idt-sh/the_godfather_of_fake_news.

[36] See https://www.washingtonpost.com/national/nothing-on-this-page-is-real-how-lies-become-truth-in-online-america/2018/11/17/edd44cc8-e85a-11e8-bbdb-72fdbf9d4fed_story.html.

Vietnam War.[37] For anyone thinking logically, this would be absurd, but many people thought it was true.[38]

The second one that he said got the most hits was that the State of California enacts the Sharia law, which is the Muslim religious law that a Muslim State can abide by. If one knows anything about California, one knows it is perhaps the most liberal State in the Union. They are having problems passing any laws, let alone the Sharia. And Christopher Blair is amazed at how many people shared the articles thinking that they were real. He has millions of shares every day and he has about sixty other journalists that think up crazy things and they post them on the Facebook page as true articles. Christopher Blair has over 44 million followers on Facebook, and every morning these followers read the articles and share them on their own pages. In the interview, the interviewer asked, "What is your normal routine?" He responded, "I wake up in the morning, I get my cup of coffee, I sit on my porch, and I ask 'what absurd material can I spew out today that people will believe is true?'"

Truth versus Falsehood: How to Discern?

The problem with misinformation is that it is very difficult to discern what is true and what is not true. Without some sort of rigorous criterion, we can arrive at the conclusion that there are no facts: everything is a matter of interpretation.[39] There are some journalists who are convinced that

---

[37] See https://www.sss.gov/history-and-records/#:~:text=From%201948%20until%20 1973%2C%20during,be%20filled%20through%20voluntary%20means. "From 1948 until 1973, during both peacetime and periods of conflict, men were drafted to fill vacancies in the armed forces which could not be filled through voluntary means. Induction authority expired in 1973, but the Selective Service System remained in existence in 'standby' to support the all-volunteer force in case of an emergency. Registration was suspended early in 1975 and the Selective Service System entered into 'deep standby'."

[38] Barak Obama was nine years old in 1970, having been born in 1961. This means that the draft was still in existence, yet it would be difficult for a nine-year old to be drafted.

[39] The phrase is attributed to the German philosopher Friedrich Nietzsche, writing in his *Notebooks* of 1886/1887: "Against that positivism which stops before phenomena, saying 'there are only facts,' I should say: no, it is precisely facts that do not exist, only interpretations".

"facts" *per se* do not exist, and that is why people need to use critical thinking when listening and watching the media.

We can take the example of the war in Ukraine in order to understand how difficult it is to discern truth from falsehood. It is very difficult to understand exactly what is going on, even for people who are there on the ground, covering the events. Just today, there was a news item about the International Atomic Energy Agency, which has sent inspectors to the Zaporizhzhia nuclear power plant and we still do not know who is shelling around the power plant.[40] Is it Russia or is it Ukraine? Both of them deny that they are doing it and the inspectors are there and they do not know. Allow me to end my introductory remarks by relating a brief anecdote.

In August 2019, I was about to enter my classroom at the Pontifical Lateran University and one of my students came up to me and said, "Father, did you hear the news? Did you hear the news? Donald Trump offered to buy Greenland!" I laughed and responded, "Oh fake news. I mean, with Donald Trump, you never know, but that sounds like great fake news." I said, "Isn't that funny?" And she says, "No Father, it's not funny. It's true. He called the Prime Minister of Denmark." I ended up doing some research on the "fact" and discovered that Greenland is a self-ruling part of the Kingdom of Denmark (which I did not know).[41] Trump called the Prime Minister of Denmark and offered a large sum of money in order to purchase the land. The news became viral and was reported in numerous media outlets. Trump was scheduled to visit Denmark a month later but decided to cancel the trip because of the indignation of the people there. This is just one example of the importance of fact-checking — to be able to discern the true from the false, taking the time for critical thinking. In this way, we will be able to get to the truth and create a better society where people can thrive and believe the information given by rigorous journalism.

---

[40] The date in question would have been September 2nd, 2022. See https://www.reuters.com/world/europe/two-iaea-inspectors-stay-zaporizhzhia-nuclear-plant-permanently-russian-envoy-2022-09-02/.

[41] See the first reliable article written on the subject here: https://www.wsj.com/articles/trump-eyes-a-new-real-estate-purchase-greenland-11565904223. A week later, *The Guardian* published a follow-up article. See https://www.theguardian.com/world/2019/aug/18/trump-considering-buying-greenland.

Chapter 5.6

MISINFORMATION IN A WORLD OF NO INFORMATION: DIGITAL BRIDGES FOR REFUGEES AND MIGRANTS WITH THE INTEGRATION PLATFORM "INTEGREAT"

Mr Fritjof Knier

Misinformation through Technology — A New World

We have all witnessed the wide and fast spread of disinformation campaigns and conspiracy theories during the pandemic, especially regarding vaccinations and health measures.

This also happened within the societies of industrial and economic powerhouse countries, which we would have considered to be well educated. The fact that democratic countries were that vulnerable to misinformation campaigns driven by just a few leading voices showed everyone how fragile we as societies are, especially in times of crisis, and these times will continually come upon us.

One would believe that the variety of information sources, from governments on a national or local level, and from journalists and other civil society actors, should have made us resilient to conspiracy theories and the spreading of disinformation, but it really has not. Social networks have been introduced as a new player in the field of sharing information and building opinions. These platforms have been ignored by those previously mentioned information providers of governments, news outlets and civil society organisations.

In contrast to the citizens of a country living there for years or since their birth, refugees and migrants newly arriving in a country find it challenging to access information that they require for their daily lives. While misinformation and conspiracy theories directed at refugees and migrants from a foreign country spread in a country's native language, they enter an almost empty playing field. This is because the dynamics of the spread of such news meant that it would be difficult for established information sources to counter these views.

What is unique in the setting of refugees and migrants is that misinformation in their communities can spread without any bad intentions due to the lack of alternative information sources. In Germany, we have learnt that refugees in reception facilities decided against being vaccinated because the word was spread that you could never be deported if you were not vaccinated. This information was not true as it had no effect on that decision. However, the result was that less than 10% of refugees in reception centres decided to get protection against the coronavirus. Other examples are information that is spread within the community or even coming from volunteers from the host society, about how a certain process is carried out, and which institution is responsible for a certain topic. Even so, this can differ from one municipality to the next, leading to disappointments and a growing distrust in the institutions, again, without any bad intentions in mind.

But new media is not only the evil dressed in zeros and ones, it does provide a great opportunity to do good, to help the less privileged and most marginalised. Without new media and growing availability and affordability of smartphones, it would not have been possible for me to write these lines, as these developments enabled us to support refugees and migrants arriving in a new country with understandable and up-to-date information that empowers them to make well-informed decisions every day, build new livelihoods for them and their families and to really become members of their host countries.

Integreat — Yet Another Information Platform. But Why?

Refugees and migrants arriving in any new country face a significant challenge in understanding local processes, support programmes and the culture as a whole. Even if the local integration 'infrastructure' such as counselling services and support programmes exists, they are not known fully by potential beneficiaries. Germany would be a prime example of a country where this is the case. Our answer to this challenge is the digital integration platform Integreat — a smartphone app, website, and printable brochure all in one, which provides a one-stop central solution for newcomers to get all the necessary information they need to integrate into their host countries.[42]

Integreat was designed in the summer of the year 2015 at a time when Europe was facing the greatest refugee movement to or within Europe since the Second World War. The outbreak of new conflicts, and ongoing wars, conflict and persecution in Syria, Iraq, Afghanistan, Iran and Somalia, among other countries, forced millions to flee to safety. Germany was about to become the fifth largest refugee-hosting country in the world hosting 1.5 million refugees by the end of the following year. Integreat's project team was developing the first version of Integreat while literally sitting next to refugees in the waiting room of a large local counselling centre in Augsburg. This enabled us to identify the needs and challenges of our users throughout the development process and learn about their usage of applications and information sources in general. A year after the launch of Integreat, we carried out an even deeper research project on how to design the smartphone and web applications for our users to address the feedback we had gathered during the development phase and the first pilot implementations. The conclusions from the research of Schreieck and colleagues[43] are still the foundation of Integreat's design.

---

[42] https://integreat.app/ | https://integreat-app.com/.
[43] Schreieck, Maximilian; Zitzelsberger, Jonas; Siepe, Sebastian; Wiesche, Manuel; Krcmar, Helmut. (2017a). Supporting refugees in every day life — Intercultural design evaluation of an application for local information. *Twenty First Pacific Asia Conference on Information Systems (PACIS)*, Langkawi.

Information is provided by local integration experts and organisations on site. Integreat enables municipal administrations and aid organisations to collect all relevant local information about processes, services, contacts, events, and points of interest in the easy-to-use Integreat content management system and push it out to refugees and migrants via the Integreat app, website, and PDF-printable brochure. Our scalable open-source platform has been implemented in over 90 of Germany's 401 municipalities.

Our team does not need to gather information from afar but instead enables the local integration experts and counsellors to directly create multilingual content for newcomers. The Integreat project team, part of a young non-profit organisation composed of both employees and volunteers, focuses on developing and maintaining the platform and supporting local Integreat implementations with project management expertise. In Germany, all municipalities share the same platform, app, and even content, as they see fit. These synergies lead to Integreat being a highly cost-efficient digital solution, where a yearly budget of 500,000 € results in roughly 500,000 refugees and migrants facing a significantly smaller barrier to finding understandable integration-relevant information.

One of the most powerful tools to succeed in today's world is information, specifically trustworthy and understandable information. With each local Integreat implementation, thousands of refugees and migrants find an understandable and complete overview of their rights, local processes, support services and contacts for the very first time. Integreat is very respectful towards our users' privacy as they belong to one of the most vulnerable groups of people. We only track very aggregated data but we know that Integreat answers 150,000 questions each month as this number represents the amount of API requests in the most recent months.

Digitisation is the gold rush of the 21st century but with the mechanisms of our current markets, the most marginalised will not profit from these developments. It needs specific projects who are making use of the tools developed during this gold rush and use them to elevate those who are traditionally left behind. Integreat has chosen to do this. A large development community was established using open-source software and frameworks, developed and used by some of the largest digital companies to build digital bridges between refugees and migrants and host societies to overcome information gaps.

Integreat's architecture is built in a way that all municipalities share the same platform which results in heavy synergies and financial savings. Additionally, content on Integreat is creative commons licensed making it reusable for new municipalities including already created translations again leading to heavy savings.

Digital Innovation in the Field of Social Services — Think Small!

A key success factor for Integreat was to think small. Usually, start-ups, even social or not-for-profit start-ups like us, look for the big hit, for market leadership, on scaling strategies and exit plans. This is not entirely wrong. A little bit of outrageous optimism paired with dedication and a small amount of self-promotion is necessary to succeed with any innovation, especially if one's organisation has not yet made a name for itself.

The Integreat team looked at the challenge at hand, at the best answer for the challenge we learned about and then tried to understand it better and better. Everything after that came organically. In social services or humanitarian aid, a small innovation may already have a big positive impact. The social sector in Germany, and for many other countries this holds to be true as well, is working in a very analogous way, with personal contact and counselling being a core value to build trust between social workers and their beneficiaries. In this setting a small digital innovation, a simple tool which is aligned with the established processes can already be a game changer. With Integreat, those service providers were able to share their knowledge and expertise with a bigger audience than ever before and answer all those questions which they were asked repeatedly in an understandable way for refugees and migrants. This is possible because of the multilingual capabilities of the Integreat platform. They were able to reach those potential beneficiaries who have not yet come to their counselling centres because they did not feel comfortable enough to do so, not knowing what they had to expect there. Service providers are able to display their services clearly and understandably, so that newcomers can select the right service for their specific challenge, and the service providers could prepare them on what to expect there, and make known the preparations to do in advance and which documents and information to bring.

Integreat answers the simple questions of many newcomers directly, leaving more time for service provider employees to focus on the more challenging problems of newcomers and working in more detail with them on building a new livelihood. Integreat directs help seekers to the best suited service in a city for their individual challenge. For municipal governments, Integreat eventually shows a transparent overview of all integration-related services within a city or region, enabling said government to identify redundancies and gaps within their services and allow them to make well-informed and evidence-based decisions, such as where to funnel and rearrange resources to strengthen their integration work in the most sustainable way.

The intervention of Integreat to achieve this is quite small. The complexity of the digital platform lies within the Integreat organisation which is responsible for designing and developing the digital components of the platform in a way that it can be used by everyone. It must be easily understandable by social workers and municipal employees with very little IT skills and by newcomers, the end users, who are faced with a new digital application and have different levels of digital literacy alike. While the innovation of the Integreat platform itself cannot be understated as it is unmatched in its field in terms of functionality and usability, it is the combination of the expertise of the various stakeholders making Integreat the success story it is today.

Organic Way of Growth

Integreat was designed by a volunteer group of students and professionals from various backgrounds. Within four months Integreat was launched in the city of Augsburg which welcomed almost one hundred refugees each week. After Augsburg, other cities and regions in Germany reached out to ask for Integreat to be used there as well. Half a year later, the non-profit organisation behind Integreat was founded. First came the solution to a very specific challenge and then a business model and then an organisation was established — this is an example of the organic way of growth.

At first, the focus of the Integreat platform was solely put on supporting refugees upon their arrival in a German municipality. The topics and the content were tailored to their challenges and needs. Integreat explained the way the asylum process works and what support services were available to them. The focus on refugees was important at the time because municipal governments and service providers felt the burden of this tall task each and every day and Integreat was a possible answer. In the years prior to the refugee movement of 2015, Germany had one million people migrating to the country. While some were Germans returning, still a large number were migrant workers coming to country. The latter could have greatly benefited from a platform such as Integreat if it was already developed at that time. In 2015, the pressure on the municipal governments to find answers to integration of the large influx of migrants was a big enough impetus to allow for the introduction of Integreat as a small, but crucial puzzle piece into the ecosystem of local integration work.

In the years following the refugee movement, despite the decreasing numbers of migrants, one municipality after another came to the conclusion that Integreat was also an ideal tool to support incoming migrant workers, many from European neighbouring countries, with understandable information to make their start to life in Germany easier. Today, Integreat is available in over 30 languages in total, helping both refugees and migrant workers from day one of their integration journey in Germany.

To put this into a little picture: Even if you steadily walk up a staircase one step at a time, over time, you end up higher and higher.

Communicating with Citizens to Build Trust — and What Stands in the Way

Integreat is often the first communication channel for municipal governments to directly address refugees and migrants, with the intent to empower them on an everyday basis. Before the app was launched, the sole interaction platform between new migrants and the government were of a bureaucratic nature, done in the form of written letters with a language so complicated local volunteers were unable to understand them. Integreat is facilitating a shift in the form of communication from governments to newcomers in order to build mutual understanding and deepen trust between both parties. There lies great potential in opening a communication space between them, as vast majorities of migrants and refugees arrive with hope and willingness to adapt and listen. Local citizens falling for conspiracy theories and misinformation tend to do so because of disappointment with the status quo.

The ultimate goal needs to be to address everyone's concerns in the best way possible, in order to guide them to a path of listening and trusting each other and shaping a cohesive society. It takes a great effort by numerous actors to achieve this and the Integreat team has chosen to address newcomers, or better help institutions from host countries and societies to address newcomers.

When entering the world of digital information services, the big social networks and technology giants come into play, both in a positive and in a negative way, as already mentioned earlier in this chapter. Facebook, Apple and Google are gatekeepers, moderators and essentially judges of information spread across their platforms while they also enable us to stay connected across distances.

When the pandemic broke out, Integreat was even completely suspended from the Google Play Store simply because it contained information about the coronavirus: what to do if one was exposed to it, and what the current rules and regulations in the German cities were. It is obvious that the information comes from trusted municipal governments all over Germany and other governmental sources. But still, these technology giants and social media companies were complicit in shutting down the free flow of information for the people whose single source of understandable information was Integreat. A study in 2022 done in Germany showed that information campaigns had the single greatest impact on reducing infection numbers, even greater than closing schools and contract tracing. Entering the playing field of social networks and big tech platforms brings various risks, but it still holds great enough potential to do good for us to play along with their game.

Refugees and migrants often leave parts of their families and social relationships behind in their home countries and they stay in touch with them through social networks and messaging services. However, the very same digital tools also play a crucial role in the spread of misinformation and conspiracy theories regarding them. The approach of Integreat is to change the rules of the game a little bit and to make use of the positive factors of these platforms and reach refugees and migrants who are active there to lead them to trustful information sources and away from the other platforms that are prevalent with misinformation.

Every time Integreat is implemented, a social media campaign will be launched with the municipal government to inform newcomers about the new information platform with reliable information for their everyday challenges. The widespread use of social networks and messaging applications can therefore be used to educate newcomers on how to both find information online and also to verify information that they find. We have found out that the promotion of Integreat on various channels is key, as the feedback from another study showed that once refugees and migrants came across Integreat, they went on to use it long term. The key issue then was that the promotion did not reach them at an earlier juncture.[44]

Educate Host Societies as Well as Newcomers — Two Sides of One Coin

Integreat focuses heavily on educating refugees and migrants upon their arrival in a German municipality in order to enable them to make well-informed decisions based on a trustworthy source. At the same time, Integreat educates municipal governments and integration-related service providers to communicate with newcomers in an understandable way. All these activities are crucial to build cohesive societies on a local and national level through cross-cultural understanding, leading to equal chances for all members of society to succeed.

---

[44] Rosenbaum Janine, Zepic Robert, Schreieck Maximilian, Wiesche Manuel, Krcmar Helmut. (2018). Barriers to mobile government adoption: An exploratory case study of an information platform for refugees in Germany. *European Conference on e-Government*, Santiago de Compostela.

However, it has become evident that over the last decade, the host society must be educated as well. We have looked at them how they are vulnerable to false information and conspiracy theories while having a variety of information sources at their disposal. Refugee movements and migration are another narrative that has been a topic of conflict and discussion throughout European countries. Politicians in some European countries have run their election campaigns by elucidating fear with made-up numbers of refugees coming to Europe. These claims, which were not only improbable at that point in time, but in the years after that, it was shown that it did not come true.

It is especially hurtful for cohesive societies if their democratically elected leaders are also the leaders of misinformation campaigns and conspiracy theories. Integreat cannot be an answer to this challenge yet, but it puts our innovation into perspective as it takes multiple efforts to counteract misinformation campaigns from various angles. Our core principle is that it is important to share information with all citizens in an understandable fashion and completely. We cannot leave out those parts that may discourage or frighten individuals. The truth is sometimes hard to hear. But if we were to look at refugee movements more closely, we can learn about what we should expect.

Refugees tend to stay within their home countries, maybe their neighbouring countries. The number of refugees is published by UNHCR on yearly basis. This number is always growing from year to year, and one of the reasons is because newborn babies of a refugee count as a refugee again without that child ever having to cross any border. The sole source of larger refugee movements is war, as we see in Ukraine right now, the refugee movement to European countries is even bigger than the one in the year 2015. But it is evidence that the theory of refugees staying close to their home country still holds. Ukrainians mostly flee East to their European neighbouring countries. During incidences such as war, it is the job of journalists, scientists and politicians to inform the society about the complex situations and challenges. Such a job could have been carried out better in the past because we tend to stay within our comfortable bubbles. However, in times of hate speech, conspiracy theories and misinformation campaigns, we need to be firm in breaking out of them. We can do this on a local level within our communities, on a national level or even global. Integreat is trying to have an impact on all three levels.

Integreat's Impact beyond Germany — Where is it at?

since piloting in Augsburg in November 2015 Integreat has been implemented in over 90 German cities and counties reducing information poverty for newcomers in almost every quarter of Germany's 401 municipalities. Integreat's technological architecture was designed to scale quickly and almost limitlessly while being highly adaptable to local needs and has been implemented in small cities, large counties and metropolises.

Currently, Integreat is reinvented as a white-label solution to support a large social organisation (Malteser Werke), operating bigger reception facilities for asylum seekers during their asylum processes (https://malte-app.de). Therefore, Integreat can evidently work in a municipal environment as well as in a camp setting. This is why Integreat is not limited to supporting municipalities and newcomers in Germany, but everywhere it is needed in this world.

Integreat's work has been noticed outside of Germany as well. A pilot project on the Greek Island Lesvos was launched earlier in 2022 with the goal ofto also bringing Integreat to the mainland, starting with the Greek capital Athens the following year. In the Netherlands, Integreat is carrying out a pilot implementation in a large reception facility, similar to that of the Malteser Werke in Germany, as a blueprint for a larger roll-out throughout the whole country. On the other side of the world, a pilot implementation was also carried out in Sydney, which we also coordinate from afar. This underlines the adaptability of Integreat in new environments. We hope to launch several of these projects within the next year, making those beacons of light for many more places in the world.

Looking at the role of governments in countries, we have to differentiate between those who are interested in making successful integration of refugees and migrants part of their agenda of a prosperous society, and those who do not have such an interest. Sometimes, Integreat needs to function independently from governmental structures in order to support newcomers and those social organisations trying to help them. Integreat is well equipped to work either way as it only changes the way a local Integreat project is governed by the parties involved. This is also part of our solution where we have done the most work in terms of scientific research: designing, implementing and running a platform ecosystem in a not-for-profit environment.

Building a Sustainable Platform — The Chicken and the Egg Dilemma

Let us talk about the chicken and the egg now. Which of them came first? If you build any sort of platform you need to bring providers and consumers onto it almost simultaneously. What would any of the two parties gain from joining the platform if the other one was not there? Platform ecosystems are well known from Amazon or Facebook where numerous companies join the platform to sell or advertise their goods and services and to reach customers while paying a fee to the platform owner to join.

Integreat also provides such a platform but the benefits of service providers and users joining it cannot be quantified in any economic fashion such as Dollars or Euros, in the way that we are familiar with. However, Integreat's team does not take on the role of the platform by itself but divides that role on a local level with municipal governments.

Municipal governments pay a yearly fee based on their size to become part of the Integreat platform and receive their separate section within it. In this step, Integreat works as the platform owner. Afterwards, the municipal government gets to decide who they bring on board to be part of the creation of local integration-relevant content. For their separate section, identified by their city's or county's name, the municipal government receives exclusive rights, so no other public or private body can be published on the Integreat platform with that same name. The municipal government then decides which individuals or organisations get access to their part of the Integreat platform to contribute.

On a local level, the municipal government becomes the platform owner. This is a key success factor for Integreat in Germany, as municipal governments have the power, as they most often are budget providers for local integration efforts and the non-government organisations (NGOs), to bring a large network of organisations together to participate in the content creation and curation process necessary for Integreat to become and stay relevant to refugees and migrants. This implementation and governance process has been subject to a new field of research on how platform ecosystems can work in a non-profit sector. As shown by Schreieck and colleagues,[45] Integreat as a non-profit platform ecosystem could not monetarily incentivise content creators and instead opted for a more centralised local platform owner who, due to its dominant position, could ensure participation from other institutions.

Looking at the metaphor of the chicken and the egg, an Integreat implementation starts with the content creation to a certain extent, which is then published and promoted in refugee and migrant communities. They are incentivised to access the Integreat platform as it holds valuable information for them. Municipal governments gain a transparent overview of all integration-related services, can identify gaps which they can address and ideally see an overall better integration taking place. NGOs reach a bigger target audience, direct help-seeking newcomers to the best-suited service provider and enable them to have an easier time communicating important information in an understandable way and in a very large scale. This is the promise Integreat gives to new municipalities and their integration service providers and how they receive an incentive to join the Integreat platform.

However, establishing a platform in the non-profit sector does not always provide one with the luxury of a natural platform co-owner such as municipal governments in Germany. It is not uncommon to research a potential country to scale to and to find that no governmental institution at local, regional, or national level has interest to take on this role. Sometimes they would even try to prevent a positive intervention in favour of refugees and migrants from happening. Instead, NGOs take on a key role in coordinating and carrying out services for refugees and migrants. A different country almost always leads to minor or major adjustments compared to the launch in Germany in the way a non-profit

---

[45] Schreieck Maximilian, Wiesche Manuel, Hein Andreas, Krcmar Helmut. (2016). Governance of nonprofit platforms — onboarding mechanisms for a refugee information platform. *SIG GlobDev Ninth Annual Workshop*, Dublin; Schreieck Maximilian, Wiesche Manuel, Krcmar Helmut. (2017b). Governing nonprofit platform ecosystems — An information platform for refugees. *Information Technology for Development* 23(3), 618–643.

platform can be implemented successfully, and again create enough incentives for all relevant stakeholders to join.

Learning from Integreat for Hate Speech, Conspiracy Theories and Disinformation Campaigns

What can we learn from the use of Integreat for our societies in our countries as a whole? Integreat is trying to build trust through transparency and providing newcomers with the possibility to make a well-informed decision by having access to the whole picture of rules, rights, and opportunities. A full picture may also include those bits of information which are not positive, which will explain that a door is closed for that person. It is important to paint this whole picture again to tailor it to different audiences. It is important to take in all perspectives relevant to a subject, especially in crises. We in Europe have a new crisis on our hands. Russia invaded Ukraine in February of 2022 which brought a refugee movement to Europe that is even greater in numbers than that of 2015 when Integreat was brought to life.

To provide these refugees with good supporting services it is highly important to include them, their communities and their associations in the development and implementation process of service designs. It is important to talk to them, not only taking the perspective of the host country's status quo. At the same time, it is important to talk about the refugees as well. It is also important to address the host society and explain the situation and current plans and emphasise that everything happening during this humanitarian response is done with great uncertainty and will be subject to change. Migration experts stress that it is a plan of Putin and the Russian regime to divide European Union member states through a large number of refugees arriving as it happened in the years prior and basically let the history of 2016 and beyond repeat itself.

It is necessary to inform and educate a country's society and prepare them that we will have to make relatively small sacrifices to fight injustice and evil and help the less fortunate. We need to be resilient to fight false information and conspiracy theories with pure truth and blatant honesty even if the painted picture is not beautiful at all. Maybe then, we do not have to ask the question about how refugees and migrants fit into our society, it is our human kindness that prevails. Hundreds of thousands of Germans have opened their homes to refugees. They have supported them at train stations and with their trips to administration to sort out their bureaucratic documents. The German people bought time for their government to find long-term solutions which they did not really deliver on. But it should give us hope and faith in ourselves as societies, on what we can collectively achieve. Humanity shows its greatest strength in making connections. Connections in the real world.

We from Integreat are trying to build bridges for refugees and migrants to the society of their host country which may become their home country at some point. An information bit from Integreat shall always lead to real-world interaction, communication or meeting. We aim at addressing them digitally and then taking them away from there quickly. Real-world connections between humans are strong and they are good.

And with Integreat, we are trying to create these connections every single day, one connection at a time. Small steps, but never stopping.

Chapter 5.7

FAITH OVERCOMING COVID-19 PANDEMIC: THE SINGAPORE MUSLIM EXPERIENCE

Dr Mohammad Hannan Hassan

Introduction

I walked into a seminar recently organised by some dear friends at a university, attended by lawyers and asatizah, without prior notice to the organiser. I quietly sat at the back of the room, dressed casually in my tucked-out short sleeve shirt without my *songkok,* or the head cover deemed appropriate and usually donned by Muslim religious leaders. I looked more like a typical young university student than a religious leader. My appearance was not unnoticed by my good friend, the organiser. As I was sitting alone at the back of the room listening to the lecture, a short message came to my handphone from the organiser. The message read, "Deputy Mufti without *songkok*? Standards are slipping these days!" I understood that it was said jokingly and with a big smile. I could not help but smile as I read the message. Instinctively, I replied, "setting new standards with a focus on content, not forms…", and with a big smiley too. He then replied, "I love it!"

On a serious note, the COVID-19 pandemic if any has emphasised the importance of focusing on principles, substance, and content, not mere forms and rituals. This does not negate the significance of rituals and forms. We recognise that rituals do play their roles in defining communities. They connect people, identify members of the community, and create ties and kinship among members of the community. They are the symbolic language that connects members of the community in their diversity and plurality. Nonetheless, forms and rituals without principles, substance, and content are mere symbols without meanings. Rather, it is these principles and substantial content that provide purpose and meaning to the rituals and forms. These rituals can and should change and be adapted, while the principles remain as the soul of the community.

Here, I argue that religions and religious traditions should focus on principles, content, and substance. I will then discuss two examples from the pandemic experiences demonstrating the focus on principles and content while remaining nimble and flexible with the forms and rituals.

Focus on Content and Substance

If there is one main takeaway from the pandemic experience, I will argue that religions and religious traditions survived and stood the test of time to this day because they have remained principle-based, nimble, resilient, adaptive, and relevant. When religions and religious traditions lose their relevance because they are not adaptive to the changing contexts and realities, they will disappear by the law of nature. Protecting and safeguarding religious traditions do not simply mean keeping their letters, but rather it is about preserving their spirit and higher purpose as they evolve through the times. While principles and purposes remain as the guiding compass and provide the direction, the forms and rituals continue to evolve and be adapted. In an increasingly volatile and uncertain environment, such as the pandemic, our attention must be on matters of principles. Faith leaders have focused on four key principles that have guided the fatwa-making and the religious life in Singapore, namely religiosity founded on the higher purposes of religion, human dignity, protection of life, and avoiding any harm (non-maleficence).

Traditions, understood as a set of beliefs, customs, practices, values, knowledge, and wisdom passed down through successive generations, serve three primary functions: to establish a sense of continuity and social cohesion (a certain identity), to render certain behaviours legitimate, and to imprint certain beliefs. To be sure, traditions, religious or otherwise, do play an important role in societies: invented or reinvented.[46]

It is this continuous reinvention of traditions that the pandemic has forced the community to do. It has also accelerated this change and reinvention deemed arduous pre-pandemic. Here, I shall mention two examples, namely the Postgraduate Certificate in Islam in Contemporary Societies (PCICS) programme, and the One-Mosque Sector (OMS) plan, introduced by the Islamic Religious Council of Singapore (Muis).

PCICS: Adapting While Not Compromising the Objectives

To set the context, all asatizah[47] in Singapore must be registered under the mandatory Asatizah Recognition Scheme (ARS) to function and discharge their roles as asatizah in providing Islamic guidance and instruction to the community.[48] From 2020, all returning graduates applying for Tier 1 of the ARS are required to successfully complete a one-year Postgraduate Certificate in Islam in Contemporary Societies (PCICS) programme, in place of the four-week Islam in Context (ICON) programme.

PCICS aims to nurture a generation of confident, compassionate, and competent professional asatizah with the requisite knowledge and skills to provide relevant religious guidance in a highly diverse, plural, and interconnected postmodern world like Singapore. Based on a holistic curriculum, it dedicates ample attention to both religious and social sciences to develop a critical-creative thinking mindset and equips the asatizah with

---

[46] I have elsewhere discussed the notion of tradition and authority in Islam. See Mohammad Hannan Hassan. (2015). Tradition and Authority in Islam. *Religious Tradition and Authority in a Post-Modern World*, pp. 12–21. Harmony Centre, Singapore.

[47] Asatizah (plural of Ustaz) is an honorific title used in Singapore, and generally in the Southeast Asia, to refer to qualified Muslim religious leaders providing Islamic instructions and guidance on Islam. Elsewhere, the term imams or mawlana is used.

[48] On the Asatizah Recognition Scheme (ARS), see Mohammad Hannan Hassan and Irwan Hadi Mohd Shuhaimy. (2018). Developing Asatizah in Singapore through the Asatizah recognition scheme. In Norshahril Saat (ed.) *Fulfilling the Trust: 50 Years of Shaping Muslim Religious Life in Singapore*, pp. 73–87. World Scientific Publishing, Singapore.

relevant 21ˢᵗ-century competencies and professional proficiencies. The curriculum is designed to equip students with a deep familiarity with the current and future contexts of Singapore society, and Islam and Muslim communities in the Southeast Asian/Nusantara region, but rooted to the rich Islamic traditions. Committed to nurturing a passion for lifelong learning and sustainable self-development, PCICS promises a student-centric experience.[49] This was and still is the philosophy and objectives of the PCICS.

Then, the COVID-19 pandemic hit the world hard, and Singapore was not spared. Soon after the Disease Outbreak Response System Condition (DORSCON) was raised to Orange in February 2020, just a level below the top category, Singapore witnessed its first case of death in March, amidst a spike in local transmission. On 3 April 2020, Prime Minister Lee Hsien Loong announced that a Circuit Breaker would be in place from 7 April 2020 to break the chain of transmission. Except for those providing essential services, most workplaces were to be closed, and schools were moved to full home-based learning. Tighter measures soon followed, including a bill on prohibiting private and public social gatherings.

PCICS was scheduled to commence on 18 April 2020. All lessons and preparations were already done for the inaugural class. The unexpected but necessary announcement caught the Muis Academy team unprepared. The team needed to brace itself to ride through this storm. All classes needed to go online. We announced the postponement of the inaugural class to 2 May. The team quickly regrouped, redesigned the lessons, reworked on the plans, and adapted according to the measures, all within less than three weeks.

To add to the challenge, the inaugural batch was already less receptive to the introduction of this additional requirement to the ARS. They now needed to go through this programme using a rather unfamiliar pedagogy, that had been adopted to respond to the volatile, uncertain, and ambiguous environment. No less anxious was the administrator, who had to manage the anxieties of participants and navigate unfamiliar terrains. Although an online and blended learning modality was considered at the early

---

[49] For greater detail of the programme and its prospectus, see https://www.muis.gov.sg/muisacademy/Programmes/PCICS.

conception of the programme, none expected it to be put to use in such an urgent and sudden manner. Mr Safwan Sulaiman, the Assistant Manager at the Muis Academy, who administers the programme said, "since its conception, PCICS has always been developed with blended learning in mind. This means that the students will not only learn during the face-to-face lessons, but also via various online learning tools as well. When the Circuit Breaker measures were announced earlier this year (April 2020), this further deepened the use of technology in our classes. The team was quick to adapt, and adjustments were made to move all lessons online for home-based learning. All these whilst still ensuring that the pedagogy is not compromised, and the experience remains student-centred."[50]

In the face of this changing environment, in an unfamiliar terrain, Muis has to adapt and adopt, within a steep learning curve and a short timeline, going fully online and guiding students to navigate this curious learning journey. In spite of the changes, the consensus was that as long as the principal objectives of the programme are not compromised, the manners and forms the programme takes can and should be adapted to the changing context and environment. To this, a lecturer, Alfian Yasrif Kuchit, expressed his concern, "At first, I was quite anxious as to how I can conduct online teaching. So, we had to rethink how we can teach and support the students better, in terms of their learning journey...and I think this accords with our role to provide a safe harbour to our students to express their thoughts and help them grow."[51]

Muhammad Faheem Abdul Khalil, a student quipped, "it was really challenging at first, to complete assignments and attend all lectures amidst working from home. Juggling all these, yes, it was tough, and also sadly there's very little time for family bonding. But the thing is, *alhamdulillah*, skills taught by our lecturers and tutors [were] very useful. Like, for example, speed reading and dividing of workloads, [and] materials. So, this really helps in reducing reading time. And it somehow allowed me to submit my assignments punctually, *alhamdulillah*."[52]

---

[50] Muis Academy. (2020). PCICS First Cohort, First Term. YouTube, August 27, 2020, 1:40 to 2:14, https://www.youtube.com/watch?v=0shgsRnrMyo.

[51] *Ibid.* 2:20 to 2:48.

[52] *Ibid.* 0:39 to 1:05.

As seen, many participants shared that juggling between work and study, and all these being done online, was a big challenge. The manner the curriculum and learning experiences were done would have certainly mitigated these challenges and made the task of new learning pedagogies bearable. Tan Nurul E'zzati Abdul Hadi, another student, recognising this struggle in juggling work and study, said, "…and I am still juggling between work and study. But looking at how the PCICS team have put in effort in structuring the curriculum, the modules, the lessons as well as the tutorials, I feel like I should also put in my best effort."[53]

Since April 2020, the team has been working continually to develop the relevant competencies, pedagogies, and technologies to fit into the new norms of learning. COVID-19 was a test of a generation. But importantly, it was also a positive impetus and opportunity for renewal, reinvention, and charting new terrains without compromising principles and objectives.

One Mosque Sector

The Mosque sector was among the most affected sector due to the COVID-19 pandemic. Due to the transmission in four mosques in the initial few weeks of the pandemic in Singapore, Muis had to make a difficult yet necessary decision to suspend all mosques, which means suspension of all congregational and Friday prayers, and all activities, starting from 13 March 2020. While initially this was set for five days, because of the unabated transmission, the suspension was extended for another nine days. Subsequently, it was extended beyond fourteen days, because the situation was not getting any better. The decision to suspend prayers and activities in the mosques was justified by a Fatwa[54] made in February 2020 on the permissibility of disallowing unhealthy congregants to come to mosque and closure of the mosque in the interest of public

---

[53] *Ibid.* 1:20 to 1:39.

[54] Fatwa is a religious ruling given by a qualified Muslim jurist in response to questions seeking religious ruling according to Islamic laws. A Mufti is the qualified jurist to issue a fatwa. In Singapore, fatwas are issued by a Legal Committee, chaired by the Mufti, as according to the Administration of Muslim Law Act (AMLA). See AMLA, s. 30–31.

health and interest and to protect lives.[55] The suspension of mosques in Singapore was arguably the first known decision in the world due to COVID-19.

The closure of the mosques and the suspension of all their activities were unprecedented. Having studied the scholarly Muslim theological and legal traditions, guided by the principles of protecting lives, public interest and safety, and the ethical principle of non-maleficence (not causing any harm), the Fatwa argued that "if there is a wider spread of the COVID-19 virus and the situation becomes more critical which would require the closure of public places, including houses of worship such as mosques, or if there is a need for public access to public places such as mosques to be restricted, this will be considered as an emergency situation.

Accordingly, the Fatwa Committee is of the view that the closing of a mosque or the suspension of congregational prayers and Friday prayers during this situation, is required."[56] Subsequently, similar principles were used in managing the safety measures as the mosques opened their doors and resumed activities safely and progressively under the Safety Measures Management (SMM). These measures include requiring a booking to perform the prayer, observing safe distancing in congregational prayers, restricting the number of congregants at one time, and various other measures. These are unprecedented and unfamiliar practices and norms brought about by the pandemic.

The Muslim community was the first religious community in Singapore to be impacted by the Circuit Breaker measures. Mosques were closed to the annual Ramadan festivities and rituals in the mosque that started on 24 April 2020, including the Eid (Hari Raya) prayers for two consecutive years. Truly, the inability to perform the weekly Friday prayer and then the Eid prayers was a significant religious and spiritual hit to the Muslim community. Following the closure of the mosques and other religious organisations, religious instructions and classes were delivered online. Increasingly, asatizah became active and creative in producing

---

[55] See the fatwa on Precautionary Measures in Dealing with the COVID-19, by the Fatwa Committee, Islamic Religious Council of Singapore, https://www.muis.gov.sg/officeofthemufti/Fatwa/Fatwa-Covid-19-English.

[56] *Ibid.*

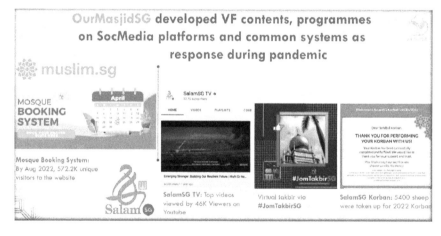

online religious learning materials, live online learning, and consequently reaching a wider audience than the physical classes were ever to reach out pre-pandemic.

Nonetheless, the pandemic has opened up new opportunities and set off new creative ways of offering religious guidance and services. Mosque leaders huddled together in a series of meetings in the face of this unprecedented crisis, seeking to turn crises into opportunities by providing

ONE MOSQUE SECTOR
SOCIAL SUSTAINABILITY PLAN

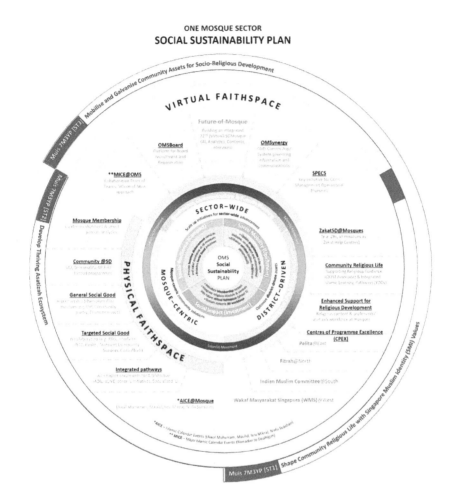

creative solutions. As a result, a One Mosque Sector Social Sustainability Plan (OMS-SSP) was developed in mid-2022. This plan endeavours to deep-dive and develop what Social Sustainability could potentially contribute within the context of One Mosque Sector. This includes enhancing physical and virtual faith spaces. More initiatives and programmes are being worked out currently. The above diagram depicts the plan.

Conclusion

As Albert Einstein once said, in the midst of every crisis lies great opportunity. COVID-19 was such an opportunity, amidst the uncertainties and adversities. The quality of a leader and the community is in the manner they act in the face of these adversities and difficulties. As Prime Minister Lee Hsien Loong said in a national broadcast on 7 June 2020, "Indeed, our nation was born in crisis...Now, at another hinge in our history, it is our turn to face the crisis of a generation. The choices that we make now will define who we are as a people, and what values and ideals we pass on to future generations. Confronting adversity, do we yield to anger, fear and bitterness? Or will we be true to ourselves, stand firm, make tough choices, and continue to trust and depend on one another."[57] The attitude and tradition of turning crisis into opportunities is our reinventing of our tradition: its spirit, not its letters. The importance of competent leadership, continuous engagement and communication, and mutual trust building cannot be emphasised enough. These were three key lessons gleaned from the pandemic, and it is during peace times that leadership and the people must invest in these qualities.

---

[57] Lee Hsien Loong. (2020). Overcoming the Crisis of a Generation. National Broadcast, 7 June 2020, https://www.gov.sg/article/pm-lee-hsien-loong-overcoming-the-crisis-of-a-generation.

Chapter 5.8

VISUALS

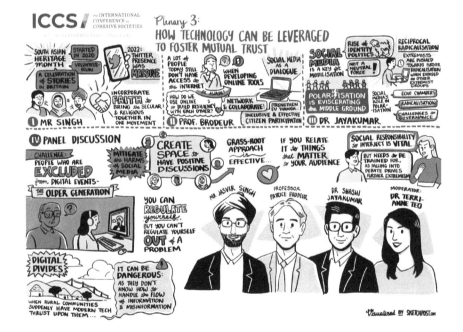

Part 6

YOUTH

Chapter 6.1

ICCS YOUNG LEADER'S PROGRAMME VISUALS

ICCS Young Leaders' Programme Proceedings

Following the footsteps of the International Conference on Cohesive Societies (ICCS) in 2019, a Young Leaders' Programme (YLP) component was held from 6 to 8 September 2022. The YLP is a platform for young local and international leaders to network and collaborate on initiatives to strengthen social cohesion and aims to develop a core of young leaders who can speak and lead with confidence on issues affecting ethnic and religious harmony today.

The YLP in 2022 continued the tradition of embracing an 'open space' facilitation format where every participant is offered the opportunity to present their views and shape the discourse in a collaborative manner. Highlights of the session included a community showcase and collaboration whitespace session, which encouraged youth civic activism and collaboration through facilitated game-play, an interactive showcase of ground-up initiatives by young community leaders, and a fireside chat with Reverend Chris Lee, Father Fiel Pareja and fashion designer Yasmin Jay on harnessing social media for social cohesion. Contemporary issues of faith and diversity were also covered at the YLP dialogues, and revolved around three main topics: faith for sustainability, faith in workplaces, and harnessing faith for community-building.

The visuals in this section summarise the proceedings from the YLP. These reflections exhibit the Young Leaders' sentiments on how cohesive societies can be nurtured in the community.

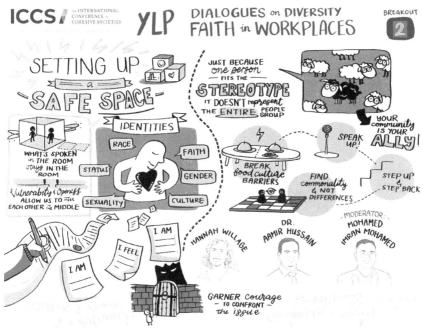

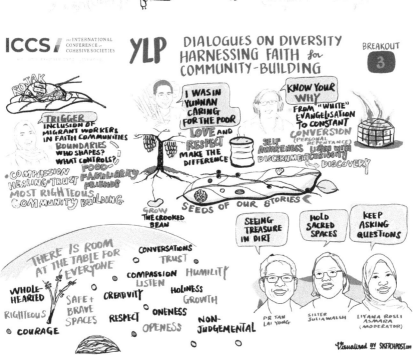

Milton Keynes UK
Ingram Content Group UK Ltd.
UKHW020750141223
434354UK00002B/35

9 789811 285370